D1506440

VETS AND PETS

WOUNDED WARRIORS AND THE ANIMALS THAT HELP THEM HEAL

Dava Guerin and Kevin Ferris
Forewords by First Lady Barbara Bush and Andrea Arden

Skyhorse Publishing

A portion of the proceeds of this book will go to Pets for Patriots, a charitable organization that helps veterans find loving companions and abandoned animals find good homes.

Skyhorse Publishing books may be purchased in bulk at special discounts for sales promotion, corporate gifts, fund-raising, or educational purposes. Special editions can also be created to specifications. For details, contact the Special Sales Department, Skyhorse Publishing, 307 West 36th Street, 11th Floor, New York, NY 10018 or info@skyhorsepublishing.com.

Skyhorse® and Skyhorse Publishing® are registered trademarks of Skyhorse Publishing, Inc.®, a Delaware corporation.

Visit our website at www.skyhorsepublishing.com.

10 9 8 7 6 5 4 3 2 1

Cover design by Rain Saukus
Cover photo credit Stephen Wallace, MD, JD

Library of Congress Cataloging-in-Publication Data is available on file.

Print ISBN: 978-1-5107-2193-7
Ebook ISBN: 978-1-5107-2194-4

Printed in the United States of America

To our nation's wounded veterans, their service dogs, companion animals, and the intrepid volunteers who brought them together. As a team, they have helped heal the wounds of war, brought love and laughter into each other's lives, and, most of all, renewed the optimism, joy, and hope of life well lived—and to my father, Dr. Martin Lewis Fleishman, a US Army Air Corps veteran and my hero.

—*Dava Guerin*

For Emily Brennan Ferris and Kieran Mandela Ferris, who make me proud every day.

—*Kevin Ferris*

TABLE OF CONTENTS

Acknowledgments   vii

Foreword by Former First Lady Barbara Bush   x

Foreword by Animal Planet Host Andrea Arden   xii

Introduction   xv

Chapter 1: Animals and Veterans in America: Their Enduring
Bonds and Healing Powers   1

PART 1: AT YOUR SERVICE

Chapter 2: The Army Specialist: "A reason to get out of bed
in the morning."   11

Chapter 3: The Marine Tank Commander: "That's what
that dog is for."   20

Chapter 4: The Army Nurse: "Some kind of a guardian angel."   36

Chapter 5: The Army Captain: "Issac has been waiting
for his special person."   53

Chapter 6: The Marine Corporal: "Gnome somehow can read me."   68

Chapter 7: The Navy Vietnam Veteran: "The dog becomes
a family member."   75

Chapter 8: The Navy Dog Handler: "This was love at first bite."   93

PART 2: MORE CREATURES, GREAT AND SMALL

Chapter 9: The Vietnam Infantryman: "Grab a bird, put on a glove, and go for a walk." 115

Chapter 10: The Army Reservist: "My God, no one is going to adopt her." 126

Chapter 11: The Cowboy Marine: "Here's how you saddle a horse." 134

Chapter 12: The Air Force Vet and Veterinarian: "Our house is a pet menagerie." 145

Chapter 13: The Navy Boatswain's Mate: "I just had to have him." 153

Chapter 14: Max, the Horse That Helps Heroes: "We have all fallen in love with him." 161

Chapter 15: The Army Veteran: "Together, they heal and grow." 171

Chapter 16: Secrets for an Enduring Bond: "Until one has loved an animal, a part of one's soul remains unawakened." 183

Epilogue 191

About the Authors 193

ACKNOWLEDGMENTS

THIS BOOK WOULD HAVE NEVER BEEN POSSIBLE WITHOUT THE BRAVE MEN and women who have served our country in the military. It is a great honor and privilege to share their personal stories of love, loss, hope, and laughter. Veterans and the animals they love have a special place in all Americans' hearts; their connection reminds us all of the power of the human spirit and the critical role that animals play in making our lives happier and healthier. We thank all of the inspirational veterans who have so openly and thoughtfully let us into their lives and enabled us to capture their stories in *Vets and Pets*. As for their special animals, their unwavering love and tenacity have changed veterans' lives in the most remarkable ways, and telling their stories has been a joy beyond compare.

We also thank Beth Zimmerman, who gave up a lucrative career to start a nonprofit organization, Pets for Patriots, that places abandoned animals with veterans. She has been a wonderful resource for us, sharing transformational stories of veterans and the animals they rescued. Also helpful with our outreach to veterans was Wallace Nunn, a Vietnam veteran and chairman of the board of the Freedoms Foundation in Valley Forge, Pennsylvania; Hal Koster, also a Vietnam vet and now executive director of the Aleethia Foundation, which has done so much for wounded warriors and their caregivers; and Wells B. Jones, chief executive officer of the Guide Dog Foundation for the Blind and America's VetDogs – The Veteran's K-9 Corps, and his organizations' communications manager, William A. Krol. John Wear, of Bucks County, Pennsylvania, who served as a tank commander and section leader with Charlie Company, Third Tank Battalion, Third Marine Division, in Vietnam, had enough faith in us to reach out to friends and fellow veterans on our behalf. Canine Companions for Independence was most generous with providing us its expertise, particularly regarding the often confusing roles that service and companion dogs play in the lives of veterans. Tania Gail Ciolko provided moral support and inspiring photography, and Amy Junod Placentra was patient and helpful when faced with a variety of technical support questions. For all of these experts, and their willingness to help us with this project, we are most grateful.

We owe a shout out to Andrea Arden, author, animal expert, and nationally acclaimed television host on Animal Planet and NBC, for her moving foreword and for sharing words of wisdom about dog training and the need to adopt shelter animals and save them from euthanasia. Andrea is also an advocate for animal adoption and knows firsthand the joy and love that abandoned and abused animals can bring. Dr. Shawn Dunn and Patrick Bradley, whose inspirational stories appear in the book, have generously taken the time to provide valuable information on animal behavior and training that readers can try on their own pets.

Without Skyhorse Publishing, which took a chance on two first-time authors four years ago, our first book, *Unbreakable Bonds: The Mighty Moms and Wounded Warriors of Walter Reed*, would never have come to life. Because of their belief in the amazing stories of mothers who have given all to help their wounded warrior children recover from devastating injuries as a result of the War on Terror, we were able to highlight the importance of military caregivers on a national and international basis. Our editors on *Vets and Pets*—Chris Evans, Joe Craig, Kelsie Besaw, and Mike Campbell—could not have been more supportive. Our agent, Lloyd Remick, Esq., an army veteran, has been with us since the beginning and has been a true partner in all of our projects.

We owe a debt of gratitude to First Lady Barbara Bush for writing her heartfelt and inspirational foreword. She is not only a champion of literacy but a dog lover, too. She and President George H. W. Bush have been supportive of our work with veterans and caregivers and have been more than generous with their time and involvement. President Bush's chief of staff, our dear friend Jean Becker, has been the driving force behind our books and has personally been involved in helping wounded warriors and caregivers in so many ways. She is our "Point of Light." President George W. Bush and First Lady Laura Bush, as well, have hosted many events for wounded warriors and caregivers. For that we are also very appreciative.

Of course there are so many people who have given us inspiration, without whom this book would never have come to pass. We'd like to give a special thanks to Ellene Fleishman, who spent countless hours listening to our stories and giving her valuable insights. We also want to thank Gary Sinise, for his dedication and tireless efforts to help our nation's veterans; Terry Bivens and Dr. Judith Jaeger for their journalistic advice; Kevin's editors at the *Philadelphia Inquirer*, Harold Jackson, Josh Gohlke, and Paul Davies, for helping him make time for this project; and the Mighty Moms of Walter Reed—Stacy, Mary, Carolee, Paulette, Tammy, Valence, Julie, Siobhan, Lyn, and Pam—the inspirations behind *Unbreakable Bonds*, who continue to inspire us. They showed us the important role military caregivers play in helping their children heal. Former Congressman Bob Clement and his wife Mary Clement gave us their stellar advice, guidance, and, most of all, friendship; Rick Fleishman and Gabrielle Fleishman were so supportive; and Gloria Camma always kept us on track. To everyone else who has helped us along this journey, we thank you as well. And, finally, the pets we cherish in our lives—Coco, Kato, Kosmo, Max, Tinkie and J.P. Morgan—thanks to you we are happier, content, and more forgiving and blessed to experience that special kind of love that humans and animals share unconditionally.

FOREWORD

Former First Lady Barbara Bush

For many of us, coming home to or cuddling with a beloved pet is one of life's great joys. No matter how your day has gone, the unbridled excitement of your pet when you walk in the door really can make your problems seem a little less grim.

Now, imagine for a moment the power of that same bond between our military veterans and their pets. For years we've all heard stories of how that relationship not only changes but saves lives. Their pets can make dark days brighter, the helpless feel helpful, the lonely feel loved.

It was a love story begging to be told.

Now, thanks to my good friend and author Dava Guerin and her coauthor Kevin Ferris, we no longer have to imagine a thing. *Vets and Pets* shares with all of us fourteen amazing love stories. And no, they aren't all about dogs. There are horses, cats, birds, and even potbelly pigs. (Note: We Bushes have always been dog people, so I am not sure what it means to come home to a cat, or a parrot, or even a snake. But a pet is a pet, even if the rest of us may not get it. Don't let anyone judge you!)

These stories will make you laugh and, of course, cry—and if you don't have one, they will make you desperately wish for a pet. I especially love the stories where the vet and the pet actually rescued each other.

Reading this book filled my heart with gratitude: for all our veterans who sacrificed so much making our world a safer place; for all the organizations whose mission it is to connect veterans with a pet who will bring joy back into their lives; for animal rescue groups that try to find and take care of the animals who have been abandoned and abused; and of course for all our four-legged (and even two-legged) friends, without whom life would be a lot less interesting.

So enjoy this wonderful book, hopefully while hugging a pet. (Mini-Me and Bibi read every page with me.) And don't forget to give thanks every single day for the men and women of our military—past, present, and future. We love and appreciate you.

—**Barbara Bush**
November 22, 2016

FOREWORD

Animal Planet Host Andrea Arden

I AM ONE OF THOSE VERY FORTUNATE PEOPLE TO HAVE CREATED A CAREER THAT revolves around animals, and I have my father to thank for this. A veteran of World War II, he struggled with many illnesses and relied on a team of caregivers and our family for support—one of the most important being his constant canine companion, Chippy. Their leisurely walks and afternoon naps were part of my father's daily routine. When he referred to his dog as his "number one son," my brothers and I would feign jealousy in a successful effort to get a big bear hug and reassurance about how much he loved us as well. Even as children, we recognized how important Chippy, and all of our animals, were to our father. This was my introduction to the healing power of our relationships with animals, something I developed an even greater understanding of and appreciation for as I moved into adulthood. This has culminated in the honor of serving on the Board of Directors of Pets for Patriots.

There are few better examples of the benefits of our relationships with animals than their role in the lives of veterans. Our veterans have been generous in their service, and here you will find they are equally generous in the telling of their stories.

Vets and Pets offers insight into and raises awareness about some of the challenges veterans face, how animals help them heal, and how we can all do more to help all around. Veterans provide an invaluable service and sacrifice. We must move obstacles out of the way for them to experience the joyful journey of friendship and love companion animals provide, and in some cases the assistance of a service animal specially trained to perform tasks.

Modern science has taught us that animals don't just fill our hearts, they also have the potential to make our hearts and minds healthier. An animal needn't be a certified therapy or service animal to lower anxiety and blood pressure. Studies show a link between animal companions and improved cardiovascular health, lower blood pressure, and easing tension in stressful situations. Spending time with animals can also increase levels of serotonin and dopamine, neurochemicals that play a vital role in overall well-being.

Animals are known to benefit people in countless ways including increasing mobility, promoting independence, mitigating emotional distress, and preventing loneliness and isolation by encouraging positive social interactions. Who doesn't love to talk about their animals? The strong inclination of animals to secure social bonds helps countless people experience greater joy in their lives and provides much-needed support to navigate through challenging life experiences.

One of the many ways we can support our troops is by supporting efforts to provide for their needs when they return home. In some cases, the companionship of an adopted animal or the support of a highly trained service animal can have a life-altering effect. Nonprofit organizations tasked with training and placing service animals, as well as those, like Pets for Patriots, that facilitate adoptions of companion animals, depend on validation of what most anyone that has shared their life with an animal can tell you: animals make a major difference.

Animals know so little of our worries and stresses, yet they offer so much of what we need in order to overcome emotional and physical challenges. They share in our joys, and when it hurts they make it better. Their friendship is truly priceless. When what you need and want is a friend to just sit with you or to go for a quiet walk, and when it might be hard to ask for help from a person, our animals are there and eager to assist. Sharing our lives with animals makes life better; they sprinkle joy into every day, and they offer an invitation for us to be needed in ways we are eager and able to fulfill.

Vets and Pets is a celebration of veterans, of the animals that are helping them heal, and of the people who have created nonprofit organizations to help assist veterans in the process of adoption.

Thank you to our veterans. Thank you to Dava Guerin and Kevin Ferris for this compilation of compelling stories created in an effort to raise awareness about the many benefits of encouraging and facilitating animal adoptions for members of the military community. Thank you to all of the people who work to make a difference for our veterans and for animals. And thank you to the animals for making all of our lives better.

—Andrea Arden

INTRODUCTION

"If there are no dogs in Heaven, then when I die I want to go where they went."
—*Will Rogers*

AMERICANS LOVE THEIR PETS. DOGS, CATS, GUINEA PIGS, BUNNIES, BIRDS, horses, hamsters, and so many others share our lives in the best and worst of times. They are our comfort and faithful companions. According to the ASPCA, there are more than seventy million dogs living in households across the United States and nearly thirty-seven million cats, not to mention millions of other animal species. And pet owners spend more than $60 billion annually on their furry companions. We love them that much!

Vets and Pets showcases the bonds between veterans and their dogs, cats, horses, pigs, and even birds of prey, and how these special relationships promote healing and emotional well-being. These are touching stories of love, loss, hope, humor, and connection between veterans of all ages, genders, and races and their beloved pets. The veterans in *Vets and Pets* face multiple physical and emotional challenges, and some of their companion animals have also suffered abuse and abandonment. Other pets have simply benefited from a loving relationship with their veterans, while certified service dogs have been specially trained to use their innate skills to help disabled veterans manage their daily lives. It is not an understatement to say that these loving relationships have saved countless veterans' lives.

We hope that these inspiring, emotional, and entertaining stories not only showcase the bonds between veterans and their service and companion animals but also the unique relationships that have enabled them to heal and even thrive. These amazing animals are helping veterans return to the civilian world and live independently, and they are bringing joy back into vets' lives.

As with all pets, service and companion animals, too, have their humorous side. When they are not on duty, they can transform from serious workers into playful pups. The book explores some of the lighthearted moments between veterans and their pets and some of the unexpected escapades they experience in their new lives together.

There is no end to the creativity, dedication, and passion generated by people striving to improve the lives of our veterans. When it comes to pairing pets and vets, these dedicated advocates have found a unique way to bring humans and animals together in an unbreakable bond.

ONE

ANIMALS AND VETERANS IN AMERICA: THEIR ENDURING BONDS AND HEALING POWERS

"I think dogs are the most amazing creatures; they give unconditional love. For me, they are the role model for being alive. For our nation's disabled veterans, they are also their lifeline."

—*Gilda Radner*

ANIMALS HAVE ALWAYS BEEN AN IMPORTANT PART OF OUR LIVES. DOG breeds were portrayed in prehistoric paintings in caves throughout Rome and Greece. They were written about extensively by ancient authors, extolling their value as protectors and companions. Dogs have gone into battle, served as guards and companions, kept herds together, hunted game, and worked side by side with man as part of one of the most collaborative, enduring, and emotional relationships on the planet.

Virgil said of the power and influence of dogs: "Never with them on guard need you fear for your stalls a midnight thief, or onslaught of wolves, or Iberian brigands at your back." His fellow Roman, Cato, (ca. 160 BC) was the first known to write extensively about dogs and agriculture. "Dogs must be kept as a matter of course, for no farm is safe without them," he wrote in *De Agri Cultura.*

1

Centuries later, the father of a new nation, and the first president of the United States, George Washington, would adopt this sage advice.

George Washington had a very deep affection for dogs. He owned many throughout his lifetime, including spaniels, terriers, foxhounds, and a newfoundland. He understood the bond between master and pet, as illustrated by one wartime incident.

It happened during the Battle of Germantown, when American forces were trying to contain British General William Howe's troops, which had occupied Philadelphia. The fight was "not going well for the Americans," wrote Dr. Stanley Coren, professor emeritus in the Department of Psychology at the University of British Columbia and an expert on canine psychology, in a 2009 article in *Psychology Today*. "Washington was encamped at Pennibecker's Mill," Dr. Coren wrote. "On October, 9, 1777, a little terrier was seen wandering the area between the American and British lines. It turns out that General Howe's little terrier had somehow gotten loose and had become lost on the battlefield. The dog was identified from its collar and brought to Washington. His officers suggested he might want to keep the dog as a sort of trophy, which might weaken the morale of the British general. Instead, he took the dog to his tent, fed him, and had him brushed and cleaned. Then, to the surprise of everyone, Washington ordered a cease fire. The shooting stopped and soldiers on both sides watched as one of Washington's aides formally returned a little dog to the British commander under a flag of truce."

Future presidents would share Washington's understanding of the value of these faithful companions. "You want a friend in Washington? Get a dog," Harry S. Truman once said.

The remarkable traits that everyone from ancient writers to modern-day presidents observed firsthand are witnessed in our lives today. Dogs are not only beloved pets and family members but are also involved in police work, military missions, farming, ranching, search and rescue, service, and therapy.

Service dogs in America were first used to aid the blind in the 1920s through the Seeing Eye, Inc. program. Since then they have evolved to tackle more complex tasks for people, including those suffering from diabetes, hearing loss, seizures, and many mobility issues. The training for service animals has also evolved, and organizations such as Canine Companions for Independence have helped set rigorous guidelines. Those efforts, coupled with federal legislation that prohibited housing discrimination against people with disabilities and gave them the right to have service dogs accompany them in public, as well as the Americans with Disabilities Act, signed into law by President George H. W. Bush in 1990, have secured the place of service dogs in the lives of anyone in need of their remarkable talents. Companion and therapy animals, too, have a tremendous impact on people. While not licensed service animals, these companion dogs, cats, horses, parrots, owls, hawks, eagles, and even potbelly pigs still play a vital role in the lives of disabled veterans, even giving some the motivation to wake up each and every day.

The US Department of Defense estimates that more than three hundred thousand veterans have been injured during the War of Terror in Iraq and Afghanistan, experiencing physical wounds as well as the devastating symptoms of post-traumatic stress disorder (PTSD) and traumatic brain injury (TBI). Add to those numbers the wounded and disabled from Vietnam, Korea, and World War II. For some of them, day-to-day living is still a challenge. No matter how many years go by, veterans can continue to relive the traumas of war and struggle to assimilate into civilian life. Some overcome these obstacles. Others, sadly, are not so fortunate.

Many veterans have caring professionals and dedicated family members to help in their recovery. And more and more, some very special nonhuman beings have barked, chirped, meowed, or whinnied their way into the hearts of these American patriots.

Service dogs have been specially selected and trained to help the wounded warrior adjust to civilian life and regain physical and emotional independence. Service dogs are trained to perform physical tasks a disabled veteran cannot do on his or her own and can assist with other chores. For instance, a Canine Companions for Independence assistance dog may pull a manual wheelchair, retrieve dropped items or prostheses, alert a hard-of-hearing handler to a sound in the environment, or turn on a light. Other assistance dogs can be trained to help people with psychological disabilities, including sensing or interrupting a panic attack or finding a safe egress for someone who needs to leave a stressful environment.

Companion and therapy dogs do not have legal service status but still play a vital role in veterans' lives, relieving stress, combatting loneliness and isolation, and providing unconditional love and support. These animals have been around since World War II, when they visited wounded service members in hospitals. That tradition continues today in VA facilities across the country. Their mere presence can lighten up even a warfighter's darkest days.

Quantifying the tremendous positive effect of animals on veterans with disabilities is no easy task, but the Department of Veterans Affairs and some nonprofit organizations are trying to do exactly that. The US Congress mandated that the VA study the efficacy of service dogs and veterans suffering from PTSD and other emotional issues in 2010. The initial VA study was curtailed after a year, but a new three-year study, with Canine Companions for Independence as a research partner, began in 2015. That effort enlisted 220 veterans with PTSD from Atlanta, Iowa City, and Portland, Oregon, in an attempt to answer the question, "Can service dogs and other animals improve the quality of life for veterans diagnosed with posttraumatic stress disorder?"

Many veterans with service dogs and companion animals can already answer the question for themselves. But research data could help make the animals more widely available, with the blessing of government agencies that care for veterans.

The VA currently does not pay for service dogs for veterans with PTSD, but they do for many with physical injuries. To obtain service dogs, the VA evaluates veterans' needs, reviews their cases, and makes a determination if they qualify. If they do, the VA refers the veterans to accredited agencies where they can obtain a certified service dog. There is no cost for the dog or its training, but the veteran does have to pay for the dog's food, grooming, board, and other costs associated with owning a service dog. Veterans who are not approved by the VA for service dogs still can secure them but often must rely on donations to purchase and train the animals, which can cost $20,000 or more. Fortunately, there are many nonprofit organizations and generous individuals willing to help or provide the dog free of charge.

For disabled veterans, service dogs must be specifically trained to mitigate the veterans' disabilities, essentially performing tasks the veterans cannot do. For example, someone who uses a wheelchair might rely on his or her dog to open doors or pick up objects, while a person who uses prosthetic legs might need a dog's physical assistance to steady him or her while walking. Once veterans and their service dogs are connected, owners can register their dogs and receive identification cards, vests, and other materials that help them understand what their dogs need in order to perform as a certified service dog, though this is not required by the Americans with Disabilities Act (ADA). However, it may benefit veterans to have their dogs identified by wearing vests to alert a passerby that the animal is working and should not be petted when out in public. While the registration of service animals is not mandated by the ADA, they, like all dogs, are subject to the same state and local vaccination and licensing rules.

Individuals with a disability are entitled, thanks to the ADA, to a service dog that can help them live their lives normally. The ADA allows them to bring their service dogs with them to most places that the public is permitted, including restaurants, hotels, housing complexes, and even aboard airplanes. They can also accompany their owners if they are hospitalized or even riding in an ambulance. The important distinction is that the dogs are trained to be working animals; they are not pets.

While a certified service dog may take as much as two years to train, companion animals are more readily available. Though not trained to perform specific tasks, these animals come in all shapes and sizes and give veterans unconditional love and support. They also help relieve anxiety, as well as mitigate panic attacks, the symptoms of PTSD, and more. Since some companions come from the many animal shelters that pair vets and pets, the newly formed teams share one thing in common—a new lease on life. The veteran now has help overcoming emotional obstacles, and the animal is saved from loneliness or worse.

Beth Zimmerman, founder and executive director of the nonprofit organization Pets for Patriots, has seen firsthand the power of the animal-human bond. "I started Pets for Patriots because I felt a calling," said Zimmerman. "I had the realization that there are two populations with complementary needs; I wanted to find ways to overcome the obstacles of bringing them together. Across our country are veterans who need a new pet friend in their lives, for any number of reasons, and there are millions of animals who are overlooked, undervalued, and facing death if not adopted. We officially launched Pets for Patriots in 2010, and we now have 260 shelter/rescue partners across the country, with more joining every week."

Pets for Patriots has helped more than a thousand veterans adopt a loving best friend and has placed an equal number of the most overlooked shelter animals into good homes. The organization also maintains a small veterinary fund to help with unexpected medical costs and assists veterans experiencing temporary financial hardship so they aren't forced into returning their pets to a shelter.

Zimmerman believes every American can contribute. "All of us have a commitment to provide the best possible care to the men and women who serve our nation," she said. "While the slogan 'Support Our Troops' is a great bumper sticker, we need to ask ourselves, 'What am I doing to make this a reality?' This includes supporting innovative organizations with demonstrable success, like ours and others, that have found efficient, effective, and meaningful ways to make life for our veterans better. We owe our veterans more than they ask for and certainly more than they get."

While dogs get a lion's share of attention as companion and service animals, they are not the only species making a difference.

Cats, just like dogs and other domesticated animals, love us unconditionally, and that can be especially true of those that were abandoned and abused. Cats also have very distinct and endearing personalities. Some are intelligent and independent, while others are in need of companionship. Regardless of their individual characteristics, each deserves someone to love them and provide food, water, and shelter. Sadly, for many that is only a pipe dream.

Another way to contribute came from Buzz Miller, a retired Philadelphia attorney who wanted to help veterans find safe and loving foster homes for their pets while they were deployed. Most people don't realize the strain on animals when their owners are overseas for long periods of time. So, in 2011, Buzz founded a nonprofit organization called PACT, which stands for People, Animals, Companions Together. PACT has more than two hundred volunteer families in Pennsylvania, New Jersey, and Delaware, with a network of foster services in twenty-three states. Hundreds of families take care of all kinds of animals, including, dogs, cats, horses, and others in need of a temporary home. PACT takes great pains to match pets with foster families, including an extensive prescreening process. Buzz also provides all foster families with the items needed to care for pets and facilitates communication between the veteran and foster family so that both are comfortable with the arrangement. Many dedicated professionals, including animal trainers and veterinarians, volunteer for PACT.

The nonprofit organization Canine Warrior Connection, founded by Rick Yount, a licensed social worker who lives in Boyds, Maryland, uses a novel approach to train dogs for veterans with disabilities: enlisting post-deployment wounded warriors who are facing their own emotional and physical challenges to train the dogs. By using what they refer to as a mission-based trauma recovery model, the warrior trainers work with the dogs from the time they are puppies through adulthood. Then, after the rigorous program is completed, they deliver certified service dogs to their fellow veterans with disabilities. Rick's work was so impressive that he was asked to establish the Warrior Dog Training Program at Walter Reed's Army Transition Brigade and was invited to be part of the PTSD and TBI program at the National Intrepid Center of Excellence in Bethesda, Maryland. In 2011, Warrior Canine Connection was formally created to provide services and research to the VA and the Department of Defense related to wounded warriors with PTSD and TBI and how training service dogs helps mitigate those symptoms.

Buzz, Beth, and Rick, and others, have dedicated their lives to finding innovative ways to make a difference. They steadfastly believe that no animal or wounded warrior should ever be left behind or underestimated.

Like dogs, parrots and other exotic pets are often abandoned by their owners. They become too large, too old, too expensive, or just too much trouble. One innovative exotic bird rescue is addressing that problem.

The West Los Angeles campus of the Department of Veterans Affairs has a program called Feathered Friends, in partnership with Serenity Park/ Parrot CARE, a nonprofit founded by Dr. Lorin Lindner. The program is part of the long-range VA study of the efficacy of service and companion animals on veterans with PTSD.

At Serenity Park, wounded veterans care for abandoned parrots each and every day in large outdoor habitats as if they were their own pets. In addition to the regular interaction, the birds get fresh food daily, including their favorites—eucalyptus, fruits, vegetables, seeds, and nuts.

"Parrots have been popular companions throughout history because they are intelligent, charismatic, colorful and musical," according to *National Geographic*. "The male African gray parrot is the most accomplished user of human speech in the animal world; this rain forest-dweller is an uncanny mimic."

It is no surprise, then, that these bright, lovable birds offer support and companionship to those who need them.

Surprisingly, rescue and care for wounded birds of prey also provides veterans a haven to enjoy nature and relieve stress. At Avian Veteran Alliance in Largo, Florida, army veteran Patrick Bradley, an expert in raptors and many other animal species, started a program that pairs veterans with birds of prey, including red tail hawks, owls, and eagles. Over the past four years, more than two thousand veterans have been able to put a bird on their arm and go for a walk. The connections formed have resulted in qualitative examples of the healing power of these majestic birds and the positive impact they have had on wounded veterans.

Horses, too, have become emotional lifelines to many of our nation's wounded heroes. In 2006, the Walter Reed National Military Medical Center worked with the US Army's Caisson Platoon to pair wounded soldiers with horses from the Third US Infantry Regiment (the Old Guard) from Ft. Myer, Virginia. They found that the soldiers benefitted from relationships with horses, and that sparked similar programs around the country. For example, Horses Helping Heroes Project helps veterans suffering from PTSD and TBI regain social skills, confidence, and trust by caring for horses and interacting with them in a peaceful, nurturing setting. Veterans have programs tailored just for them and feel more connected to and excited about life by interacting with these majestic animals. Another innovative program, the Jinx McCain Horsemanship Program, has helped dozens of veterans regain confidence and social skills while working as cowboys.

As the VA accumulates data to confirm that animals can have a positive effect on veterans with PTSD and other disabilities, thousands right now are experiencing the healing powers of their canine, feline, equestrian, and avian companions firsthand. From helping open doors to calming frayed nerves and making them laugh, or by just being by their sides, these special animals and heroic veterans are redefining the animal-human bond.

Most of all, vets and their pets are helping each other heal from the horrors of war, loneliness, isolation, and abandonment. Together they are stronger. They are living their lives as they should, with love, hope, acceptance, and defiance!

PART I

AT YOUR SERVICE

TWO

THE ARMY SPECIALIST

"A reason to get out of bed in the morning."

H E'S KNOWN AROUND TOWN BY JUST HIS FIRST NAME. HIS PIERCING GOLD eyes penetrate everyone he meets like a dagger. With his head the size of a basketball and erect ears pointing toward the heavens, this 150-pound phenom knows how to make an entrance. Grown men shudder when he walks down the street, running to the other side for fear that their lives might be in danger. Unlike some of his furry cohorts, he's a dog on a mission. He's named for the Greek god of music, poetry, art, oracles, plague, medicine, sun, archery, and knowledge, and he takes his job seriously. After all, he's responsible for helping a dashing young wounded warrior recover after having both of his legs blown off in a mucky field in Afghanistan.

Meet Apollo. The handsome and powerful red European Doberman pinscher that gave retired US Army Specialist Tyler Jeffries his life back.

Owners of European Dobermans will tell you that their dogs are very loyal, intelligent, and fiercely protective of their families. The Dobermans have elegant bodies that are a joy to behold. Their movements can be graceful and at the same time project a powerful determination that often belies their gentle souls. And like their fellow canine breeds—pit bull terriers and Rottweilers—they are not generally the type of dogs that are chosen as service dogs for people with disabilities. "That's a damn shame," according to Tyler. "I like Apollo just because he's different. So many people think Dobermans are mean and aggressive, but it's all in how you bring them up and train them. I like proving people wrong by telling them what these amazing dogs have done in battle over many years and what my Doberman has done for me."

Dobermans, along with German shepherds, played a significant role in both World Wars. They protected soldiers in bunkers, alerted them to danger, found casualties, detected landmines, and more. "The Dobermans were the first dogs in battle to claim over three hundred confirmed kills," Tyler added. "They would sit in the foxholes with the sleeping soldiers so they could hear any potential threat. The marines also had their own group of dogs who were specially trained in battle and they were called the 'Devil Dogs.' They were far from devils in my opinion." In the South Pacific, twenty-five Devil Dogs were killed in the Battle of Guam in 1944. Today these remarkable dogs are remembered in a memorial devoted to their bravery, sacrifice, and heroism.

The truth is European Dobermans do make wonderful service dogs thanks to their rich history of service, intelligence, and obedience. They love to work and are happiest and at their best when they have a job and know what is expected of them. Stephen Parsons, the owner and trainer of Family Dobes in Salt Lake City, Utah, who has been breeding Doberman pinschers for more than twenty years, says, "Dobermans will not be dogs that just lay on the front porch and bark at strangers. Dobermans want a job. Dobermans want to please you. Dobermans have a deterrent look to them that keeps the bad guys at bay, but they are not the mean, vicious dogs that Hollywood has convinced people they are. Rather, they are smart enough to be good actors, and Hollywood chooses them over some of the harder-to-work-with breeds. Dobermans are everything I want in a dog for the lifestyle I lead."

For Tyler, getting to know Apollo was his lifeline to recovery from catastrophic injuries that almost killed him on October 6, 2012. Tyler had been in the US Army for four years and was in Kandahar Province in Afghanistan. As an army infantryman, Specialist Jeffries was a jack of all trades, working as a vehicle gunner, minesweeper, or whatever else was required. The job requires smarts, flexibility, and quick thinking.

Tyler, like Apollo, has never met a challenge he didn't embrace. On that clear Saturday morning, Tyler was about to leave on a mission when a soldier in his platoon who was supposed to sweep for landmines volunteered for another job. Tyler, the consummate team player, volunteered to take the man's place. He grabbed the minesweeper and off he and his buddies went to complete the day's tasks. After sweeping most of a village and clearing it of landmines, Tyler and his platoon took a quick break, sitting on the side of the road for a few minutes. It was a welcome relief from a grueling day. Suddenly, Tyler heard his lieutenant say, "Let's get this done." Tyler replied, "Sure, let's go."

Tyler grabbed his gear, stood up, and took only three small steps when he heard a loud *boom!* A remote-controlled improvised explosive device (IED) blew up without him having any idea it was there. "It was like it wasn't even real," said Tyler. "I was afraid to look down at my legs, and I remember thinking that I didn't want to die in this god-forsaken place. There was blood everywhere, and it wasn't long before I heard my buddies screaming and running toward me through the smoke from the blast."

What they found wasn't a pretty sight. The IED blew off Tyler's legs—his right one below the knee and his left at the knee. He also sustained severe burns on his arms and nose; his prognosis was not good. "I was one of the few guys blown up by an IED who was awake and conscious through the whole thing," said Tyler. "I was laughing and joking with my guys as they were applying the tourniquets and trying to keep me awake and talking. But deep down I was really scared and wasn't sure if I would ever go home again."

He did come home, but not before a harrowing emotional and physical experience. As he lay on the murky, cold dirt, still bleeding through the three tourniquets on what was left of his legs, Tyler pleaded for his life. "I kept telling my guys, 'Hey, don't leave me here; I don't want to die like this.'" They reassured him that the medivac chopper was on its way. The closest it could land, though, was in a field on the other side of a small pond; the soldiers didn't miss a beat. "These guys didn't even stop to look for IEDs. All they cared about was just getting me to safety," said Tyler. His buddies lifted Tyler up over their heads, keeping a close eye on the tourniquets, and carried him slowly across the water to the landing site. Almost as soon as they crossed the bank, the chopper arrived.

After being stabilized in Afghanistan, he was sent to the US military hospital in Germany and then to Walter Reed in Bethesda, Maryland. There, his mother, Pam, and other family members helped him during his long and painful recovery. Tyler was an inpatient for more than four months and then moved to Building 62—an apartment building on the hospital campus where wounded warriors and their families live during their outpatient rehabilitation. "I remember the doctors and nurses telling me to take it slow and get used to walking on my prosthetic legs. I would be lying if I said it was easy, but I'm kind of hardheaded and wanted to get out of the hospital as soon as I could," he said. Within one and a half months, Tyler was up and walking on his new legs. All told, Tyler would spend nearly two years at Walter Reed.

He faced even more adjustments after returning home to North Carolina. "It was tough for me in the beginning," Tyler explains. "I had just retired from the army and was having trouble adjusting to my new reality. Not only did I not have a job, but I also had no legs, and getting used to my prosthetics was rough. The legs are really heavy and I have to stop and sit down because of the pain. Plus, all of us wounded warriors experience what they call phantom pain in our legs, even though we don't have any. I wouldn't wish this on anyone."

As with many wounded warriors, being away from their buddies and returning home to civilian life can be daunting. "I had a tough time even going out to the store or the gym because people would always stare at me and that was really annoying," Tyler added. "It made me so self-conscious that I didn't want to go out of my house many times. I remember signing up for a gym and walking in for the first time to stares and people looking away from me. That's why I wanted to buy gym equipment and have it installed in my house, to avoid all of those kinds of people."

Over time, though, Tyler fought through the emotional and physical pain like the tough soldier he is. But no amount of therapy or medication could ever measure up to the healing power of the very special relationship he was about to have with an intelligent and sometimes willfully disobedient Doberman, Apollo.

"I fell in love with European Dobermans when I went to a benefit held for me in North Carolina," Tyler said. "That's where I met Clay Burwell, who was a former army guy. We hit it off right away. He showed me some pictures of his dog, named Zulu, who was a European Doberman. I told him I wish I had a dog like that." Clay responded, "Hey, man, I can make that happen for you. And since you need a service dog, I can ask my friend Brandon McMillan to see if he can help too."

Clay made good on his promise. The next day he called Brandon, who by that time had popular television shows on both Animal Planet and CBS. Clay explained Tyler's situation, and without hesitation, Brandon volunteered his time to train any dog that Tyler purchased. "I was hoping I could get a Doberman like Clay's dog, but they were so expensive and I just didn't have that kind of cash," Tyler said. "As luck would have it, Clay knew a breeder, and that breeder actually had a puppy that turned out to be Zulu's cousin. Clay showed me a picture of the only red Doberman in the litter. I said, 'I want him.'" But the cost for that gorgeous puppy was a whopping $18,000! He came from a very good bloodline, Tyler was told, and was especially elegant, a model of the breed—hence the high price tag.

"I loved that dog, but I was afraid he would be out of my reach financially, so I was heartbroken. But before I knew it, Clay found a woman from New York City to pay for the dog. She donated all of the money and then sent a check to the breeder almost immediately. So between the cost of the dog and the cost of the six-month training, I figured Apollo was a $55,000 dog."

Once everyone was on board, and all the details worked out, it was time for Brandon to create a training program that would ensure Apollo was ready to help Tyler with his physical and emotional needs. "Between Brandon and that woman who paid for Apollo, I can honestly say they both saved my life," Tyler said. "I could not be more thankful, and it's because of them that I have a reason to get out of bed in the morning."

Brandon McMillan has spent his entire life training and living with animals. Both his father and uncle were trainers with Ringling Brothers, and his love of animals began almost from his birth. In addition to hosting the popular shows *Night*, on Animal Planet, and *Lucky Dog*, on CBS, he has also worked on many films and trained a wide range of animal species. His passion, though, is helping dogs by rescuing them and finding them permanent, loving homes. So it was no surprise to anyone who knows him that he would agree to train a service dog for Tyler, as well as other wounded warriors.

Tyler was eager to meet Apollo, but he would have to wait six months during the pup's initial training with Brandon. It was the longest six months of Tyler's life. "I called Brandon every day to see what Apollo was doing and how he was," Tyler said. "It was funny, that the first thing Brandon did when he picked him up and brought him back to California with him for his training was take him to Home Depot."

One of Brandon's first concerns was to make sure Apollo had what it took to become a certified service dog. He put him through a series of tests at Home Depot, such as walking up and down the aisles and seeing how he interacted with people. Brandon even put the Doberman in front of a giant mirror to see how he related to his reflection. There were many more tests, and luckily for Tyler, Apollo passed with flying colors. "Believe it or not, I didn't meet Brandon or Apollo until the training was almost done. Brandon asked me to send him a hoodie and three T-shirts, which he put in Apollo's crate so that he would remember my scent and would know it was me when we finally met." The long wait was worth it. "I went to California for a week of training before I got him," said Tyler. "When I first laid my eyes on him I was speechless. I waited so long to see him. I swear I have never seen a more beautiful dog. We clicked right away, and it was like we belonged together; I couldn't be happier."

The initial week-long training focused on helping Tyler when he was using his prosthetic legs. "We worked to train Apollo to be able to make sure I don't trip going up and down the stairs. I use his back as my brace, and when I give him the command to 'Brace,' he knows what to do," said Tyler.

Tyler and Apollo, along with Brandon, would take long walks along Venice Beach, the famous "Muscle Beach." It was there that all of the skills Apollo learned with Brandon could now be applied to his new master. Apollo could help Tyler pick up objects and open doors, as well as alert him to strangers and be his steady sidekick in case of a fall. By the end of the week, the dog was ready to head to Maryland, where Tyler shared a home with his mom.

On the flight east, Tyler and Apollo were clearly bonded. Apollo wouldn't leave Tyler's side. The first night they slept together, Apollo was a bit shy. Tyler was sure that it was because he was adjusting to him plus being in new surroundings. By the next night, the two of them spent hours playing on the bed, wrestling with each other and just horsing around. They had a great time. "The one thing I learned in my training with Brandon was that when a service dog has its vest on, something clicks inside them and they know it's time to work. When the vest comes off, the dog becomes a normal dog again. He knows that he can chase a ball or do whatever he wants to do," Tyler said. "It is amazing to me that when Apollo is in full-focus mode, his eyes are locked on me waiting for a command. That's when he knows it's all business." Apollo was so tuned in to Tyler that soon he didn't need a specific command to "brace." Apollo could sense Tyler's need for stability and was there to catch him if he was about to fall.

In the four years that Tyler and Apollo have been a team, Tyler has been transformed. No longer is he afraid to be seen in public, fearing ridicule and piercing stares from people. "Thanks to Apollo, I have grown so much. He got me out of the house more, helped me become more independent, and took the pressure off. Now, when I walk into a room, people run up to

Apollo. They could care less about me! They say things like, 'Oh my God, can I pet him?' Or they say, 'Oh man, let me back up and walk away. Your dog is scary and big.' Other people just stop us so they can take pictures. I used to say before I got married that Apollo is a chick magnet. Now I believe he is a magnet in general."

The one quality about these giant dogs that people don't often get to see while they are working is their very human-like and intuitive side. Tyler recalled the first night back in the apartment he shared with his mom off-base. It was a terrible sleepless evening. So, the next morning Tyler tried sleeping in, with Apollo snuggled under the covers with him. Around eleven in the morning, Pam knocked on the door. As she turned the doorknob to look in the room, Apollo poked his head out of the covers and growled fiercely. Pam, frightened by the sound and the sight of the big Doberman, slowly backed up and left the two boys alone to continue their nap. "That was amazing to me because I could tell that all Apollo wanted was for me to get some extra sleep," said Tyler. So the two of them cuddled back under the covers, with Apollo's giant head and paws resting peacefully against Tyler's body.

In just a few weeks, Apollo learned to love Pam, even taking some commands from her. This family of three was well on its way to recovery.

Soon other members of the family would get to know Apollo—Tyler's young daughter, Ella, and eventually, his fiancé and soon to be wife, Lauren.

The first night Lauren spent with her new boyfriend, was, as she recalls, "A trip." Apollo, according to Tyler, has this habit of "stalking." He lowers his massive body almost down to the floor, perks his ears even higher than they already are, and slowly slithers toward the person or animal he is focused on. "I was freaked out," Lauren said. "He was actually stalking me. I was terrified the first time I saw him do that, so much so that I went outside to sleep. That was quite a night!" Despite their rocky beginning, Lauren and Apollo have their own special relationship. Lauren says she thinks it's because she is the one that feeds him. "He protects everybody, especially Tyler, but he sure does listen to me when he wants his breakfast or dinner."

Strangely, Apollo has formed a bond with a nonhuman member of the Jeffries family: their cat, Bullet. "One day we saw Apollo and Bullet chasing each other around the house. We just cracked up," said Lauren. "The two of them take naps together, cuddle up on the couch, and Bullet even walks along Apollo's back sometimes. He doesn't even blink."

Ella, too, thinks nothing of jumping on Apollo's back and riding him like a horse. "Apollo's obedience training and natural tolerance allow him to do things that he may or may not want to do," Tyler said. "Sometimes I can tell that he doesn't want to do something and he is not happy about it, either. You can hear him sigh, or complain a little bit. But when he wants something, like a big monster bone, he will nudge you forever just to make sure you know that he is serious."

With Apollo by his side, Tyler's life has turned around dramatically. He is having an accessible smart home built for him in North Carolina by the Gary Sinise Foundation. Gary called him personally to let him know he was chosen to receive the custom-made house, which can take up to a year to build. Tyler also has a plan to help other wounded warriors through a program where they can hunt, fish, and shoot. Of course, the greatest change in his life is that he is now a happily married man.

Tyler experienced the thrill of a lifetime when, in August 2015, he was among a group of wounded warriors and their moms who were invited to visit both Presidents Bush—41 and 43—and First Ladies Barbara and Laura Bush, at their summer home in Kennebunkport, Maine. It was a hot August afternoon when the group descended upon Walker's Point. They were at least twenty strong, including warriors on wheelchairs and on prosthetic legs. The Bush family couldn't have been more gracious. Despite George H. W. Bush being in a wheelchair and wearing a neck brace after a recent fall, he was delighted to see some of the warriors and military mothers that he holds dear to his heart. As everyone was chatting and getting to know each other, someone from the group mentioned to George W. Bush that Tyler was planning to propose to Lauren later that day at a popular waterfront restaurant in town. Suddenly, President Bush said to Tyler: "Hey, where is your fiancé?" Tyler said that Lauren was about five minutes away with Ella and Apollo. "Well, get her over here," the president said.

One of the moms turned to Tyler and asked him if he could muster up the courage to propose to Lauren right then and there. He was speechless but managed to mumble, "Sure." As Lauren arrived, it was obvious that she, too, was nervous. As she walked up the long driveway, Tyler was beginning to sweat. Wounded warriors missing legs tend to sweat more than the average person anyway, but this time was worse. It is nerve-wracking enough to propose in private, let alone right in front of a group that included two presidents and first ladies. As Lauren approached Tyler, she reached out to give him a big hug. Then, Tyler, with the help of his wounded warrior friend

Jeffrey Shonk, got down on his prosthetic knee. Before he could get even one word out, Lauren shouted, "Yes!"

The following April, Tyler and Lauren were married at a beautiful North Carolina lakeside resort. The Bushes were all invited but couldn't attend because of previous commitments. However, they sent Lauren and Tyler a beautiful letter, which the happy couple quickly framed. As they said their vows, Apollo was there by Tyler's side. Ever the loyal service dog, Apollo was working that day. But it was a labor of love—a testament to the deep bond between man and dog that has stood the test of time.

The fierce red European Doberman pinscher and the intrepid wounded warrior found each other by accident and pain. Their love and devotion to each other, though, is nothing but pure bliss.

THREE

THE MARINE TANK COMMANDER

"That's what that dog is for."

JIMMY DIDEAR WAS BACKED INTO A CORNER, WITH AN ELEVATOR BEHIND him, a glass partition to his left, and a wall to his right. Directly in front of him—almost in his face—was a VA police officer. He was asking questions, lots of them, about Jimmy and his service dog, Max. Not getting the answers he wanted, the officer kept pushing. And the more he pressed, the madder Jimmy got.

"I don't know if you've ever been in a situation where you're up against the wall and you can't get out of it," Jimmy said. "You're gonna come over the top of somebody. I know how to do it. I know how to put this guy down and make sure he doesn't come back."

Max is a ninety-four-pound mix of chocolate Labrador and American bull terrier that Jimmy had brought with him to his weekly Tuesday morning group session at the Corpus Christi VA Specialty Clinic. As he and other vets waited for the counselor to arrive, Jimmy was letting Max stretch his legs and get some water. The officer spotted them and approached.

"This guy corners me and starts asking me a bunch of questions about the dog," Jimmy recalled. "Like, 'Is he a service dog? What is his job? What is he trained to do?' And all this other stuff. The more he talked, the madder I got. And I told this clown, 'You can only ask me two questions. The Americans with Disabilities Act and the VA say you can only ask me two

20

questions: Is he a certified service dog and what is his purpose? You cannot ask me what my problem is. You cannot ask me why he's with me or any of these other things.'"

Jimmy could see his fellow group members watching the confrontation from the other side of the glass partition. Jimmy, a hot-tempered former marine tanker who had served twenty-two months in Vietnam, was steaming.

"You do not want to corner me," Jimmy stated matter of factly in his smooth Texas accent. "It was embarrassing as hell, and I was getting madder and madder. I was at the point where I was fixing to go over this guy—and one of us was not going to get up."

Instead, Max acted. He reached up with his mouth and took hold of Jimmy's hand. It wasn't a bite. It wasn't meant to cause pain. He just gently applied pressure, trying to redirect Jimmy's attention.

"And I snapped out of it," Jimmy said. "I came back down, and I looked down at him and he was looking up at me. And I see that he had positioned himself in between me and this guy."

As the argument heated up, the officer had inched closer and closer. But Max had stepped between them, nudging them apart, without either of the men realizing what was happening. And the touch of the dog's mouth on his hand had calmed Jimmy down, focused him. He looked the officer square in the eye and declared:

"That's what that dog is for."

Jimmy was still shaking when he and Max joined the group. The other vets had told the counselor what had occurred, so they all took time that day to talk it through, with Max attentively by Jimmy's side. In some sessions, when Jimmy is calm, Max will lay on the floor next to him, maybe even sleep. Not today. Jimmy was agitated, and Max was on high alert, ready to be the calm presence his handler needed. "I threatened I was not coming back to group," Jimmy said. But no one wanted that, neither his fellow vets nor the VA staff.

The Vietnam veterans in the support group know from experience how valuable Max is. "The guys want me to bring him because if they are having a problem, if they are getting upset in the session, Max will go up to them and put his head in their laps or crawl up on them," Jimmy said. "He gets them to pay attention to him, and then they start coming back to reality, back to the States. So he's working for me and the rest of them."

The staff is equally welcoming. And they went out of their way after the incident by the elevator to assure Jimmy that they wanted him to keep coming to the clinic.

"They sent me a whole bunch of emails, telling me that everything is covered, don't worry, come on back, don't mess up what you got going," Jimmy said. "So now, every time I go over there, everybody wants to know, 'Where's your dog?' Even the doctors will ask, 'Hey, where's Max? How come you didn't bring Max? We don't want to see you, we want to see Max.'"

Behind the teasing is something that they and Jimmy understand: since teaming up with Max, the combat vet has come far in his decades-long battle to live with post-traumatic stress disorder (PTSD).

Jimmy Didear has spent most of his life in Corpus Christi, Texas. There was a time, before he turned two years old, when he lived in a much smaller community, what he calls a "poke and plum" town. As in, when you poke your head out the window, you're plum past the town.

His father was a truck driver and his mom a waitress. When his dad opened the United Van Lines agency in Corpus Christi, his mother went to work in the business, as did Jimmy and his four sisters, even down to picking up nails off the driveway. While attending W. B. Ray High School in the early 1960s, Jimmy was into ducktails, motorcycle jackets, fast cars—and girls. He found them so distracting that he wound up repeating ninth grade. "I didn't study a whole lot and got into trouble," he said. After graduating in 1964, he hauled furniture all over the country for his father but also worked part time for a funeral home. (One of his tasks was driving an ambulance, which was needed for emergencies at the local racetrack. That was perfect for Jimmy, who got to attend races for free.) The long-distance driving wasn't for him, though, so the next year he headed for Houston to attend the Commonwealth School of Mortuary Science. While he finished the one-year course of study, the war in Southeast Asia was heating up.

"At that time, Vietnam was rocking and rolling and people were getting drafted," he recalled. "I decided I was not going to get drafted. They were putting everybody in either the army or the navy, and I didn't want to wear bell bottoms or hip huggers. I wanted something that looked cool, so I joined the Marine Corps."

A month after graduation, in September 1966, he was headed to boot camp in San Diego, California—a Hollywood marine, he says. He vividly recalls the screaming drill sergeants who met the recruits at the airport late on that first night and the civilian onlookers pointing and laughing. "You're thinking, 'You can't talk to me like that around these people,'" Jimmy said. "But, yes, they can."

On base, there was the ritual assembly line for haircuts, one right after the other, with the electric razor so hot from continuous use that it burned Jimmy's scalp. They were issued yellow sweatshirts emblazoned with "US Marine Corps" and marched to their Quonset hut barracks. It was two or three in the morning by then, and they thought it was finally time for some well-deserved rest. "Ha," Jimmy said looking back, laughing at their naiveté. "Five o'clock came and we were up and at it. Then the fun started."

Weeks of grueling physical training and mental toughening followed. Jimmy remembers the fence that separated the marine base from the San Diego airport, and the stories of recruits scaling it to escape boot camp. "I thought about it," he admits. "Boot camp was rough. But every night when I went to bed I told myself, 'If I'm here tomorrow morning, then I'm going to try one more day.'"

Of course there was a reason for the Marine Corps to induce all that anguish and conditioning. "They needed to see how far they could push you," Jimmy said. "It's all psychological. Sure there might've been a little pain to it, but not something that was long lasting. They are there to break you down and rebuild you into a person who can possibly survive in a war. That's their main objective, to make sure you come home."

That point about endurance, and never quitting, was driven home to Jimmy after a day at the rifle range. The recruits had been driven the five miles or so from their barracks to the range, and the plan was to have them march back. It was a forced march, not quite a run but using a fast-paced, forty-inch step. Once back at the barracks, they were ordered to run around the parade ground. After three laps, the drill instructor announced that anyone who wanted to take a break was welcome to do so. Jimmy and two others took him up on this uncharacteristically generous offer.

"That was the biggest mistake I ever made," he said. Not only were the three required to run three more laps, but for the rest of the week they had to pack everything they owned in their duffel bags—including sheets, pillows, and bedding—and carry it with them wherever they went. "That taught me a valuable lesson: you don't ever quit."

"That's one of the main things I got out of the Marine Corps, besides the camaraderie and togetherness," Jimmy emphasized. "You don't quit, even if you have a hole in your shoulder or your leg. Don't quit. Just keep going."

By graduation, just a few short months later, Jimmy was a changed man.

"They made a different person out of me," he said. "I was a spoiled little kid. My parents had money and were able to give me what I wanted or needed—though of course I had to work for it. The Marine Corps was different. It taught me to depend on people, how a man's word is his bond. You learn who you can trust and who you can't trust."

And there were lessons in selflessness and sacrifice as well: "You will die for another person. You won't even think about it. I saw it. We saw it every day and we lived it every day in Vietnam."

Jimmy arrived in Da Nang, the port city in what was then the northern end of South Vietnam, in late March 1967, part of the First Tank Battalion, First Marine Division. Before his permanent assignment to a gun company and tank crew came through, he spent a few weeks at the headquarters company pulling guard duty and on day and night patrols. And there he saw how the lines between friend and foe could quickly blur in that war.

"We had a barber who cut hair for us on the base," he said. "One day he was cutting hair, and then one night we killed him coming through the fence with a satchel charge. He was Vietcong. They were all over."

By May Jimmy was with Charlie Company, Fifth Platoon. Each platoon had five M48A3 "Patton" tanks, armed with a ninety-millimeter gun and a crew of four (commander, gunner, loader, driver), and one "flame" tank, an M67 with a crew of three that carried 360 gallons of diesel or napalm. Tanks, with a maximum speed of thirty miles per hour, were used for infantry support, accompanying patrols and crews clearing roads of mines. There were security details too. At night, a tank might be posted at each end of a village, along the main road, to ensure safety for the locals. But regardless of the mission, no day was routine.

"They put mines all over the place," said Jimmy, who initially was a driver. A mine might break a tank tread, or worse. Sometimes the crew could do the repair on site with spare parts, ever watchful for further attacks. "I hit seven mines while I was there. They can really rattle your cage."

"So you lived under that fear all the time," Jimmy said. "When am I going to hit something? Or when am I going to get overrun? You're on heightened alert from the time you land until the time you come home—and even after you come home you're still hyperalert. You're always watching your surroundings."

In December and January they were hit hard, while on search-and-destroy missions near the DMZ, the strip of no man's land that separated

North and South Vietnam. They worked along the coast from ships—landing, clearing an area, and then reboarding. In late December, a rocket-propelled grenade hit one of their tanks, killing a crew member named Clarence Willis Obie III. A month later, maneuvering through burial mounds in a cemetery in Quang Tri, they were hit again. One RPG smashed into Jimmy's tank, and moments later, another struck the vehicle to his right. Only moments before, his tank commander had told Jimmy to "drop down and button up," meaning drive without his head sticking out of the tank, the latch above him securely fastened. Jimmy obeyed, but the tank on his right had not buttoned up, and David Dodson was killed.

Jimmy was rocked by the blast his tank took, but otherwise okay. However, he was on his own. The tank's intercom was down, and in those first seconds after the RPG hit, he didn't know if his fellow crew members were alive or dead in the smoky confines of the tank. He did know he had to get out of there, fast. He had seen how an RPG could chew through metal and was expecting more hits on his tank.

"When you're sitting in there and you're fixing to get hit again, and you can't see behind you because of all the smoke, and you can't get anybody to answer you on the intercom, so you don't know if the other guys in the tank are alive or dead, it's a lonely, lonely feeling," Jimmy said. "How I got the tank out of there I have no clue. I guess the grace of God."

He'd had to back out to the safety of the tree line, careful not to expose the more vulnerable rear of the tank, where the motor is, to another RPG. "If you're hit in the back, where the engine is and where we kept our ninety-millimeter rounds, it's over," Jimmy said. And while backing to safety, he'd had to avoid the burial mounds around him, for fear that he'd get hung up and make his tank a sitting duck.

That was harrowing enough. But then, once safe, his commanding officer came over with news: he was now in charge of a tank and its crew.

It was dark, so Jimmy still couldn't tell then who had survived the attack and who had not. He does remember seeing bodies wrapped in ponchos waiting to be taken away by helicopter. One thing was certain, though: there were enough casualties so that he, Lance Corporal Didear, was now in charge of a tank and its crew.

"You go from being a crewman to somebody who is in charge of three other people's lives. That's a hell of a responsibility for someone who was just twenty-two," he said. "That was the day my life changed totally."

Having studied mortuary science, Jimmy was no stranger to death. His fellow marines knew of his background and had nicknamed him Digger—he still answers to it today at veterans' reunions. And having been in the country for almost a year, he had seen what war could do. But those two months of combat, and the deaths of Obie and Dodson, hit home. These were people in his own unit, people he knew, people in a close-knit circle of marines who were there to keep each other safe.

He responded to those casualties, and the challenge of command, with a vow. "I made a promise that I'd do everything in my power so that I'd never lose another crewman," he said, "and to accomplish that mission I had to learn how to not show any fear so the guys could trust me." From that starting point, the face he would present to the world was of a no-nonsense hard ass: "If I caught you smoking dope, or you couldn't handle your deal, you didn't have to worry about the enemy because I would send you home in a bag. You were not gonna hurt the rest of us." He believes that discipline paid off. "We became a good team," he said. Most important, while he was in charge his people stayed safe. They were occasionally banged up, but no one else was killed.

Jimmy, though, came dangerously close to death not long after, while trying to drive his tank off a landing craft during the monsoon season. The tank ahead of him drove straight off the gate and safely onto the shore. But before Jimmy could follow, the waves had shifted the boat and he drove his almost fifty-ton vehicle right into a hole. The driver's compartment quickly filled up with water, making escape through that hatch impossible.

"I remember trying to get a breath of air, but there was no air," he recalled. "And then I left. I wasn't there anymore. I drowned."

He vividly describes an out-of-body experience, seeing a hand turning the crank that maneuvered the turret manually if the tank lost power. It was something he could have only seen from the turret, which was physically impossible because a screen inside the tank would have prevented him from moving from the driver's seat to the turret.

"Everything went dark, and next thing I know I'm seeing this hand crank this thing and it can't happen," he said. "We're under water. Nobody could've dove in there and cranked it."

Miraculously, though he can't say how, Jimmy survived. When he came to after this near-death experience, he was on the beach. He heard enemy rounds coming from farther inland onto their position. Then suddenly he was being carried on a stretcher to a helicopter. He spent a few days on a medical ship recovering, and then rejoined his unit, which soon moved south to continue operations near Da Nang.

"A lot of other things happened during my time in Vietnam. There was a lot of blood and guts out there, and we all lived this every day," Jimmy said. "People just don't know what we have been through. That's why I think a lot of us came back and just hid." Physically they come home, he said, but they're caught in a time warp. "I feel like I never left Vietnam," Jimmy said. "I'm still there. I live it every day."

Jimmy married his high school sweetheart when he returned to the States, and the couple, as well as a baby daughter from her first marriage, moved into a trailer near Camp Lejeune, North Carolina. One night the baby was crying, and with the bed up against the wall and Jimmy on the outside, his wife's only way out of the bed was to crawl over him. Neither she nor Jimmy was prepared for what would happen next.

"When I woke up I had her on the floor and I was trying to cut her throat," recalled Jimmy, who had been awakened by her screams. "I didn't have anything in my hand but I was going through the motions. I think that's when a lot of this PTSD started coming out."

Many years later, a counselor would compare PTSD to being on a flight from which some never come down. As he described it to Jimmy, when a traumatic situation occurs, your endorphins, your senses, every part of your being, are at a dramatically heightened level. With the passage of time, and some distance from the dangerous situation, those levels usually return to normal. But that's not always the case for veterans. "A lot of us have gone up and our brains have locked in that position so we can't come back down," Jimmy said. "So we stay in that heightened state of alertness at all times."

To this day, Jimmy watches his back—always—and the people near him. He knows what's going on around him; he knows where the exits are. He can sense the slightest noise—something he learned while listening for people crawling through the bushes toward his position—even when he's asleep.

"That's the life of Vietnam veterans and other people who have been in the military," he said. "You're always living this life. And that's why they end up being by themselves so much."

That night in the trailer, Jimmy snapped out of it at the sound of his wife's screams. After that, if she had to crawl over him to get out of bed, she always woke him up first.

There were debriefings for Jimmy and others on their way home from Vietnam. But that was mostly about what they were allowed to bring out of the country, what was okay to talk about, what photos they could share with family and friends. There was nothing about PTSD, about the difficulties of transitioning from almost two years of combat tanker duty to the real world, where you are not in constant danger of being attacked or overrun, and where every waking minute isn't dedicated to keeping your men alive.

Jimmy described the overall military attitude of the time: "You didn't have a problem. If they didn't issue it, you don't have it. Period."

Not that Jimmy would say there was a problem. He just considered the hyperalertness—like getting up in the night to ensure the perimeter of his home is secure—as normal. The same for the distance he put between himself and others, all others. It was a self-defense mechanism he'd adopted in Vietnam. "You put enough of your friends in a body bag or you send a bunch of your buddies home with parts missing, and you don't connect to anything," Jimmy said. "I had a wall built up around me so that nobody could get to me."

He could sometimes appear connected, as a husband and a father, or at work in the funeral business dealing with clients and bereaved families. "I was out there and able to be around people," he said. "I could pretend that I was being nice or that I was happy. But I wasn't."

Day or night, deep down, part of him was alert for the unexpected. "You're waiting for an explosion," he said, "for someone to pop up and take a shot at you, or just to irritate you, something."

Those closest to him, and those who lived with him, saw behind the facade and bore the brunt of his disconnect. His first marriage ended after twelve years, his second after five. There was distance between him and his children.

"It wasn't any of their faults, it was my fault, but I didn't know it was my fault," he said. "Like my ex-wives always said, I had no heart and I was cold. But I just thought everyone else was crazy, or everyone else had problems, or everyone else didn't understand."

They couldn't possibly understand, in part because he never talked about the war, or what he saw, or what he did.

Compounding the isolation was the reception that many Vietnam veterans had received on their return home, often during their very first moments back in the United States. "When we came back we were called murderers, baby killers, rapists," said Jimmy, who, on his way home, encountered demonstrators at the airports in California and Texas. "We were young kids being called that. So you go into hiding. You don't ever want to tell people that you went to Vietnam. You don't want to talk about what went on over there."

The difficulties of being around others meant that he could only join family gatherings for short periods of time. He wouldn't stay the night—he never knew when he would wake up screaming or how he would react if someone inadvertently approached him while he was sleeping. If there was a loud noise and his instincts told him to jump or dive for cover, he knew people would think there was something wrong with him. He recently read the riot act to a young Iraq veteran who laughed when he saw a spooked Jimmy hit the ground because of a noise. "He should've known better and I let him know how I felt," Jimmy said.

All this was forever nudging, at best, toward withdrawal, from everyone and everything. "I lived in my own little world," he said. "My little world was my security blanket."

Much worse were the occasional thoughts of suicide. "I had thought numerous times about how to end it all," Jimmy said. "What's the old saying? Suicide is a sign of weakness. No, it's a survival mode. But I was not going to give up. Just like when I was over in Vietnam, I was not going to let them beat me."

But he was miserable. He couldn't sleep. He couldn't eat. He was crying all the time. Almost thirty years after coming home, he finally decided that he needed, and was ready for, some help. But his initial contacts with the VA weren't encouraging. He remembers being told to toughen up and learn to live with it. "Ain't happening, brother," he replied. "I am not gonna live this life anymore."

He finally reached out in 2001 to a neighbor's daughter, who ran a VA clinic in South Carolina. She contacted some colleagues in Corpus Christi and that same day Jimmy received a call. They wanted him in the office the next morning. It was the start of a regimen of medication and one-on-one counseling. The drugs were too much, he thought—"Hell, I felt like I could walk out of my second-story building and never touch the ground." He still wasn't able to open up about Vietnam, though, and was finally persuaded to join a three-month post-traumatic stress residential rehabilitation program at the VA hospital in Waco. Even there, Jimmy hesitated to talk about the war, but he did write the requested autobiography, which his sister transcribed and sent to him. His reaction after reviewing it? "I read it and I'm going, 'Damn, I am screwed up, aren't I?'"

Waco was a turning point. Afterward, Jimmy agreed to join a local group, his medication was adjusted, and—most significantly—he met an Iraq vet who had a service dog. He asked his counselor about the animals and was encouraged to apply for one. Though he was initially unsure about having a dog in his small apartment, he joked, "What the hell, I may as well find something I can have a relationship with."

He connected with an organization called TADSAW (Train a Dog Save a Warrior) out of San Antonio, which brings together rescue dogs and veterans suffering from PTSD in hopes of creating "a positive, nonjudgmental, unconditional relationship desperately needed by both."

It's not for everyone. As TADSAW warns potential clients, acquiring a service dog is a significant change in lifestyle and a huge commitment, a mantra that Jimmy stresses over and over to others: "You have to realize that if you're going to commit to this, you've gotta commit 24/7. You can't just do this halfway. The dog is not going to fail you; you're going to fail that dog."

Jimmy's commitment began with a local trainer in January 2015. They rejected seven dogs before Jimmy found Max, who was just days away from being put down. The trainer was skeptical. The dogs have to meet a list of criteria, and Max didn't appear to be a good fit in a number of areas. But the trainer agreed to let Jimmy try the dog out for a weekend. "He came home with me in February and we've been together ever since," Jimmy said. "Max and I just kind of clicked."

Four months of training followed. The first is basic obedience school, where dogs learn sitting, walking, standing, staying, and coming. School is in session for two hours a week, normally an hour on Monday night and a second on Thursday. In between is homework, from one to two hours a day. Dog and handler practice what was learned Monday in order to be ready for tests on those commands Thursday. The standards are high, even during this first training, because what the dog learns at this level contributes to the quality of service it can provide later.

"They'll start you out having your dog walking on a leash," Jimmy said. "You walk in a circle and go ten to twenty feet and then stop. When you stop, he's supposed to sit down right there beside you. Not lean against you, not go behind you or in front of you, but beside you. And when you go to walk again, he walks with you. When you stop, he sits beside you."

At the end of the month, the dog is put through its paces, seeing if it will obey commands despite distractions from other dogs, people, and an assortment of noises (including gunfire, and those with PTSD are warned in advance about this exercise). "They even have a guy who has a pet chicken," Jimmy said. "They put it in front of the dog to make sure it doesn't react to it." The dog must stay put, even as its handler walks away, even as others let cats walk all over it. The dog must stay until called by its handler.

That first month set the pattern for Jimmy and Max's training time, which continues to this day. An hour in the morning and about the same in late afternoons or early evenings—a schedule designed to beat Texas's grueling summer heat, and one that benefits both dog and handler.

"He and I train every day. It made me start getting out in public and not being locked down in the apartment," Jimmy said. "It made me take him out in order to work with him. So all my focus is on him."

The next month of training shifts the focus from one-on-one to more public settings in what's called learning canine good citizenship, from riding in elevators to going up and down the aisles of the local Walmart. In such settings, the dog learns to, among other things, ignore food he finds on the floor, a skill that is essential before it can be brought into a restaurant or meat market.

"He sits and you put food on the floor," Jimmy said. "In the beginning the dog will have a tendency to go for it. So you teach him that food on the floor is bad, but food from your hand is good. So, now, at a restaurant, if the waiter drops some food, Max knows not to touch that food."

Throughout, dog and handler are learning to read each other's emotions and body language. For Jimmy, that means being aware of when Max is thirsty or is ready to go out. For Max, it's sensing when Jimmy is happy or upset. "He sleeps alongside my bed, and he will get up in the middle of the night and nudge that bed until I reach over and pet him, and then he'll go back and lay down," Jimmy said. "It's to make sure I'm okay. Maybe I've been having a nightmare or maybe I've been squirming a lot or talking out loud. He'll come over to make sure I'm all right."

The last two months of training are more of the same, on an even more demanding level in preparation for a multiple-part public accessibility test (PAT). The dog must successfully complete each task, or keep retaking that part of the test until he gets it right. Jimmy remembers going to a local Whataburger with Max and the trainer. The dog was told to stay down and was supposed to remain prone while Jimmy walked away out of Max's field of vision. But when Jimmy left, Max instinctively stood up to see where he'd gone. They tried again. Max lay down and Jimmy walked away. This time

Max stayed down. Another test that day was having Jimmy walk to another part of the restaurant, again where he couldn't be seen by Max, and then call the dog to come. The dog is supposed to immediately obey the command. And Max did. Once outside, though, the trainer informed Jimmy that he couldn't pass Max on that stage of the training because the dog had failed to stay down the first time Jimmy walked away. They'd have to repeat that part of the test another day.

Having the dog stay when the handler leaves is a challenging—and somewhat confusing—lesson to master. "The dog is supposed to follow me everywhere," Jimmy said. "He's supposed to be with me at all times in case I have a problem, or to protect me, or if I pass out or have a seizure." In other words, the dog is trained to never let the handler be out of sight. So of course Max stood up the first time Jimmy walked away.

When the retest came around, Jimmy was already nervous enough. That feeling worsened when he found out the test would take place in Spohn Memorial Hospital, where his trainer was in intensive care.

"I had Max's vest on that said 'dog in training,' and I walk into the hospital waiting to get arrested or get run off," Jimmy recalled. "But nobody said a word to me. I get to the second floor, coronary ICU, and ring the doorbell. No one answers, so we walk in and there are all these people with their IVs, and their tubes, and all this sterilized stuff. I'm thinking, 'When am I getting locked up?'"

When a nurse approached, Jimmy was sure he'd be asked to leave. Instead she directed him to where his trainer was, surrounded by family and himself hooked up to IVs. He told Jimmy to set the dog down and walk to the other end of the ICU. Jimmy complied, all the while giving Max a "Don't you move or I'm gonna kill you" look. Max complied, and he passed the test. A bit later, when the trainer's doctor arrived and casually stepped over Max to go about his business, Jimmy understood how accepted service dogs were.

"And he's been with me ever since," Jimmy said.

There is regular dog Max, and there is service dog Max.

"He's a dog, and he tests me every day," Jimmy said. "He can make me angry real quick because he pulls stunts. He'll run off and play when I take him to the park and let him run around. But sometimes I'll give him the command to come back and he'll just give a look like, 'Huh, what do you want?' After I holler at him a couple of times he'll come back, but he pushes you like that. Not a day goes by that he doesn't push my buttons, but you have to learn not to be angry, or work through it, and that helps you deal with human beings."

You can tell Max is on duty by the vest he wears. It not only lets people know he is a service dog, but it has also been customized with insignia that clues passersby into his handler's Marine Corps connection. "You put that vest on him and he's an entirely different animal," Jimmy said.

In the last stages of his training, Max had the vest on whenever they were working. It came off when he was allowed dog time.

"When I get that vest on him, he automatically knows it's time to work," Jimmy said. "As far as how he knows, I don't know. He just does. But when that vest is on, his attitude changes, his demeanor changes. You can see it in the way he walks and carries himself."

Part of that attitude comes with being attentive for Jimmy, who is still on hyperalert when out in public. Having Max with him, knowing he too is paying close attention to their surroundings, helps take some of that edge off.

"He's always watching around when we're walking," Jimmy said. "He'll come behind me if someone is coming up behind us. Or he'll stop and stare at something and it makes me stop and look, and say, 'Okay, what's out there?' He sees things that I don't see. If you and I are talking, he would get on the floor between the two of us and just lay there until I'm ready to go. He's not gonna let you get right up next to me unless I tell him it's okay. He does that just automatically."

Max will let Jimmy shake someone's hand, or hug another person, but chances are he'll step in between the two, just as he did during the incident at the VA clinic. "To me that's kind of like security because I know he's watching out for me," Jimmy said.

Regular dog Max can be even more protective. In walks around the neighborhood, Max has, as Jimmy says, "gone crazy" when a hoodie-clad teen has stepped out of his home and seemed to be headed toward Jimmy. "He wanted that kid," Jimmy said. "He was growling, his hair was up, and he was pulling. Finally, the kid turned around and walked back into his apartment. And then Max went right back into being normal, wagging his tail, going down the road."

That security blanket covers the members of Jimmy's Tuesday group at the VA, who will call to Max if they're having a bad day or difficult moment. Still, Max is constantly aware of his primary mission. "He always comes right back to me," Jimmy said. "He has to know where I am at all times."

The combination of being pulled from the comfort zone of his apartment and feeling just slightly more secure in public has taken Jimmy a few steps closer to his family. Over the course of two weeks in August 2016, he attended two family celebrations, a reunion and his grandson's birthday party.

"Before having Max, I wouldn't have gone to two family events in a row like that," Jimmy admitted. "I would've found an excuse not to go. I might've lied and said I wasn't feeling well."

Previously, if Jimmy did attend an event, he would've been focused on all the people in the room and found an excuse to leave. With Max drawing so much attention from people, Jimmy has a chance to relax, just a bit.

"At the reunion, people were coming up and asking if they could pet the dog and things like this," Jimmy said. "Some of the relatives mentioned they had a dog that needed to be trained and wondered how I did it. I get kind of proud talking about him and showing him off.

"One relative has seizures and she stayed pretty close to him. I let her know that if you have a problem, Max will come up and try to get your attention and will even sense that something is going to happen before it does. So she stayed kind of close."

Jimmy and Max stayed for about four hours, and part of that time was spent outside, where they could be by themselves and Max had an opportunity to play. The same happened at the birthday party. "It's just that, getting in there and staying around crowds for a long period of time, I don't normally do that," Jimmy said. "But he is making me get out. I know it doesn't sound like much, but Max has helped me reconnect with my family."

Service dogs are by no means a cure-all for PTSD. But they allow vets a chance to refocus and help them—and their family members—live with issues that may never completely go away.

"I can go to an event for a little while, but then I have got to get outside. I've got to get back to myself, back in my little security blanket," Jimmy said. "From what my counselor and doctors have told me, that's just a sign of PTSD, and that's something I have to learn to live with for the rest of my life."

The difference now, he said, is that after his stay in Waco, and his counseling, and with having Max, his family is more aware of what creates the walls that Jimmy raises. "They know I have a problem, and I guess they've accepted me," he said. "And some other people they know I go to VA, and they know I have a service dog. When people ask me what he's for, I say he's a medical dog. When they ask, 'What's your problem?' I tell them it's a result of things that happened a long time ago in faraway country. I don't say much beyond that because I'm not looking for sympathy, and they wouldn't be able to handle it if I did tell them what happened over there."

The beauty of the relationship with Max, or any service dog, is that the veteran doesn't have to worry about being judged for his actions in wartime, or for his behavior postwar, whether nightmares or hyperalertness or being distant.

"He depends on me, and I depend on him. That's why we're a team," Jimmy said. "He and I are closer than even my family because he's with me all the time. I can talk to him, or I can have a situation, and he is still here. I'm sure my mom or my sisters would still be there for me, but I always wonder if they'll be scared of me if I have an episode, like if I wake up in the middle of the night screaming, or act like I'm fighting somebody, or worrying that someone is looking at me through the bushes. Are they going to understand all that? They may. But I *know* this dog will. Even when I have a bad time and holler at him, he still wants to be my buddy."

Max not only keeps Jimmy grounded, but he, and all service dogs, act as a bridge between the people who make unimaginable sacrifices for their country and a society that sometimes doesn't know what to make of its veterans.

"These dogs will accept you for who you are and what you are regardless of what you've done, and they don't judge you," Jimmy said. "All we want is to be accepted. We'd like to come home, but some of us are stuck in time. We have to learn to live with that for the rest of our lives. There's no fix. There's no medication you can take. There's nothing anybody can do but accept you for who you are and what you are."

If success for Max is measured in his ability to get Jimmy out of his apartment, the fall of 2016 might be the time to, at least partly, declare mission accomplished. That's when Jimmy purchased a three-bedroom home after thirty years in an apartment. Jimmy thinks it's kind of cool to have a garage to pull his truck into when the weather is bad. But a bigger home also gives Max more room to roam, both indoors and out in a new yard.

"Silly, isn't it?" Jimmy asked. "Hell, I'm seventy years old. What the hell am I buying a house for? I kept asking my mom and my sisters and they said, 'Oh, just go do it and quit worrying about it.'

"I guess I'm still trying to grow up, still trying to reach out more and more."

That's what that dog is for.

FOUR

THE ARMY NURSE

"Some kind of a guardian angel."

S HANDA BEAR TAYLOR ACCEPTED GOD AS HER PERSONAL SAVIOR WHEN SHE
was in eighth grade. At the time, her single mom was raising five girls
while living up on a hill in the notorious Oak Street projects over-
looking Coatesville, Pennsylvania, a once-bustling steel town about thirty
miles west of Philadelphia. Shanda remembers going to church with her
grandmother as early as age four or five, and later her brother and two of
her uncles were lay ministers. She attended Wednesday prayer meetings and
sang in the youth choir and then the combined choir of youths and adults—
"Always with a group, I was never brave enough to sing solo," she said. The
church, and her belief in God, would be a touchstone throughout her life.
"It was really responsible for a solid infrastructure to my faith even to this
day," Shanda said.

It's no surprise, then, that Shanda believes she has always been blessed
with guardian angels watching over her. "I believe God put these people,
who were so pivotal, in my life back then," she said. First, of course, was
her mother Joyce Taylor. Her mom was a chronic asthmatic, and Shanda
has a clear memory of her and her siblings huddled around Joyce, preparing her for a trip to the hospital while she struggled for breath. Her illness
made working full time difficult, but still she had resisted moving to the
projects—"Her worst nightmare," Shanda said. "My mom knew there was
so much trouble her girls could get into over at Oak Street."

36

The kids thought it was great, moving from their little duplex on the outskirts of the city, to a home where the two older girls would have their own rooms. But Joyce understood how dangerous the crime- and drug-ridden Oak Street could be. She knew there would be less-than-desirable influences there and how her own brood could get caught up in things. Shanda even remembers a popular joke from the time, which is still used today. "If somebody would bother another person," she recalled, "we'd say, 'Don't make me go Oak Street on you!'"

Joyce fought back by being a protective parent and great role model. Shanda remembers a woman who didn't drink or smoke and whose home was immaculate. The children were always neat and well-dressed. There were new outfits for the start of the school year, and holidays like the Fourth of July and Easter, and Joyce was a regular at the lay-away counter of the nearby Kmart or Jamesway. "My mom always kept the house spotless, even in the projects," Shanda said, "And she was always neat and tidy; her hair was always done."

And Joyce had no intention of letting the family's financial situation or other circumstances stand in the way of her children's dreams. Years after Shanda had graduated from Eastern College, an elite, four-hundred-student private school on suburban Philadelphia's Main Line, she asked: "Mommy, when I said I wanted to go to this school, you never said, 'Where do you think we're going to get that money?' or 'We can't afford that.' Why didn't you say something?" Shanda recalls, "Tears welled up in her eyes and she replied, 'I was just so happy you wanted to go to college.' Never a negative word whatsoever. Never."

Shanda's grandmother, a hard-working custodian in the local school district, was guardian angel number two. "She'd give a person the clothes off her back," Shanda fondly recalls. "Whenever kids came over—and we never knocked—there was always pie or something, always food. She'd say, 'There are some collard greens on the stove.' She was always asking if we wanted anything to eat. I mean, she was just the best grandmother in the world." Shanda moved in with her grandparents, Onetta and Herman Taylor, when she was in middle school. She had always been well behaved and a good student, but something changed for her with this move. "I felt like I had an even greater sense of purpose," she said. "I always wanted to do the right thing because they counted on me. They didn't put pressure on me or anything, but my grandfather was becoming ill and my grandmother was still working." For a young girl who would one day aspire to be a nurse, it was good training in being responsible for others and offering compassionate care.

One of the treats of living with her grandparents was visits from their youngest son Robert, a career army man and Vietnam veteran. He was always in shape, and Shanda remembers him jogging while home on leave. He was a role model for his niece. "He always talked to me about life, and he always spoke to me like I was an adult," she said. "He was the epitome of an all-around amazing person and really was a mentor to me. He saw things in me that, of course, I never saw in myself."

In addition—though she wouldn't learn this until after his death many years later—he regularly sent money to Joyce and her children. What Shanda did know was how pivotal he was at two important points in her life. During middle school, Shanda had signed up for an architectural engineering course, but she quickly decided it wasn't for her. But by then, the only option available was Junior Air Force ROTC. Post-Vietnam, the 1970s was not a popular time to wear a uniform, but because of the influence of Uncle Robert, Shanda saw the military as a source of pride. She not only signed up but also was squadron commander by the time she completed the four-year high school program. Several years later, fearing she would have to leave college for financial reasons, Shanda sought Robert's counsel, and his advice was crucial to her exploring the US Army ROTC scholarship opportunities that enabled her to stay, and ultimately graduate, from Eastern.

There were many other guardian angels along the way. A first-grade teacher who would encourage the young girl with "Shanda, I know you can do this," and another who shushed the other students with this admonishment: "Can you please be quiet? Shanda is trying to read." A school counselor who once told Shanda's mom, "Joyce, don't give up on Shanda, she's college material." And Hershal Bailey, the head of the Upward Bound program at Lincoln University, which helped prepare economically challenged students of color for college.

"People have always believed in me, from the time I was a little girl," Shanda marveled today, remembering the shy child who didn't share people's confidence in her. "I still struggle with it, wondering how they saw so much in me. I remember my brother Fred used to say, 'You're so smart,' and I'd reply, 'No, I'm not.'" Still, others saw what she could not. "They take you under their wing, they believe in you," she said.

And here's something else she couldn't have envisioned back then but came to appreciate much, much later: guardian angels sometimes come with four legs and fur.

In army basic training at Fort Jackson, South Carolina, Shanda had good reason to believe that her first name had been changed to "Drop!"

"Why are you smiling?" the drill sergeants would shout. "Drop, Taylor, and give me twenty"—as in twenty push-ups.

"Why are you always so happy? Drop, Taylor!"

"Why do you look like a cartoon? Drop, Taylor!"

Shanda giggles at the memory. "I was always a happy kid, always," she said, and she saw no reason to stop just because a bunch of tough guys—and the occasional woman NCO—were screaming at her day and night, whether outside during formation or inside a chow hall. "They were smirking. I could see them wanting to laugh."

Most important, they didn't break her: "They never made me stop smiling."

Shanda had learned to stick up for herself growing up in Coatesville. After switching to a new junior high school, she asked to be transferred to an advanced class when she found the work wasn't challenging enough. Her friends thought she was crazy, trying to add to her workload. "I just had a craving to learn," she said simply. Once, when she was being punished for talking in class—and she most definitely was not—she walked out of school and home to Oak Street rather than put up with an unjust punishment. She reported a substitute teacher who spoke to students in a way that Shanda considered disrespectful. Joyce was often supportive, even though she spent her share of time in the principal's office discussing the head-strong Shanda.

It was that kind of confidence that later served Shanda well as a brand-new second lieutenant taking charge of a military police (MP) platoon in Germany. She was able to smile—on the inside—at the first question the mostly male group had of their new five-foot-four, 110-pound boss: "Hey, when you gonna turn sixteen?" Shanda might wonder herself what she was doing in certain situations, but she was more than well prepared that day when she took command as a US Army officer. "I'd like to think that I was somebody who always respected others," she said. "Great people make everybody else feel significant and important and valued and appreciated. That's the sign of a true leader."

Her four years in Junior Air Force ROTC, and her Uncle Robert, inspired her to join the US Army Reserves the year after graduating from

Coatesville Area High School in 1981, entering under a program that allowed her to delay active duty while she earned a college degree in psychology. She attended basic training in the summer of 1982 after her freshman year at Eastern. Though she enjoyed the challenge—why else would she smile throughout?—it occurred to her that a military career might be easier if she were an officer—a goal she would attain. The low crawl under barbed wire, with her face in the ground, was the clincher. "I thought I'd have to do that the rest of my life if I remained enlisted," she said. The summer after her sophomore year of college, she was sent to Fort Benjamin Harrison in Indiana for training in her first military job, personnel administration specialist. And here, again, her potential was noted, even if she didn't feel ready for such recognition. She was chosen to be the class leader and promoted to acting corporal, which meant, among other things, that she had her own room in the barracks while the rest of her unit bunked in large open "bay" areas. "I wanted to be with everyone else," said Shanda, who didn't see herself as a leader at that time, "but that wasn't the way it worked."

It was a successful summer, but her return to Eastern wasn't assured. Neither she, nor her family, had the resources that would allow her to continue at the small Christian school. She considered dropping out and going on active duty. But when she reached out to an army recruiter—a guardian angel in uniform—the woman urged Shanda to use enlistment as a last resort. Exhaust all financial aid possibilities first, she advised. That's when Uncle Robert, who was an ROTC instructor at the University of Indiana, suggested applying for an army ROTC scholarship. "Shan, there's a lot of money out there," she remembers him saying.

She applied and went through the process. But right before the final step, appearing before a board of ROTC cadre for a determination of eligibility, Shanda's grandfather passed away. In the depths of her mourning, she considered skipping the interview. "It was just a tough time," she recalled. "But something inside of me said, 'Shan, you have to do this for grandpop. He would be proud of you and he would want you to do this.'"

She remembers standing before the panel, three people in uniform, but not what she told them. "It's all a blank, just because I wasn't really there," she said. "It was just my heart that was speaking. But, whatever I said, it must have been acceptable."

It was a hectic final two years of college. Three times a week she was with her ROTC unit at Valley Forge Military Academy and College, not far from Eastern, at six a.m. for physical training. Back at Eastern, she ran cross-country, sang in the college choir—a group named, appropriately enough, Angels of Harmony—and studied, constantly. "I was very dedicated to that," she said. So dedicated, she was an honors student. Dashing between two worlds, her Eastern friends wondered how she could do it all. At Valley Forge there was the added pressure of being the only woman in the program. The college itself wouldn't go coed until 2006.

"Of course, I was the only female whenever there was something going on at Valley Forge," she said. "I was the only female during PT, in the big gym. But at the time I didn't see any of that. It wasn't a big deal and I didn't feel special. I didn't feel like they didn't accept me or anything."

In fact, it was just the opposite. She would earn the American Legion award for academic excellence, be named distinguished military graduate, and earn a coveted opportunity to attend airborne school.

"When I received the American Legion award, the whole corps of cadets was on the parade field," she recalled. "My two grandmoms attended it, and my mom and sister, and three members of the Angels of Harmony. I still have that picture. It's so special. I didn't realize how important that would be for this little Black girl from the projects." Still, she kept it in perspective, understanding her new mission-oriented role in a much larger world. "I didn't see myself as special on that parade field," she said. "I saw myself as a cadet."

Shanda was always mission oriented. That was evident during her twenty-three-year military career, as first an MP and then an army nurse. And during her seventeen-year marriage to Danny Boyd, the West Point graduate and fellow MP officer she met and fell in love with while they were both stationed in Germany. He would go on to a high-profile career in the FBI's foreign service program. (The family's first beloved dog, Hoover, was named not for the vacuum cleaner, as many people assumed, but for the famous FBI director.) Her most important mission was being a mom to three beautiful and now successful young ladies, whom Shanda even home-schooled for a time.

This busy military family would move from Germany to New Jersey to Seattle to Germany and then return to Washington State. On top of her bachelor's in psychology, Shanda would graduate from the prestigious nursing school at the University of Washington and then earn a master's degree in human relations. It was the hard-earned nursing degree that allowed her to finally fulfill her longtime goal of being an inpatient psychiatric nurse at the Madigan Army Medical Center near Tacoma. "I had planned to be a nurse for a very long time," she said. "And one of the reasons I wanted to become a nurse, especially an army nurse, was that I always wanted to take care of our nation's heroes and their family members."

Shanda also ran almost daily for at least an hour and then more on weekends—it was her "me time," along with a good hot bath, what she calls her "magic potion." In fact, her daughters would sometimes suggest she go for a run. "Because they knew I was a different person after I ran," she said. Her house was immaculate—just as mom and grandma had taught her—and she cooked meals for months in advance, keeping the freezer stocked for both family meals and, when needed, to give away to friends and neighbors. She was super mom, super wife, super athlete, super nurse, super army officer, all rolled into one bundle of perpetual motion.

Until May 22, 2004.

Shanda was heading home in the family's Volvo station wagon on Highway 520 near Redmond, Washington, when she spied a speeding vehicle entering the highway in her direction. "I saw how fast he was going, and I still remember thinking, 'Oh, my gosh, I better move over,'" she said. It wasn't enough. He crashed into her, violently enough to total both cars. She has a vague recollection of being pushed over several lanes, and of being asked if she was okay. Miraculously, she was not bleeding and had no visible wounds, but okay she was not.

She awoke in a hospital, still in uniform, and she clicked into complete-the-mission mode. "I looked perfect," she said. "and I felt like I could go to work. I had to get to the dry cleaner to pick up my uniform, and I had a meeting in the morning. That's the only thing I was thinking about, the work. That's how we're programmed. I had four years of junior air force ROTC, three years of army ROTC, and at that point twenty-one years in the military. So that's all I knew was 'mission first.'"

Despite the severity of the crash, and what she remembers as an unsteady gait and head and neck pain, she wasn't admitted. Instead, Shanda demanded that Danny get her a rental car so she could go to work. He was concerned, but as Shanda said, "He knows I'm very mission oriented so, to him, it's like, 'Okay, she's just being herself.'"

When she did go back to work, she wasn't herself. First, and most excruciating, were the headaches. "I started having the headaches almost immediately after, and I was at home with all this pain," she said. First she sought relief at a doctor's office, but within a few days, at her daughters' urging, was in an emergency room. She was sent home with pain medicine. But the next day, at home, she couldn't even feed herself. The family was going for a bike ride, and she assured them she'd be fine by herself for a while, just needing rest and a good hot bath. She made it up the stairs, but immediately got sick in the sink. When she raised her head and looked in the mirror, she saw how "really, really pale" she was. She called 911. "I don't know how I sounded to them, but they knew something was really wrong too," Shanda said. "'Stay with us on the phone,' they said, 'We want to keep talking to you.' When the paramedics arrived they said if I had waited five more minutes I would have spent the rest of my life on a respirator or ventilator—if I had survived. I was minutes from death."

Had she made it to the tub, it's likely she wouldn't have been alive when her family returned home. "If I hadn't looked in the mirror, I would not have seen my face and realized how sick I was," she said. "And at the ER, the first thing the doctor said was, 'I don't like the way she looks.'"

This time she was admitted, at Evergreen Hospital Medical Center and, upon release, was provided with a home health visiting nurse for several months. She had survived. "Dying then wasn't God's plan for me," she states today—but the super mom that everyone knew and relied upon was gone.

Just a year before, from Germany, she had preplanned the family's return to the States, down to signing up the girls for soccer. She could juggle her ER nursing job and going to school for her master's and her time as a Red Cross volunteer. She and Danny were attending high-level diplomatic functions, and she was in the thick of things when her medical unit was activated to prepare soldiers for deployment after the 9/11 terrorist attacks. Now, after the accident, she was a changed woman.

"I went overnight, like in an instant, to not even being able to wash the dishes or being able to read," she said. "I knew the words, but I couldn't put them together long enough to read a sentence. I stopped watching TV because I didn't understand it. On family movie nights, I would pick out films that we had already seen and I had forgotten. And when I did understand it, I'd be halfway through a program before I realized that I had already seen it. I used to clean the house every Monday, I did all the laundry, and I helped handle the household budget. I went from all that to not being able to do anything. I couldn't even write a chore list."

In addition to suffering from a traumatic brain injury (TBI), Shanda was diagnosed with fibromyalgia, which is characterized by chronic pain, sleep problems, and memory issues. She was also experiencing post-traumatic stress from the accident. "Remember that movie *Talladega Nights*, when the race car driver played by Will Ferrell gets into an accident but decides to get right back out there?" Shanda asked. "He thinks he's driving fast but he's really just creeping along. That is what it feels like. When I was driving, it's like the entire world was in a hurry and anytime that anybody got close to me I cringed and thought, 'Oh, my gosh, please don't hit me. Please don't hit me.'"

In 2006, she was medically retired from the army. Not long after, Shanda and Danny divorced. She was suffering from depression, and the physical pain was relentless.

"I still remember being at home, on the floor, in the dark, with the headaches, living with them, not wanting to do anything, not wanting to go anywhere," she said. "You think about what it would be like not to be in that kind of pain."

Not fully understanding what was going on with her medically, and unable to function as she once had, Shanda blamed herself during this bleak time. "There was no explanation. It looked like I just quit," she said. "In 2006, I was at the lowest, lowest, lowest part of my life. I was always so hard on myself. Why can't I do this? Why don't I remember that?"

Fortunately, in that wilderness there were some guardian angels. Her daughters, ages ten, twelve, and fourteen when she was injured, ran the household as she had taught them and kept a close eye on her too. Also crucial were her health-care providers at the Seattle VA, from the Women's Clinic to the Ploytrauma Center to the Women's Trauma and Recovery Center. And there was also support from the Disabled American Veterans, the University of Washington, her alma mater, and other organizations. Most miraculous of all was that Ranger, a sixty-seven-pound golden retriever, had fortuitously entered her life just months after the accident on Highway 520.

Consider just one chapter of their lives together: Shanda and Ranger were in the checkout line at the University of Washington's bookstore. Shanda was buying a planner, a concession to the reality about her memory issues. Normally, Ranger waited patiently in line, quiet and seated. Not that day. He was pacing, back and forth, back and forth. "I was asking him to sit, and he wouldn't," she said. "That wasn't like him." Something was up, and Shanda learned that as they were almost out the door. She had a minor seizure—and was told later that Ranger sensed the change in her body chemistry. He would have the same reaction before other seizures as well.

Such incidents made her VA provider realize that Shanda would benefit from having a service dog, and he decided that Ranger was the perfect candidate.

The family had always known he was smart, even as a puppy. "We were having a family night or something," Shanda said. "And we thought, 'Let's see if he can ring a bell when he needs to go out.' And he did, he started ringing the bell! Yes, he rang the bell and trained himself. I didn't have to potty train him."

They weren't the only ones who noticed his intelligence. When she and Ranger took obedience classes together, the trainer would tell Shanda that he was the smartest dog she'd ever trained, and she kept using him as an example in the class. "That was a little uncomfortable," Shanda admitted, "because obviously there were other dogs there. But she kept it up."

And Ranger was calm, almost unnaturally so. "When other children were over, or when the neighbors and I had a get-together at the house, he would just lie there, very calm," Shanda recalled. "And the joke was that I had him on puppy downers. But he was like that the entire time we had him, almost as if he was just intuitively, instinctively, a service animal."

But first he was a family pet, almost in service to them all. Shanda believes his calming presence was crucial for the girls during the stressful time after her accident and during their parents' divorce. And he not only supported Shanda physically—alerting her to seizures but even helping pull her up hills during the regular walks that she used for exercise now that she could no longer run—but he was also there for her emotionally. When she was at her lowest, a "Let's get with it" look from Ranger could help her get up and face another day.

As she became more involved with veterans organizations, the unflappable Ranger made it easier for her to travel. "He would fly with me across country. He's been to funerals. You name it, he's been there," Shanda said. "I bet we had at least forty flights together, from 2009 to 2014, and never one single accident. Not one. And people never even knew he was on the plane because he was so quiet. They'd come up afterward, fascinated, because they hadn't noticed him with me. That's how good he was."

There were times, however, when he made his presence known. For the longest time, the family thought that he couldn't bark—he just never did. But in 2013, while Ranger and Shanda were attending the Disabled American Veterans (DAV) National Convention in Orlando, Florida, he let loose. "I think he barked three times in his life," Shanda said. "And the first time was at that DAV convention. There were something like four thousand veterans, and we were checking in, and right in the midst of all that he let out a bark. It was unbelievable. Why are you doing that? I wondered. But he did it twice more, at another veterans' convention in Las Vegas and then again at the Washington Women's Veterans' Summit. He just loved veterans and wanted to make sure they knew that we were there."

He could also be mischievous. Shanda had been invited to Las Vegas to participate in a Ms. Veteran America competition. Though she often has people marvel at how young she looks, she didn't think a pageant was right for her. Somewhere deep inside still dwells that not-so-confident child from Coatesville. But she let herself be talked into it, in part because the contest isn't solely about appearance. "I finally agreed," she said, "because I wanted to send a message to little Black girls growing up in the projects that one day they can do something like this. But I also wanted to send a message to women with TBI that they can do this too."

So off they went, quickly making friends with the reigning Ms. Veteran America and others. During the lunch break, Shanda had to step away. She gave instructions to Ranger to stay and wait for her and then left. When she returned, her fellow contestants were laughing themselves silly. "Soon as you turned that corner," one told Shanda, "Ranger tore up that pizza. He grabbed that so fast." Even Shanda laughed. "Oh, they just loved that," she said. "Because they had seen how well-behaved he was with me, so great, so wonderful, so obedient. But at that point he was nearing retirement age, and I guess he figured that once I wasn't looking, he was going to gobble down that pizza."

Turns out he had a fondness for the ocean too. The family didn't realize it at the time, but during a family outing, he was lapping up sea water when Shanda and the girls weren't looking. They learned the hard way on the trip home. "We didn't know that Ranger was drinking that water, but on the way back, oh my gosh," she said, laughing at the memory. "He was passing gas so much we thought it was going to knock us out. That was the funniest thing ever. We loved that."

By age ten, Ranger was still hard at work, always by Shanda's side. But friends were mentioning how tired he looked. Shanda saw it too but wasn't ready to let go. Finally, Ranger's vet suggested that he travel less and be allowed to take life a little easy. Shanda reluctantly agreed and gradually retired him. He would join her for local events, but she would have someone stay with him at home if she went farther away.

In 2015, after a hot summer, Ranger was more tired than usual. He wasn't bouncing back from the lethargy that seemed to have overtaken him. At that point he had been staying more and more with Shanda's friend Joan Myers. When Joan took Ranger in for a checkup, the vet discovered three tumors. He was bleeding internally and wouldn't have long.

Shanda was at church when she got the call about Ranger's condition. Immediately, she slipped into mission-oriented mode. She had to see him, but she also wanted to make sure that two of her girls in nearby colleges had a chance to say goodbye too. The oldest, Olivia, was then an army first lieutenant at Fort Drum, in New York, preparing for deployment to Iraq. But Tay, the youngest, was nearby at her mom's alma mater, the University of Washington, and Danielle, Shanda's middle daughter, attended Western Washington University in Bellingham, about ninety miles north along Puget Sound.

It was a solemn drive, but one that Shanda will never forget.

"I'm telling you, Ranger was still in service animal mode," she said. "When we were driving up, even though it was very uncomfortable for him to lie down because his tumors were so big, he laid down and put his face in the middle between the seats, where the arm rest is. That entire drive up there, he sat like that with his eyes on me, every move I made. It was like he was saying, 'I'm still here with you, I love you, and I got you.'

"I just couldn't believe it. He was still in touch, still in tune with me, until the very end."

Danielle was already crying when she came out. "They had a special relationship," Shanda said. "When we had the divorce, he was just there for us, and, Danielle, she often talked to him and stuff. He really helped everybody."

Shanda thought Danielle would resist the idea of taking Ranger to a veterinarian so he'd no longer be in pain. Instead, she said, "Mommy, I can't let him suffer like this." "That's how much she loved him," her mom says today. They found a place nearby, and the veteran in Shanda took some solace when she saw a military recruiting station, flags flying, close at hand. Inside the veterinarian's office, they were briefed on the procedure. Ranger was resting in Shanda and Danielle's laps. When the woman was ready to do the injection, she paused. He was already gone, surrounded by his loved ones. "He died on his own," Shanda said. "He was at peace."

The vet took his paw prints, and gave them copies. One went to Danielle and the other to Joan. The vet also sent Ranger's ashes to the family. In the summer of 2016, Danielle and her boyfriend went camping in Bellingham and spread the ashes of this beloved family member in the lake where he used to go swimming.

"Danielle used to say, 'Mommy, Ranger was not a dog. He was something beyond,'" Shanda recalled. "She really believed that. It's almost like she was saying he was some kind of a guardian angel. And it's true. After all that stuff that happened, he truly saved our family."

There wasn't going to be a replacement for Ranger. This was decided before he even got sick. How could there be? He had seen Shanda through so much. The initial months recovering from her accident. Her discharge from the service. Her divorce. He had been there for her as a single parent, had stood by her girls through the ups and downs of their growing up years. He had been a good and faithful friend, a family member. So once he'd been retired, and Shanda had to adapt to life without him, she was determined that there would be no new service dog. "I didn't want to go through that pain again, of having to get used to not having a dog with me," she said.

And then she was in Washington, DC, for an event on women veterans. It was the day after her fifty-second birthday. She remembers being in front of the Russell Senate Office Building on Constitution Avenue, waiting for a niece, Charlisha Williams, to pick her up, when her phone rang.

"Hello, Shanda? This is Teresa Morkert from Northwest Battle Buddies. Remember that little golden retriever puppy, the one you and Ranger played with when you were down there?"

Shanda did remember. Timber, who had been donated by an organization called Council House Golden Retrievers. A lively little pup, the color of English cream, that she and Ranger had enjoyed meeting.

"He's your new service animal, if you'll have him."

Two months later, they were training together, in Battle Ground, Washington, three hours away from Shanda's home. She and other vets in the program—all of whom had PTSD and some who had TBI—stayed in a hotel near the kennel. The experience, led by founder and trainer Shannon Walker, with help from trainer Ovie Muntane, brought back fond memories of Shanda's years in the army. "As cold and rainy as it was, we had each other," she said. "It reminded me of being in the military. We would sit there and joke around. It was awesome, just so amazing."

It was a more extensive training for a service dog than she'd had with Ranger, teaching Timber not to flinch when someone approaches to shake Shanda's hand or if there are loud, distracting noises (they trundled a wheelbarrow through during training). The dog must also learn how to pass raw meat in a grocery store without "scenting," acting as if the food isn't even there. "One of the tests is they drop food right in front of the dog, sometimes something hot and delicious like Chinese food with chicken," Shanda said. "We have to watch and be ready to grab them, get their attention if they so much as look at it. So how they react is—and it's the cutest thing—they completely turn their heads away, like, 'I don't see that.' Isn't that amazing?"

Shanda found much of the training very practical, appreciating it more and more as she applied the lessons in real life. One example was learning to go through a checkout line. The handler brings the dog up to the line and puts him in the down position, always ensuring his tail is protected so that no one could step on him. "It's all about awareness," Shanda said. "And it actually helps me with my brain injury to focus on him. So then my mind is not everywhere. I have to focus. I'm not just responsible for myself but for him too."

She is as disciplined with Timber as she was with herself and her troops when she was an MP officer. If she meets someone out on the street when she's with Timber, she'll stop them before they run up and hug her. "Excuse me, please, let me get him situated," she tells them. She makes sure he's in the down position and nonreactive and then lets the person approach. "It's not that he will bite or do anything," she said, "but it's easy for them to form bad habits."

Timber does have one bad habit, dancing, and Shanda takes full responsibility. At the many events she's invited to for veterans, there is often music. Well, Shanda likes to dance. And she'd often take hold of Timber's paws and have him dance with her. "Now when he hears music," Shanda said, a bit of guilt creeping into her voice, "he either wants to stand up on his back legs so I can hold his paws to dance, or he does this thing on his back and starts doggie break dancing with all four paws in the air."

He has even performed, quite unexpectedly, before singer Lee Greenwood. At a recent veterans' event in Atlanta, Greenwood was singing and Shanda was crying. Patriotic songs in general, and Greenwood's "God Bless the USA" in particular, often move her to tears. Timber, ever sensitive to his handler's emotions, was trying to distract and comfort her. He opted for his break-dancing routine. Shanda was captivated by Greenwood's performance and not looking down at Timber—until she noticed fellow veterans whispering and pointing, "Look at her dog! Look at her dog!"

It's cute, for sure, but Shanda is well aware that handlers must always keep their dog focused and on the job. It's for the same reason that people are discouraged from petting or giving treats to service animals while they are on duty. "It is critical to understand that if the dog is focused on them, he's not paying attention to his veteran handler," Shanda said. "The vet can have a panic or anxiety attack, or worse, a seizure, and maybe hit the ground and hurt herself while the dog is distracted."

That's partly why Shannon Walker insists that the dogs she's trained be recertified every six months, to review the handler-dog team and to refresh and reinforce the highest standards for the Public Access Test. At one recertification, Shanda learned that Timber was starting to focus on the smells of other animals that he would pick up on people walking by him. "People have their own dog's scent on them if they have a pet at home," Shanda said, "and Timber was trying to sneak a 'scent' when they went by. I hadn't even realized it."

Fortunately, like Ranger, Timber is quite adaptable when it comes to training.

"Timber is very, very, very bright," Shanda said. "I almost joke that God really felt bad for me so he gave me two dogs with genius IQs; both very, very, very brilliant. Oh, my gosh, so smart."

Some tasks take more getting used to than others. Ranger took to airplane flights fairly easily, but Timber had more of an adjustment. He wasn't even a year old when he started flying, where Ranger had been more mature. Initially, Timber was reluctant to lie down during takeoff—he could feel the vibrations on his belly when the engines started. Landings, too, brought him to his feet. "He'd try to stand up or crawl into my lap," Shanda said. "And you feel bad for them, but you are not supposed to coddle them." She got that exact advice from Northwest Battle Buddies when Timber was freaking out during a thunderstorm. Shanda called them for guidance and was told: Do not coddle him. "It makes sense," Shanda admitted. "If he's scared of things, how is he supposed to take care of me when I'm afraid of something?"

All in all, they are partners—and not just on the dance floor. From the moment she wakes and throughout her day, Timber is by her side. "Timber blesses me by forcing me to take in things and notice things that I probably would never have done before, just because I have to take him out," she said. "Now I look forward to taking him out because it's good for my mind. I see it as an opportunity to have some therapeutic time." The everyday challenges of invisible injuries can sometimes feel overwhelming and entice her to stay inside, but Timber won't allow it. "Once I'm outside, especially in the winter, and I feel that fresh air, I realize that's what I need," she said.

Shanda is grateful for the opportunities that each day brings. "I see how God is using tragedy. Something that could have destroyed me has made me stronger," she said. "Ranger saved me; Timber too."

And there are no regrets about going back on her pledge to never have another service dog. "It is so much work, especially when they are sick or there are other things going on," she said, "But having that responsibility teaches discipline, and that helps build devotion and dedication. You know how in the military we have a 'battle buddy' during training? You make sure that person knows you have their back. That's how I feel about Timber. No matter what, I'm there for him. And I wouldn't have it any other way. I can't see my life without him."

Recovery from a TBI can be painstakingly slow. The army nurse who used to juggle so many duties during a shift now might need two hours or more just to book a flight. It was only two years ago that she was able to write things out and start using an at-a-glance calendar. This for a mom who used to plot out a whole year of activities and special dates for her busy family. She used to cook meals six months in advance and organize them in her freezer—dress right dress, as they say in the military. Today, in her new home for a year, she has yet to use her stove, relying instead on her microwave and crockpot.

"I made a salad yesterday and I was so proud of myself," Shanda said. "Just because it takes so much thought. You have to get the ingredients. You have to have a little cutting board and the containers. Every single step you have to think about, like slicing the cucumbers, the celery, and the olives. It's not second nature. Nothing is that has to do with any type of organization or sequencing."

But she's getting there. Shopping for furnishings for the new townhouse was difficult, largely because of all the choices, but parts of her well-appointed home are a reminder of the old Shanda. "It can be difficult," she said. "Choosing a pillow, or deciding which wall hanging to put up, it's like studying for an examination. But I have my townhome in order, at least the downstairs. People can't believe I did it, especially my children. But I'm still not completely unpacked because everything takes really long."

She celebrates these moments, what she calls tiny, tiny victories, ever mindful that she must be "gentle to myself, kind to myself." And that means ensuring she has time to laugh and play. "It's difficult," she said, "but I'm getting better at it. Timber helps me laugh at myself, and he reminds me to take breaks. And that is so powerful."

Through her work as an advocate for veterans, she knows she is not alone, and she can understand what others must endure every day.

"There are so many veterans and family members and caregivers going through all this," she said. "You struggle and you struggle and you struggle. They feel like no one understands them and that they can't get help. They don't know where to turn, or how powerful a service dog can be. Not everybody thinks they can push ahead to make it through. But I tell them, 'Don't give up.'"

Being able to empathize, to feel, tells her that she is recovering. And her advocacy work keeps her connected to that longtime passion of being a nurse.

"I still get to spend time with veterans, and actually care for them, maybe not as nurse, but care for their hearts, care for their emotions, and just loving on them," she said. "I want them to feel that they are valued and that they are appreciated, and how honored I am to know them and to know their sacrifices. That is still getting to be a nurse to me. That is part of what it means to provide quality care."

And if healing should occur, she knows who is ultimately responsible.

"I know I have nothing to do with this," she said. "I really believe that it's all part of God's plan to help survivors of TBI, or those living with PTSD, who want to have some hope.

"When love is your cornerstone, and knowing also that God loves you, I mean, what else do you really need? That's what gets you by."

FIVE

The Army Captain

"Issac has been waiting for his special person."

FOR LESLIE NICOLE SMITH, SECOND CHANCES ARE HER REASONS FOR waking up each and every day. Like a ray of sunshine, each beam of light brings her hope and the promise of better days ahead. It wasn't always that way, though. Fifteen years ago, she was given only twenty-four hours to live. Leslie was so gravely ill that she was medically retired from the US Army and placed on imminent death status, while lying in a hospital bed with social workers planning her funeral arrangements. However, thanks to a medical miracle, and the love and connection of an abandoned dog that also was given a second chance, Leslie's life took a dramatic turn for the positive.

Despite her stellar career as a public affairs officer in the US Army, she was not immune to being affected by serious health issues that forced her left leg to be amputated below the knee and devastating vision issues that left Leslie legally blind. But with her handsome golden Labrador-mix service dog, Issac, by her side, there is nothing she can't do. And, ironically, just like Leslie, Issac was also only given twenty-four hours to live. He was saved from being euthanized in an animal shelter. He knew he had a greater calling—to be Leslie's eyes and ears and her lifelong companion. Luckily for both, they found each other in the nick of time. Second chances brought them together; they've brightened up each other's lives ever since.

A public speaker, veterans' advocate, champion for wounded, ill, and injured warriors, ambassador for the Gary Sinise Foundation, aspiring actress, and tireless volunteer, Leslie is on a new, nonmilitary mission—one that she hopes to share with anyone and everyone who will listen.

Leslie Nicole Smith is a spitfire. This attractive petite brunette with sparkling brown eyes, almost perfect diction, and an infectious smile has military blood flowing through her veins. Since she was a little girl she listened intently to stories her father told her about his military and government service. She knew she wanted to follow in his footsteps.

"My love of service really stems from my dad's own service in the army," said Leslie. "He would tell me stories from his army days working in the White House Communications Agency during the Kennedy administration. They were captivating! One of them that really stuck in my mind was the story about Jackie Kennedy, among the most admired first ladies of her time. Here's how my dad related the story: 'I was working in our office in the basement of the White House, and Leslie, like I told you many times, it was a no-frills space. We were all at our desks, and all of a sudden who should come walking through the door but the First Lady. This was a very rare occasion. You could have heard a pin drop. After she acknowledged us, she looked around the room and remarked that the grey paint on our walls looked very dull and dingy. They next thing we knew, painters were on their ladders, covering up that dull grey paint and brightening up the place with a blue color. That was one of the benefits of being so close to power, to actually see them as real people, realizing they are just like us and they care. That was one day I'll never forget.' My dad's enthusiasm and passion for service showed me that you're capable of doing anything in this life that you want and never taking no for an answer."

Leslie learned so many other valuable lessons from her father, as well. "After he graduated high school, my dad worked in a shoe factory in Newbury, Pennsylvania, a rural working-class town, pounding nails into shoes on an assembly line. One day it dawned on him that there had to be more in life than just hammering tiny nails into shoes. That one moment of clarity changed his life, and each and every time he told me that story, I found it inspiring. I have that same spark in me too, and I always knew on some level that there was more out there for me," Leslie said. That spark must have really worked since her dad went on to serve in the US Army, working in the White House and later providing communications services to the old

Walter Reed Army Hospital in Washington, DC, and other locations around the world.

But finding that potential and knowing what path to take were Leslie's personal challenges. "My dad always told us that people who go into the military want to do something bigger than just for themselves. They want to help others and give back, and they live and love to serve. My dad had that inspiration, and his influence on me was so empowering," said Leslie.

So it was no surprise to any of Leslie's friends and family that she sought a scholarship to the ROTC program when she entered Marymount University in Arlington, Virginia. She decided to apply there because it was close to home but far enough away that she could spread her wings and become her own person. "When I was in high school I had that mind-set to venture out and see what's out there to discover," Leslie said. "In high school I was always trying to have more leadership roles, so I could understand as much as possible and to start preparing for the next steps of my career. It was naturally inherent in me to always want to volunteer, run for school offices, and try to be out in front leading as much as possible. That was my comfort zone and it motivated me. As a result, I became student body president, senior class secretary, cheerleading captain, homecoming queen, and year-book business manager."

When Leslie arrived at college she kept asking herself, "What more can I do?" Marymount was officially founded as a finishing school to prepare girls to marry midshipmen from the Naval Academy. Ironically, the first year when Leslie arrived, in 1987, was also the first year that the college became coed. Not only was Leslie not the typical Marymount student, but she also stood out because of her choice to be part of the college's ROTC program. "There were a few of us in army ROTC, and looking back, we were definitely in the minority," Leslie said. "There were so many times that I felt different because, when the other girls were making plans to go out, I would be preparing for military classes and drills by getting my uniform ready, getting my boots shined, and prepping for drills."

Leslie loved her college days. She especially was thrilled to be able to meet other ROTC students from colleges all around the region who would converge on Georgetown University in Washington, DC, to attend military classes. "Georgetown was the army ROTC host school at the time, and there was a mix of cadets from so many other local colleges. I didn't feel different at all and in fact, we stood out in a good way. Sometimes when I would walk around in my uniform at Marymount, I wondered what the other girls were saying about us. I often thought that what they were saying wasn't at all positive."

But giving up in the wake of doing something different was not in Leslie's DNA. Oh no. She had greater plans, and they certainly didn't involve a wedding ring or a house with a white picket fence. "When I was close to graduation, I had a clear career path," said Leslie. "I wanted to join the army and that was that. Before my commissioning, I submitted my branch request, but at the time the needs of the army didn't consist of my major in college, which was communications. Because we were in the very beginning of the Gulf War in January, 1991, and I graduated in May, 1991, the army had a shortage of nuclear biological chemical officers. So I resolved to become a nuclear biological chemical officer, because what the army needed was what I was more than happy to do."

Leslie attended the officer basic training course at Ft. McClellan in Alabama and was there in August, 1991. "My class was filled with people just like me," Leslie said. All of the officers in training were liberal arts majors, and there was only person who was an actual chemical engineering major. "I was happy to put the needs of the army above my own," said Leslie. "Everyone was bonded, and I always say that your military family sometimes surpasses even your own family. It is an amazing camaraderie and connection with fellow service members that I can't even explain." Leslie said that even though it was challenging to learn a new field, every job is as important as the next in the military. "If there were a nuclear, chemical, or biological attack on our country, your quick and accurate response is what is going to make the difference between how many lives are saved," said Leslie.

And it was a quick and accurate response to a noncombat medical emergency, a blood clot in her leg while she was stationed in Bosnia, that would save Leslie's life.

It was September 28, 2002, when Leslie finally awoke from the surgery that would forever change her life. It was surreal. "I think about if anyone would have told my dad in 2002 that his daughter would be taking her dying last breath in the same hospital where he spent most of his career working, well, it really puts things in perspective," Leslie said. "For me, it kind of all came full circle—realizing that everyone is connected in some way or another. As a result of a devastating blood clot—deep vein thrombosis—when I was in Bosnia, I lost my left leg. It was amputated below my knee. I always felt the safest when my dad was there in the hospital room with me. I believe that things happens for a reason, and when my dad was there I felt an amazing sense of calm—that everything was going to be okay." Leslie attributes the blood clot to tying her boots too tightly. Why? Because in her role as a public affairs officer, she was on duty 24/7, always having to look her professional best as she hosted distinguished visitors who came in country to visit troops. Tying her boots too tightly actually put her at higher risk for developing a clot from Factor 5 Leiven, which is a serious blood disorder. "Representing the army was so important to me, that I wanted to make sure my uniform looked sharp and tailored because the public affairs officer is one of the first people any visitor meets upon arrival," she said.

Leslie said that being in the military, and learning so many important life lessons from her dad, laid the foundation for her to overcome the loss of her leg. "Understanding that in the military, no matter what you are faced with, you do the best to complete the mission. That means never giving up, never being the victim, and adapting and overcoming challenges to turn your life around. Even though I had a massive blood clot during my deployment to Bosnia, I was medically retired from the army because no one expected me to live, and now I am legally blind. In some strange way, I believe it has been a blessing for me to learn and grow."

And she met the love of her life in the process. He's tall, blond, and handsome. No, he's not a Naval Academy graduate, and he doesn't drive a Corvette. He's so much more than that. A golden Labrador/retriever mix named Issac. "I always tell people, 'It's all about Issac,'" said Leslie.

Unlike Leslie, Issac didn't come from a loving and supportive home— quite the contrary. He was found wandering the streets of Myrtle Beach, South Carolina, alone and afraid. He had no collar or identification, and it was clear to the people who picked him up that he was either neglected, abused, or both. "It makes me so sad to think about Issac living on the street all alone," said Leslie. "But for me, it was fate."

Leslie's decision to even think about getting a service dog didn't come lightly. "I truly feel you have to be ready in heart, mind, and soul alike to make that kind of commitment; but I knew finally I was ready," she said. "My hesitation all along was that I felt that there was someone else out there who was more in need than me. My thought at the time was that there were other warriors who were more deserving, and I needed to wait my turn. I especially felt that way because I never served in Iraq and Afghanistan." But Leslie's service was exemplary, having been deployed to Bosnia and working as a public affairs officer with the responsibility of taking care of high-level government officials, flag officers, and famous celebrities visiting the base, communicating relevant messages to the media and to internal audiences, and making sure anyone who visited was given all of the information and anything else they needed during their trip. But upon her return to the United States, after suffering the life-threating blood clot and losing her left leg, she began to realize that she in fact was worth it.

"No matter what people tell you, it is traumatic losing a limb," Leslie said. "But on top of that, in 2005 I lost total vision in my left eye too. The doctors were really baffled and had no idea why this was happening. After many tests and seeing medical specialists, I was referred to Johns Hopkins. The doctor came up with a probable cause that was my possible exposure to chemical agents or a toxin in Bosnia. I asked him what he meant by toxins, and he said, 'The gases emitted from the mass grave sites, and Leslie, those toxins can lay dormant in your body until it attacks again.' It was shocking to hear that possible diagnosis, and it was frightening to realize that this will always be in my body and I'll never know when it will act up."

To make matters worse, Leslie would, without warning, periodically lose all vision and then have to be rushed to Walter Reed for immediate treatment. She has special medication to administer herself, but each and every time it happens, Leslie is scared and afraid that she will lose the very small remaining amount of vision in her right eye.

"The other big reason that pushed me to get a service dog was I already lost all the sight in my left eye and was missing my leg, and that made me very unsteady in public. I was continuously bumping into things in the house and in public places. In the supermarket I would do the same thing, and when I would bump into someone's shopping cart accidentally, they would get mad at me. I found myself apologizing all the time saying, 'I'm so sorry I hit you, but I'm blind and I didn't see you.' I could never figure out why they were irritated. But I'm convinced that everything happens for a reason, and this was my timing to apply for a service dog."

Subconsciously, Leslie knew there would be a dog somewhere that would be perfect for her. "Something just clicked in me, and I decided to call and reach out to Canines for Veterans. One of my fellow wounded warriors had a service dog from them. I called and said, 'Hey, I'm Leslie, and I met Ed and his service dog, Gabe, at Walter Reed. He had a service dog from your organization, and I think it's time for me to get one too," said Leslie. "It's time."

Canines for Veterans, a program within Canines for Service, and its founder and CEO, Rick Hairston, couldn't have been happier to help Leslie once she told him her story. "The unexpected thing is that Rick Hairston responded to me right away. He asked me to fill out an application that had one main question about what my daily activity was like. He said once they evaluated it, he would match me up with a dog. He was wonderful, supportive, and understanding," she added. To Leslie's surprise, in just one week Rick called her back and said, "Leslie, congratulations, we have the perfect dog for you. His name is Issac, and we feel he is the best, biggest, and strongest dog we have and can give you what you need in terms of adapting to your changing environment and active travel schedule. In fact, everyone at the Canines for Veterans felt that Issac has been waiting for his special person, and that is you." Leslie couldn't believe her good fortune.

Leslie could hardly wait to meet Issac. Rick said he was about two years old and done with his training, which had taken approximately one year. Rick introduced Leslie to Issac on a brief visit to DC, because she couldn't make the in-person training right away. She would have to travel to North Carolina and work with Issac, along with his trainer.

At the time, she learned that her trainer was a marine who was incarcerated in a military prison, for what offense she didn't know and that didn't matter.

"The split second I saw Issac, I thought, 'Oh my gosh, there's my dog, he's going to help me.' Electricity went through me. It was the same feeling I had as a child when the lights first got turned on our Christmas tree. It was an overwhelming sense of pure joy and happiness and an instant connection all at once," said Leslie.

It was as if Leslie and Issac had known each other all of their lives. The connection was immediate, emotional, and joyous. "The first time we met, I knew it was meant to be. There was absolutely no hesitation on Issac's part, and he right away positioned himself on my left side; it was as if he had known me forever," she added.

Leslie would soon learn more about her new best friend. Rick explained to her that Issac was trained at Camp Lejeune by a marine serving time in the brig. "Wow, that was quite an introduction," Leslie said. "I was very anxious to meet the marine that spent an entire year of his life with my new dog, and I was excited to go there in person as part of my training with Issac. It was funny because, even though I knew he was in the brig, I wasn't nervous. I didn't think any differently of him, because he was a fellow service member," Leslie said. "But the reality was there was a sense of extra apprehension, because I was the very first female veteran to receive a service dog trained by this nonprofit."

"After working with him for a few times, I asked the guard after the training was completed if, at the end of the meeting, I could give the marine trainer a hug; they thought I was insane. I could tell it was really hard for them to understand the gift I'd been given in Issac. I was touched that he devoted his time to train Issac for a year. For me, the least I could do was give him a hug."

But there was no hug—not even a handshake was allowed; no physical contact at all. She never even knew anything about him. She couldn't even share pictures of Issac as a way of showing him how the dog was doing. It was heartbreaking for Leslie not to be able to let the marine trainer know that what he was doing in the brig was changing lives.

After her first meeting with Issac and Rick, Leslie traveled to North Carolina to begin her one-week, one-on-one training with Issac. They would do many exercises and command training, and soon the pair would go out in public to PetSmart and local restaurants. It was obvious to everyone that Issac and Leslie were a match made in heaven, and as a result, they were allowed to leave training early because their relationship was that good and so natural. "We fell right into place when we got home for the first time," said Leslie.

"The biggest thing when we first came back home was a nervous excitement. I was worried that I would give him a wrong command and mess up his training. I didn't want to confuse him either. But that was me, not him. Issac was really confident on his own, and over a short period of time, I wouldn't have to give him commands because he wouldn't seem to need them. It was like he anticipated just what I needed." One of Leslie's main challenges was her vision and mobility. "A huge thing for me is always dropping things. When I did, Issac would pick them up automatically, even if I didn't give him a command. Then, after he picked up the object he would hold it, position himself in front of me, and hand me the object. I think that comes from the bond and connection we have. We understand each other and are truly a team and partners for life."

As time went on, Issac and Leslie's bond became even more solidified. She got him in 2009, and he adapted to her changing health conditions with marine precision. She often wondered if he learned that from his marine trainer, and perhaps his compassion and gentleness came from having been abused and abandoned.

"There is so much I love about Issac, I can't put it into words some-times," she said. "I know it sounds strange, but sometimes I think that I hope I go first because I couldn't imagine my life without Issac. We are that much in tune. I often say that Issac is a goofball. That's why I love him, because he always makes me laugh." In fact, Leslie said that Issac has been nicknamed the "friendliest service dog ever" by so many people around the country who have met him. Leslie said that Issac has some very funny facial expressions and mannerisms, and when she is having what she calls a blah day, Issac knows just the right remedy. "I sometimes look at him, and he'll be on his back with his legs right up in the air, and he gives me this big smile. One ear will be up or flopped down, and when his little gum line gets caught in his teeth, it catches me off guard. I just have to laugh, and I say to myself, 'It's going to be okay because I have Issac. That's why Mommy loves you.'"

Another thing Issac tends to do, according to Leslie, is sense her needs even before she sometimes does. She is fascinated by how dogs can think, reason, and act on their conclusions. "Even when I take a bath, Issac, all on his own, will bring me my shoes, and I think he has to be processing in his mind, 'There's mom's leg, so that mean she needs her shoes.' He always adapts and figures things out. He's working 24/7, trying to make me happy and always doing his best."

Leslie believes that Issac is even more amazing because he was a stray in Myrtle Beach. He was picked up, taken to the Grand Strand Animal Shelter in South Carolina, and not considered adoptable, let alone a candidate for service dog status. "When Issac was first brought to the shelter, he was a bit wild and set in his ways," said Leslie. "People weren't interested in adopting him, and he was scheduled to be euthanized just twenty-four hours before Canines for Veterans picked him up." Canines for Veterans scouts out animal shelters for potential service dogs. When they spotted Issac, a Labrador/retriever mix, they knew he would be perfect, but first they had to find out if he could handle the potential command test. Issac passed with flying colors and went from possibly being euthanized to starting a new life as a service dog in training.

Leslie, day after day, year after year, has been continually amazed by Issac's intelligence, compassion, and the bond they developed.

While she knew that Issac probably had been abused as a puppy, she never really knew what that abuse was until one Saturday afternoon while shopping with him at Bed Bath & Beyond. "When we moved into our new house, Issac and I went shopping for a new broom. I saw one hanging on the wall and lifted it up off the rack to check it out. In the split second after I grabbed the broom, I saw Issac cowering. His tail went between his legs, and I could see the fear in his eyes. I'm sure he was thinking that I was going to harm him and hit him with the broom. It broke my heart, so I bent down and I said to him, 'I'm so sorry, Issac. Mom's not going to hurt you.' I put the broom down. I was torn apart knowing that in his previous life he was obviously abused, and probably by a broom or something similar. I got down on the floor and hugged him. 'Issac, it's okay, mommy won't let anyone hurt you ever again.' We bolted right out the door, leaving any traces of the broom behind."

Over time, Issac realized that, though his job is to protect Leslie, she is there for him as well. That's probably one of the reasons that he is totally devoted to her. "I think the reason he is who he is, is our connection. He never stops working, but I make sure he has plenty of play time. He actually is quite a goofball and loves to make me laugh, and I do the same for him," Leslie said. "His personality totally ties in to a story I heard from Rick. He said that when the dogs are rescued and start training, the marines rename them based on the Bible. He was given the name Issac, and one day I googled its meaning, and it said that Issac meant 'to laugh.' I think he's goofy because he does make me laugh; that's what I love most about him. He knows when to be silly and, at the same time, when to help me with my daily needs. But don't let him fool you. He's always working, aware, and alert. And every night before we go to sleep, I tell him how much I love him in baby talk—the way most dog owners do. 'Mommy loves you, and Issac, you can't get any older because I need you forever. You are my hero, and I'm where I am because you are here.'"

About eight months after Issac and Leslie were paired together, Leslie faced another medical trauma, and she had no idea how he would respond.

In November 2010, Leslie was rushed again to Walter Reed. The sight in her right eye was now gone too. "On the third day, the doctors were doing rounds, and they looked at my right eye and asked how many fingers I could see. I only saw a small line across the top of my right eye. I could look through that little crack and I was so excited that I could see my family again!"

Even though Leslie was in the hospital, the doctors said it was okay to bring Issac in every day to visit. She was thrilled, and when he was there she felt that everything would be all right. "When I finally came home, my parents stayed with me because I couldn't drive and needed to heal. When they first brought me home, I came in and sat on the couch and Issac was right there with me," said Leslie. "The sofa was low, and Issac was sitting in front of me, face to face and eye to eye. He stared at me for what seemed like eternity with a dead-hard stare; we locked eyes. It felt as if he were taking everything in. My eyes were a mess. They were swollen because of the minor surgery I had, and they were horribly black and blue and severely bloodshot from the trauma. I knew that Issac could feel my emotions and sense my pain. Then, in a split second, he snapped out of it. It was like he was telling me, 'Okay, I got it.' The next morning when I got up, I went into the bathroom as usual. We have one sink and a vanity, and when I first walked in I was discombobulated. I remember thinking what am I going to do? I couldn't comprehend the fact that I was almost totally blind. So I sat on the vanity bench, leaned over, and started crying. Why was I blind? It's so finite, I thought. You can get a prosthetic leg and you can walk again. But doctors can't replace eyes at this point to help you see again."

Issac obviously saw that Leslie was in pain. Normally, when he kisses Leslie, he slobbers all over. His big, wet tongue knows no bounds. This time, when she needed him the most, he instinctively knew to go easy. "Issac gets up, puts himself right in front of me, and began to lick away my tears with the tiny tip of his tongue. They were like baby kisses, and I swear he was saying to me with his kiss, 'I've got you, Mom. I understand. I know there is a difference with your sight, but don't be afraid; I'm here.' That moment just proved beyond a shadow of a doubt that the bond between a person and their service dog is priceless," said Leslie. Leslie could tell that Issac, the kisser with the sloppy big tongue, knew that she needed the baby kisses. He could see her face was different. He knew she was in pain. "What I needed in that moment was care and compassion," Leslie added. "Isaac didn't receive any additional training to adjust to my legal blindness, but he changed on his own in the way he did things. In the past, if I dropped something, he would get it before I would tell him and he would wait for me to take it. Now he picks it up and nudges me. I think he is saying, 'Mom, I'm here and I know you can't always see where you drop things or where I am. Don't worry, I'll be your eyes.'"

Another example of Issac's love and devotion came the same day that Leslie was told by her doctors that she was legally blind. "Hearing the words *legally blind* caused me to lose hope that any of my vision would come back. I truly understood at that moment how much I would need to rely even more on Issac to be my guide and help me deal with this devastating condition," said Leslie.

Leslie recalled that day vividly. While she was troubled by getting the bad news about her vision, having Issac there was comforting. Little did she know that later that day, her love and devotion to Issac would be profoundly revealed.

After Leslie, her parents, and Issac went on a long therapeutic walk to help her cope with the news, they eventually returned to the house to talk about—of all things—Leslie's yard work that needed to be done. Anything to divert her from thinking about her new diagnosis. "The last thing I wanted to talk about was my trees and flowers," said Leslie. "But I knew it was taking my mind off what my doctors said, so that was good for me at the moment."

During her conversation with her dad, she felt a numb feeling in her soul and describes the feeling as if she were in a trance. Suddenly, through her limited vision, and out of nowhere, she saw a strong, muscular, brownish-colored dog charging toward her, Issac, and her dad. The dog bolted into the front yard, breaking Leslie out of her half-conscious state of mind. "Issac immediately stood to a full-on defensive position and moved himself in between me and the aggressive dog. The dog lunged at Issac with all of his might; Issac's screams were horrifying," Leslie said. Leslie's heart sank as she heard Issac's frantic cries. Issac kept twisting and contorting his body to get away from the biting dog. With her limited vision, Leslie tried to follow the sounds she heard in an attempt to save her beloved Issac. "I knew the dogs were right in front of me so I jumped in to try and separate the two dogs. I kicked my right leg up to the dog's face, hoping he would latch on to me and bite me instead. I thought, 'Hey, I'm already missing one leg, and I would rather lose my other leg than let anything happen to Issac.' I was afraid Issac was going to die,'" she said.

Leslie was frantic. She knew Issac was in a dire situation and tried another strategy. "The dog never bit my right leg, so I twisted myself around and more or less reached out and without hesitation, grabbed for Issac to physically get him away from the other dog. In a split second the two dogs were in a serious and dangerous brawl, and I was screaming and at the same time doing everything I could to rescue Issac, but the dog was relentless," said Leslie. "He surged at Issac and Issac did everything to avoid his vicious attack. The last time he lunged, I grabbed Issac by his collar, but his frantic contortions twisted my arm and caused a partial rotator cuff tear and a broken finger. I couldn't hold on any more and Issac, in a panic, managed to get away and run down the street. I was terrified. I ran down the street after him screaming, and my dad started running, too, though he tripped. I was scared to death for Issac's safety and I remember feeling like I was on the top of a cliff and holding on to Issac, but my grip wasn't strong enough and he was slipping away."

About thirty minutes later, Leslie was beside herself, not knowing where Issac was or if he was even alive. He had run into dense woods nearby, and she feared the worst: that he would die alone and she would never find him. Still, not even her broken and mangled right finger could stop her from searching through the neighborhood.

"Suddenly, I heard a tapping sound and I stopped in my tracks. When I turned around to hear where the sound was coming from, there was Issac. My heart melted. I dropped to my knees when I saw him. I gave him the biggest hug and couldn't stop crying for joy. It was truly a remarkable moment that solidified our bond even further. It was reminiscent of the ending of a *Lassie* episode, where the young boy and his dog were always reunited. Once again I realized how much I needed and relied on Issac. The veterinarian who treated his wounds—he had a puncture wound in his groin area, and the pads on his paws were ripped open—said that Issac wasn't running away from the aggressive dog to save himself, but rather running to get the dog away from me," said Leslie. "His injuries were so severe that his paws had to be bandaged and changed, confining him to bed rest for almost a month. This prevented Issac from helping me, especially in public. When he wasn't with me I felt like I was missing a part of me. That's one of the many reasons I tell Issac every day that he is my hero."

Leslie's vision is akin to a roll of the dice. Some days it is bearable, and the next it might completely disappear. She can only see in three parts of her right eye. "I have to watch things in three parts and I never see a full face," Leslie said. "I've been trying to adapt by taking classes at a great blind rehab program at the VA. It's helped me get better at doing the simple things that people take for granted like styling your hair or putting on makeup." Some mornings, Leslie says it takes her three hours to get ready. She has a system in place to tap her face with a makeup brush and get the blush in just the right spot. After all, Leslie freely admits that she is a fashionista at heart. "When I was at Walter Reed in 2010 and was told I was totally blind, in my subconscious I said to myself, 'Oh my god, who is going to do my hair and makeup? Oh no, my mother. She always put into my head that you don't leave the house without makeup.' But when I realized that I was blind for good, I had another more motivating thought. I said to myself, 'Whatever small gift I'm given, even just seeing this little sliver of light, I promise to never take for granted the ability to learn and figure it out. If I go blind tonight, I don't ever want to say to myself that I didn't give 150 percent. Sight is a gift.' And when it was taken from me, and then a little bit given back, I came to appreciate what seeing meant and how important it was to overcome my fears. Something inside me kicked in that day—a determination to not wait, never quit, and never say to myself that I didn't try hard enough. I will never be in the darkness. I used to feel guilty when I couldn't work anymore, feeling that I'm not contributing. I worked for six years for the government and the USO after my military medical retirement, and my leg being gone didn't stop me at all. But being blind is an entirely different proposition."

That's where Leslie's bucket list kicked into high gear.

"When I was in college, I always wanted to be in plays; high school, too. I regretted in college not trying out for drama and plays; I thought that I would do it later, but I always had an excuse. Something inside of me kicked in, and I decided to give it a try. Plus, a big part of my personality likes to get involved, and I was figuring out my new normal and feeling like myself again. Luckily for me, I met the actress Deidre Hall, from the television soap opera *Days of Our Lives*, in Los Angeles at the first event I attended after being teamed with Issac. Two years later she called me and asked if I wanted to appear as an extra in a special veterans' episode of the show. I jumped at the chance."

Leslie got the acting bug and enlisted the help of a professional acting coach and actress, Lisa Regina, whom she met through a headshot photographer, Barry Morgenstein, in New York City. Leslie took classes in Philadelphia and Long Island and did get a couple of acting jobs. She played a zombie in a movie called *Chernobyl Diaries*. "I guess I wasn't the best zombie," Leslie said. "They said I wasn't scary enough and the scene I was in was cut." She has also appeared in the TV shows *Project Runway All-Stars* and *Criminal Minds*.

But after being cast as an extra in the show *House of Cards*, Leslie had an epiphany.

"I was in full dress blues standing in a field and thinking, 'It's six thirty in the morning and its freezing, and we are repeating these scenes over and over. But I wouldn't trade this experience for anything.'" Later that night, after warming up and putting on a dress and a pair of her favorite sparkly heels, Leslie was part of a panel on disabled veterans in Baltimore, Maryland. "Having two different experiences in one day—acting and public speaking—made it the perfect day for me."

Now Leslie had a new direction in life and dedicated herself to advocacy, serving on many boards and veterans groups, becoming an ambassador for the Gary Sinise Foundation, and living her life the way she had dreamed.

Then, in December 2015, another episode with her vision knocked her for a loop. She could feel her vision fading in her right eye and knew just what to do. She had to immediately take medication, call 911, and make sure she got to the hospital right away. When the paramedics arrived, they asked, "Is your dog coming with you?" Leslie was barely conscious and in no shape to take him by his leash, but she nodded her head yes, and Issac jumped in the ambulance. When they arrived, the ER doctors immediately connected Leslie to many IVs; her pain was off the charts. "I wasn't holding Issac's leash, and it was chaos in the room. I could hear the nurses saying how incredible Issac was because he positioned himself at the end of my bed; he knew they were working on me and knew to stay out of their way. I remember them giving me morphine, and that made me physically sick. Issac saw my distress and looked to see where my hand was. He gently started licking my hand and comforting me. He needed to let me know he was there, but then he would return to his tucked-away spot on the floor at the end of the bed," Leslie said.

Issac never left her side. He knew he needed to stay out of the doctors' and nurses' way. Leslie said that his thought process is amazing.

Issac, the goofball, isn't so goofy after all. On the contrary, while he enjoys lots of good lovin' and too many hugs and kisses to count, not to mention the thrill of playing with his overload of squeaky toys, he knows he has a job to do. Not because he has to. He wants to. Neither he nor Leslie will ever quit. She sees his beauty inside and out. He sees her gigantic heart. Together, they see the world the way it should be seen—with love and devotion, or as Leslie and Issac say, "A *pawsitive* attitude."

SIX

THE MARINE CORPORAL

"Gnome somehow can read me."

THE NOUN *GNOME*, ACCORDING TO THE MERRIAM-WEBSTER DICTIONARY, means: "An ageless and often deformed dwarf of folklore who lives in the earth and usually guards treasure." Don't tell that to Marine Cpl. Justin Crabbe (ret.). His Gnome has sparkling brown eyes, a smooth yellow coat, and muscles that even Arnold Schwarzenegger would envy, as well as a thick, blocky head and a body as evenly proportioned as a bright-red Ferrari. And, no, this Gnome has never spent even one nanosecond under the earth. Five years ago, Justin could never have imagined he would have to rely on his Gnome for doing everything he used to do with abandon. Things such as reaching for a cup in a cabinet, retrieving dropped items, or opening doors—simple, ordinary tasks that most people take for granted. But Justin's life was far from normal. Everything he knew before was gone.

It had been just another grueling day for Cpl. Justin Crabbe, who, like many young marines, was serving his country in the rough and rugged Afghanistan terrain—August 26, 2011, to be exact. As he and his platoon were patrolling near a dam, Justin stepped on an underwater improvised explosive device (IED). It had been missed by the sniffer dog on patrol with them, likely because it was under the water. All IED blasts are devastating, and they are made worse by the nails, debris, and other items packed inside to maximize damage.

Justin lost both legs in the blast, as well as his right thumb and fingers on both hands. Almost drowning in a pool of blood and water, his first concern was for his buddies' well-being. "Were they hurt?" he asked. "Are they okay?" The next thing Justin knew, he was on a Medevac helicopter to the military hospital, and after five days, he was flown back to the United States to begin a long and painful recovery at Walter Reed.

"I thought I knew what happened at first, and that I just lost my legs," said Justin. "But I had a different reaction stateside when the doctors woke me up. I was on a ventilator for nineteen days, and I was so happy when they slowly brought me out of sedation and I was able to see my mom. Her face was so comforting to me. She asked me if I knew what happened, and since I still couldn't talk because of the ventilator, I just pointed down to where my legs used to be. She calmly moved closer to me and said: 'Justin, do you know anything else that you lost in the blast?' I just shook my head from side to side. 'Son,' she said in a very matter-of-fact tone, 'Your thumb is gone on your right hand, and you are also missing some fingers on your left hand.' I couldn't believe what she was saying at first. 'Wow, I'm missing fingers on both hands, too. I knew about my legs, but this is crazy.'

"I knew right there and then that that was bad news, and honestly I was really mad," said Justin. "The thing about losing a thumb is that it is so important to everyday function. Can you imagine not being able to button your shirt, or picking up a glass, or even writing a letter without one? And the worst part is that I'm right-handed."

He didn't stay mad for long though. "Once they woke me up for good and took the ventilator out, I was able to talk to my parents and sister. I thought to myself, 'Why am I so upset?'" That thought led Justin to an epiphany. "Something started clicking in my brain, and I realized that, even though I lost my legs, my thumb, and some fingers, I still have Mom, Dad, and my sister. I realized that they were so selfless and took time off to be with me, so there is no rational reason, if I still have them, that I should be upset. I'm alive, after all."

Justin didn't know that much about prosthetic legs at the time but was aware that some of his buddies and other wounded warriors were using them with great success. "At first I thought, 'Oh, this sucks that I'll be getting fitted for prosthetic legs.' Then it occurred to me that, hey, I'm still normal and can do things that everyone else can do. Why should I bitch and moan? That won't make my legs grow back," Justin said. With the support of his family, and realizing that he was still alive and could live a full and productive life, his mood began to quickly improve. "It only took a couple of weeks for me to get back to being me again," said Justin. "I can't let this slow me down. I have to adapt and overcome."

Justin was only twenty-two at the time, and his mother, Maureen, became his full-time caregiver. She left her job and home in California to spend the next year and a half by his side at Walter Reed. "I don't know how I would have done it without my mom," said Justin. "She gave me strength every day and always instilled in me and my sister a positive mind-set. We learned that if life throws you a curveball, you take the ball and run with it. You don't hide or run away. That can-do spirit was a lifesaver."

Maureen was one of the caregivers known around Walter Reed as a mighty mom. She, and many other mothers, moved to the base to take care of their severely wounded children and never gave up on them. They were rocks and advocates who would do anything to protect their children. But Justin's mom went a bit further. Maureen reached out to other parents who were arriving at Walter Reed lost and in a panic. She would take them under her wing, giving them the information they needed to navigate the complexities of the military medical system. She also gave them a loving shoulder to cry on. One of those grieving mothers she helped was Tyler Jeffries's mom, Pam, who Maureen heard about on Facebook. "That's my mom," Justin said. "She's amazing. And when I think about how she stopped her life for me and never asked for anything in return, that is incredible. I couldn't ask for anything more. My parents and sister kept me going, and who knows where I'd be without them."

After a year and a half at Walter Reed, Justin finally was able to return to California, where he lived with his parents for about two years. "My parents completely renovated their house to make it accessible for me. They widened all of the doorways, made me a roll-in shower, had bars installed on the front access door, and so much more," said Justin. "It was my mom who researched everything I would need as an amputee, including what nonprofits would be able to help, like Homes for our Troops, which builds smart homes for wounded warriors, and Canine Companions for Independence, which provides service dogs for qualified disabled Americans, including wounded warriors. She found out about all of them."

It was obvious to Justin, his doctors, and his family that he not only would need an accessible home but also a highly trained service dog. He contacted Canine Companions for Independence while he was still in Bethesda. One of the oldest service dog organizations, Canine Companions carefully breeds and expertly trains assistance dogs. They provide the dog, training, and ongoing follow-up services. Soon, Justin was having an interview with the group, which assesses a potential dog handler's needs and personality to ensure the best match with a dog.

Justin was more than excited to take part in Canine Companions' two-week training course. "It was a neat experience, and I learned a lot about what to expect and got to know the dogs they thought would be good for me, and vice versa," Justin said.

The first dog Justin met he really liked. But it was dog number two that wowed him!

"I only spent a few minutes with Gnome and that was it—I knew he was my dog," said Justin. "It felt like we knew each other forever. He obeyed every command, and he wouldn't leave my side. The trainers couldn't believe it, and they were surprised that he and I matched up with all the requirements—pretty cool."

According to the American Kennel Club, Labrador retrievers are strongly built and possess a sound, athletic body that enables them to function as a retrieving-gun dog. They have the substance and soundness to hunt waterfowl or upland game for long hours under difficult conditions; the character and quality to win in the show ring; and the temperament to be a family companion. They are well suited as a breed to be certified service dogs. In addition, as anyone who has ever owned a Lab knows, they are also highly intelligent, enthusiastic, sensitive, and empathetic.

For Justin, Gnome's main tasks were to pick up the keys he was always dropping, push buttons on the doors to open and close them, turn lights on and off, and open and close cabinets.

But the real challenge for Justin was dealing with other people.

"Before I got Gnome it was difficult to go out in public. Actually it was terrible," Justin said. "People were very rude and would stare at me all the time. They would say, 'Oh, what's wrong with you?' I didn't like that. Once Gnome came things totally changed. Now when people first see me they ask, 'Oh, what does your dog do? What kind of dog is that? He is really handsome.' Then I tell them my story, and their entire body language changes. They want to know more about me and my service and that makes me feel really great. It also takes the pressure off of me, and the focus is put on Gnome."

One of the many surprises of getting to know Gnome, Justin recalls, is the special role he has taken upon himself to make Justin's life better.

"Gnome somehow can read me. When he sits by me, he makes me feel better. He senses if I'm in a bad mood and comes right over to cheer me up," Justin added.

Soon after Gnome became a permanent part of Justin's life, he met Casey, the love of his life and the woman he would soon marry. She lived in Singapore and was working there as an interior designer for international hotels. They met by accident on a dating website, when Casey by mistake put the location of where she wanted to meet someone as California rather than her home state of Arizona. Justin responded to her profile, and soon the two met. The rest is history. "Casey is an amazing, intelligent woman and I am the luckiest man in the world to be her husband," Justin said. "I love her to death."

Life was going great for Justin. Other than having some medical issues, he moved into his smart home, got married, and was soon expecting a little girl. "Gnome had a sixth sense about everything and everyone he loved," Justin said. "When Casey was pregnant, he would put his nose next to her belly and just lie there. He would rest his head on my chest when he saw I was down or just not my normal self. But when Oakley was born, Gnome was scared at first. I think he didn't want to accidently hurt the baby because of his size, and so he stayed away. But after about a month they became the best of friends."

Justin and Gnome are inseparable. In fact, his wife says, if Justin leaves the house without him, Gnome becomes despondent. Like the time Justin was taken by ambulance to the hospital because of his ongoing stomach problems. As Gnome watched Justin being put on the gurney, Casey said she could see the pain on the dog's face. Once Justin was on his way to the hospital, Gnome sat dutifully by the door, looking distressed, and didn't leave that spot until Justin returned home.

Other than that hospital stay, Gnome goes where Justin goes. "He flies with me and sits below my feet on the plane, goes with me to hotels and restaurants, and I take him everywhere," Justin added. "The only places I won't take him to are air shows or events where there would be extreme noise, like a fireworks display. But, no matter where we go in public, if he has his vest on, he means business."

But he's still a dog, and when his vest comes off, watch out! "Gnome loves my parents, too, and it's fun to take him over to their house where he can just be a normal dog," Justin said. "It's like a light switch goes off in his head and he says to himself, 'Yippee, I can play now.' He can literally spend all day running around with my parents' dogs and playing with his favorite toys. I love to see him like that, and I make sure he has plenty of down time to enjoy his life."

Justin said he cannot underestimate the positive emotional effect that Gnome has on him. "He's my buddy and I love him so much. I wouldn't be as good as I am without him by my side," he added. "Sometimes when I wake up I remember having that bad day back in Afghanistan. I don't have PTSD, but I have bad memories—not super good memories. But my positive outlook all goes back to my family, everything ties back to that. Gnome helps me get through those days when I feel that way, and my family plays a big role in that as well."

But no dog is perfect, and Gnome has his moments. Sometimes, Justin says, when Gnome isn't working he gets a tad jealous. "Gnome and I have this bond, and I can see when he's feeling neglected," Justin said. "If I'm spending too much time with the baby he gives me this look and I know he's thinking, 'Hey, don't just hug and kiss her. I'm still here, look at me.' But when Gnome is working, he won't do that. He might come over and gently nudge me with his nose and remind me that he's still here. His amazing sensitivity is just something I think he was born with."

Justin has made sure Gnome has a great life. Everyone in his family are animal lovers, and Casey and Oakley consider Gnome as a brother and a son. "He is my little boy, and left to his own devices, he would just be a lover who would lick you all day and lie on your lap," Justin said.

Justin plans on keeping Gnome, even after he is no longer able to perform as a service dog. They are often retired at age nine or ten. Roughly every two years, Gnome will be tested to maintain his certification and to check on his health and his ability to respond to commands in public. Canine Companions provides ongoing support as a way of maintaining their relationship with recipients and their dogs. Often, these certifications are good problem-solving sessions and a time to eventually discuss plans for a dog's retirement. "I won't get another service dog as long as Gnome is alive. I want him to be happy and feel loved regardless if he is working or just being my son. I've talked to many people who've said that the old dog would become very jealous of the new dog. If they can't wear their service vest and are not allowed to go out anymore as a service dog, they often feel that they're being abandoned. It's like they are saying to you, 'Oh, you don't like me anymore; maybe I'm a bad boy?' That's when the bad attention-seeking behavior starts. I never want Gnome to feel that way," said Justin.

In the meantime, Justin and his wife would love to have another child. He also plans to take some courses in motivational speaking and help encourage other wounded warriors as well.

As Oakley sits on the floor and tugs at Gnome's ears, he keeps his cool and gives her way too many wet kisses to count. Casey keeps a close eye on her baby daughter but knows she is in good hands—or paws—with Gnome. Justin, Casey, Oakley, and Gnome are a family of four that relishes the unconditional love they feel for each other, something so precious and deep that it can only be realized by wizardry. After all, gnomes, while they come in many shapes and sizes, can't compare to the yellow, furry Gnome, with the soulful brown eyes whose earthly powers are simply magic!

SEVEN

THE NAVY VIETNAM VETERAN

"The dog becomes a family member."

SERVICE DOGS BECOME MEMBERS OF THE FAMILY. PERIOD. YES, THEY ARE primarily there to work and offer support in innumerable ways. But they are also emotional creatures that are irrevocably bonded to their handlers, living with them for years and learning to empathize with them during both joyful and sorrowful times. Never was this clearer to Paul Mimms than in the months following the death of his wife Catherine in May 2016.

Catherine, like Paul, was blind. Each had a service dog. In fact their story together began at a service dog training school in 1989, where they both had gone for their very first dog. But in 2013, hobbled by a broken ankle and having had a pancreas transplant that failed, Catherine decided to retire her dog and not get a replacement.

It hadn't been the best of matches. It happens. Some combinations work, dog and handler in perfect sync, and some simply don't for a host of reasons. But it was clear after her surgery that she would no longer need the dog. It was time to return her to the school.

Paul decided he would make the trip from their home in Kansas City to New York City, leaving his own service dog, Brook-Lyn, a mix of golden retriever and yellow Lab, at home. He wasn't gone long, it was just a day trip up and back, but he was clearly missed.

"When I came back, my dog went berserk," Paul said. "She seemed to be saying, 'You did come back. You didn't leave me.'"

But something was clearly different. "You could tell she was looking around for the other dog," Paul said. "And then eventually it sinks in. She got to where it was, 'Okay, I guess I'm the queen here.'"

Without a dog of her own, for the first time in decades, Catherine was interacting more with Brook-Lyn, and the dog returned the affection. "She would come up to her and sniff her, and she would just as often plop down beside her chair as my chair," Paul said. "If anyone petted her—and it didn't matter which of us it was—she wanted to flop on her back."

Looking back now, what's clear to Paul is the close relationship that Catherine and Brook-Lyn shared, even though she was his guide dog. "The dog becomes a family member, even a service dog," he said. "When they get home, they are essentially just a dog. So they are around you and family members who pet them without going overboard."

And Brook-Lyn, too, would mourn for Catherine.

"When my wife passed in May, that was an adjustment for the dog, too, as well as for me," Paul remembered. "Just like when my wife's dog left, Brook-Lyn was running around the house sniffing and looking for her. You could just kind of tell what was going on."

After five years together, Brook-Lyn and Paul were tight, a good team whether close to home or in their many travels around the country together. Now they would grow even closer.

"It was just her and me after that. Of course, I had my episodes of—oh, no—tears," he said, starting to break down, "and I don't know what she thinks of that. It's an anxious moment, an anxious time, for her. She gets really boisterous and she wants to play, and so I'm not sure how she is interpreting the crying and tears. But she's right here with me. If I cry and she hears me crying, she comes and she wants to play and she wants to be petted and flops on her back.

"I was already close to her, but in those kinds of moments, you realize that the dog is another family member. You realize also what a great amount of support she gives as you go through something like this."

Paul was born just two months shy of Victory in Europe Day, in 1945, the closing year of the Second World War. He grew up in Washington, a small town in Iowa, with two sisters, his mom, and his maternal grandparents.

He remembers a garden—a sizable one of about a quarter of an acre. "As I came up, I learned how to plant it and harvest it. So I got that lesson early that tomatoes actually come from somebody who grew them. Some of the kids now think that they just come from a grocery store."

One other distinct memory—more unique, as he described it—was the way chores were handled by him and his sisters. They were not assigned by gender. "We divided everything up into three parts as much as we could," he said. "One of us would have to wash the dishes, one would dry them, and one would put them away. One of us would sweep the kitchen floor, one the dining room floor, and one the living room. I did the same things my sisters did."

He learned how to iron, to cook, to clean the house. "A lot of the things that are supposed to be 'girls' work,' well I learned that too," he said. "And I can say that having that foundation helped me out later."

"When I was a young person I was sighted, so I didn't have to learn things as a blind person," he said. "I lost my sight as an adult, so I just had to relearn how to do things as a blind person. It was quite a bit easier, I think."

He was a scholar-athlete, eventually graduating eighth in a class of about four hundred. He lettered in football, basketball, and track. Visiting a coach many years later, he was reminded that at one point in his life he was always running.

"I didn't have that vivid a memory of that until he said it," Paul recalled. "Then I remembered it. I used to run to school, run back home."

It was his favorite sport, the one in which he most excelled. By fourth grade he was already faster than anyone in his school, all the way up to the sixth graders. In sixth grade, only one other student in his small Iowa town had a better time in the hundred-yard dash—a high school kid—and Paul would eventually beat him too.

Athletic skills ran in the family. "My sister was probably a better athlete than I was on a comparative basis," he said, remembering that he was the only person who could outrun her. "But there was no chance for her to compete, so she got out of all that by freshman year."

He persisted, even after the family moved from small-town Iowa to Kansas City, Missouri, in 1960, when he was fifteen.

"Sports were a lot of what I did growing up, and I appreciate the value that it lent to the building of my character," Paul said. "There was a saying that they had in the gym: 'When the great scorekeeper comes to write against your name, he writes not whether you won or lost, but how you played the game.'

"That stuck with me. I realized the value of team membership, team playing, and fairness. There's a time to win and a time to just enjoy competing. There are some valuable lessons that come from athletics if you're so inclined to apply them. I still apply them."

Unlike today, when being an athletic standout, a National Honor Society member, and among the top ten graduates would attract the attention of college recruiters, there were no schools lining up with scholarship offers for Paul. And the family had no college fund. The superintendent of schools saw Paul's potential, though, and steered him to Antioch College in Yellow Springs, Ohio. A school board scholarship was available if he went there. "That was the clincher," Paul said. The down side was the lack of intercollegiate sports at Antioch, effectively ending Paul's athletic career.

Though he'd always done well in school, college was a new experience. Testing well and winning awards, as he'd frequently done, weren't enough to prepare him for college-level work. Still, he persevered, at least until the scholarship money ran out after year two. "I just couldn't come up with enough of the money to make up the difference," he said. When he returned to Kansas City, Paul was soon hired for an assembly-line position at Ford Motor Company. He worked underneath the cars as they rolled down the line. It wasn't one of the most sought-after jobs, but Paul liked it. And he soon learned that he had the skills needed, which weren't necessarily shared by all his coworkers. "One of the things we had to do was put a clip on the rear axle to hold the brake line in place," he said. "And the guy on the other shift could just never get that thing right. He would try and the clips would just pop off and go flying—*Bing!* His area was littered with those clips."

It wasn't hard work, and the pay was great. "I enjoyed it, but it wasn't challenging," Paul said. He started in July 1965 and, just three months later, received his letter from Uncle Sam informing him that he was now eligible for the draft and should report for a pre-enlistment physical.

"Shortly after I found out that I was number four in the draft lottery," Paul said. "So I decided to enlist in the navy rather than be drafted into the army." It wasn't so much a love of the sea that inspired his choice, but something far more practical. "My picture of the army was me digging a foxhole," he recalled. "Then I weighed about 195 to 210 pounds, and I was about six foot two and a half—I ended up being six foot three. That's a big foxhole. I thought I wanted to be doing something else while in the service rather than keep digging a foxhole deep enough to provide for my own protection."

Paul hit the ground running in Vietnam. Literally.

He was a year and a half into his enlistment and traveling on a commercial flight to Saigon on Valentine's Day that was packed with service members coming from Clark Air Force Base in the Philippines. He remembers an otherwise uneventful crossing of the Pacific, with the flight attendants—then called stewardesses—in miniskirts serving sodas. Once over Vietnam air space, the pilot announced that their landing would be delayed because of congestion on the ground. Translation: the air field was being bombed.

When they finally received permission to land, around midnight, the plane went into almost a flat-out dive. Once on the ground, Paul had his duffel bag and another bag to carry off the plane, and he remembers the stewardess's additional attire at the door as the troops prepared to disembark.

"She had a helmet and flak jacket on and was saying, 'Good luck. When you hit the ground, don't stop running until you get to the terminal.' She was saying that repeatedly."

Paul had every intention of following that advice. On departure from the Philippines, the officer of the day had the sailors wear their dress white uniforms, which would make them—and especially someone as big as Paul—stand out on a tarmac that was being illuminated by the magnesium flares the enemy was firing over the airfield.

"We got to the bottom of the steps of that rollout Jetway and started running," said the former track standout. "I was passing people."

There were no casualties that day. Everyone made it safely inside, and Paul spent his first night in Vietnam sitting on the floor of the terminal, leaning against his duffel bag.

The first time he held an M16 in his hands was while on guard duty at a former hotel turned into a transient barracks in Saigon for troops awaiting assignment to a permanent duty station. The navy didn't use M16s in training, so Paul simply never had a reason to use one. That night in Saigon, he was on watch from 2000 to 2400 hours (eight p.m. to midnight), behind a pile of sand bags in front of the hotel. He was one of two sailors out there, along with some soldiers, one with a machine gun, as well as others on the roof of the building.

When he was handed his M16, Paul also received ammo and a quick briefing on how to load and fire the weapon. "They showed me where the bullet went, and then they said, 'Anything coming down the street, shoot at it,' because it was after curfew," he said.

Fortunately, over those four hours, all was quiet. When his shift was supposed to end, he learned that his relief wasn't available. He'd have to stay another four hours. "There's a general order in the military that you cannot leave your post until properly relieved," Paul said. "So I wound up standing an eight-hour watch." Traveling and not sleeping in the days leading up to his watch caught up with him at about three in the morning. He dozed, and dropped the M16. "It hit the ground and the bolt slipped home, arming the weapon," he recalled. "So I had to check with the army guys to make sure I could eject that round and put it back in the clip."

So he was fully awake when, about five minutes later, a motorcycle came roaring down their street. "The guys on the roof saw it first because it came around the corner," he remembered. "And then it flew past us and the guys on the roof opened fire. You heard the engine race, as if it had been hit or it skidded or something. So there I was in live combat, watching tracer rounds go toward this guy on the motorcycle. That's when it hit home that I was really there."

The next day, when a call went out for volunteers to work in the chow hall on the top of the hotel, Paul raised his hand. "I said, 'I think I'll take that,'" he said. "If you were on mess duty, you didn't have to stand watches, though I still wound up standing a couple just out of necessity."

A month later he was aboard his ship on the Saigon River, one of the amphibious landing crafts that were the primary means of transporting tanks across water. The crafts' flank speed—engines all out—is about eleven knots, or twelve miles per hour. "They're about the slowest thing the navy has other than lifeboats," Paul recalled. That made them tempting targets for enemy troops along the river.

One day the warning signal for general quarters came: battle stations. Paul was ordered to make sure a fellow sailor who had worked twenty-eight hours straight was up and ready. The man had just finally been able to stand down ninety minutes before the alarm sounded. Understandably, the exhausted sailor slept right through the noise.

"I went down and got him," Paul said. "I had to pull his feet out of the rack and stand him up, grab a handful of his T-shirt to make sure he didn't fall over, and get him to where he knew where he was."

Paul had the sailor's shoes, shirt, and hat in his hand as he led him through the door. Just as they passed that hatch, there was a loud bang behind them. That woke the sailor up. "When he heard that he grabbed his shirt, his shoes, and his hat and he was on his way," Paul said. "He knew what was going on then."

Only later did Paul learn that the loud bang was from a rocket crashing into the side of the ship. "That hole was wider than my wing span, which is like six foot six," he said, "And that sailor's rack was right in the middle of that. One minute later and we were both toast."

President George H. W. Bush, Barbara Bush, Mini-Me, and Bibi spending an afternoon at home. *Photo credit: family photo*

Mrs. Bush reads one of her favorite books with her two Maltipoos—Mini-Me and Bibi. *Photo credit: Richard J. Carson, USA Today*

Animal Planet host, author, and animal adoption advocate, Andrea Arden

Apollo relaxes when he can be just a regular dog. *Photo credit: Michael Anderson Photography*

The happy family—(*left to right*) Lauren, Ella, Tyler, and Apollo. *Photo credit: Michael Anderson Photography*

Tyler proposes to Lauren with Presidents Bush 41 and 43 and First Ladies Barbara and Laura cheering him on. *Photo credit: Evan Sisley*

Apollo can't get enough of Tyler. *Photo credit: Dava Guerin*

(*Top*) Jimmy Didear on the tank he commanded in Vietnam. (*Bottom*) in the DaNang hospital in October of 1968, with his friend John Maxwell. *Photo credits: family photo*

Jimmy and Max. *Photo credit: family photo*

Max. *Photo credit: family photo*

Shanda Taylor dancing with Timber at a veterans' event. *Photo credit: family photo*

Shanda with her two guardian angels, Ranger (*left*) and Timber (*right*). *Photo credit: family photo*

The captain in uniform. *Photo credit: family photo*

Timber the editor. *Photo credit: family photo*

Leslie and Issac in their formal US Army portrait. *Photo credit: Barry Morgenstein*

Leslie, Gary Sinise, and Issac attend an event for the Gary Sinise Foundation; Leslie is a foundation ambassador. *Photo credit: Leslie Nicole Smith*

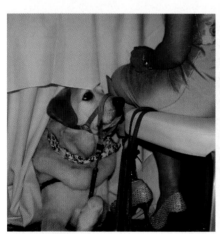

Issac never takes his eyes off Leslie, even under a table. *Photo credit: Leslie Nicole Smith*

Issac comforts Leslie when she was hospitalized at Walter Reed. *Photo credit: Leslie Nicole Smith*

Gnome, Justin, and Casey in Yucaipa, California. *Photo credit: Canine Companions for Independence: Stephen Wallace, MD, JD, photographer*

Gnome and Justin taking one of their regular walks in Yucaipa. *Photo credit: Canine Companions for Independence: Stephen Wallace, MD, JD, photographer*

Gnome gives Justin one of many wet kisses. *Photo credit: Canine Companions for Independence: Stephen Wallace, MD, JD, photographer*

Justin and Gnome share a sunrise together on the beach. *Photo credit: Canine Companions for Independence: Stephen Wallace, MD, JD, photographer*

Paul Mimms and Brook-Lyn out for walks. *Photos courtesy America's VetDogs*

Aaron and Yuma training at Al-Waleed in
Iraq. *Photo courtesy of Aaron Haglund*

Traveling by helicopter. *Photo courtesy of
Aaron Haglund*

Down time in Fallujah. *Photo courtesy of
Aaron Haglund*

Patrick shows a veteran how to hold Sarge on a glove. *Photo courtesy Avian Veteran Alliance and Patrick Bradley*

Patrick and Lucy, the wounded screech owl, have a strong bond. *Photo courtesy Avian Veteran Alliance and Patrick Bradley*

Patrick Bradley and his wounded bald eagle, Sarge. *Photo courtesy Avian Veteran Alliance and Patrick Bradley*

Patrick and Liberty. *Photo courtesy Avian Veteran Alliance and Patrick Bradley*

Air Force veteran Steve Dittbenner and his wife, Lynn, visit with an injured red-tailed hawk, with the help of an Alliance volunteer. *Photo courtesy Avian Veteran Alliance and Patrick Bradley*

Jonathan and Tessa chilling out at home.
Photo by Jonathan Hedrick

Tessa holding hands with Jonathan. *Photo by Jonathan Hedrick*

Jonathan and Tessa's 2016 Christmas card.
Photo by Jonathan Hedrick

Ziggy's memory lives on in Jonathan's heart. *Photo by Jonathan Hedrick*

Tom McRae on horseback during the Arizona Ranch Challenge in the fall of 2016. *Photo courtesy Jinx McCain Program*

Vets participating in the Jinx McCain Program. *Photo courtesy Jinx McCain Program*

Stefanie Mason and Emily at the stables in Delaware. *Photo credit: family photo*

Stefanie Mason with her partner, Bo. *Photo credit: family photo*

Crix and Teeny check out Crix's Walkin' Wheels mobility device. *Photo courtesy Shawn Dunn and family*

Teeny and Pigs prove that birds and dogs can get along. *Photo courtesy Shawn Dunn and family*

Shawn and Crix: a match made in heaven. *Photo courtesy Shawn Dunn and family*

Shawn takes Crix for a walk. *Photo courtesy Shawn Dunn and family*

There's nothing that Cossack loves more than hugs from Molly. *Photo courtesy Molly Taskey and family*

Cossack loves his daddy, Molly's fiancé Marlon-John, especially on Christmas morning. *Photo courtesy Molly Taskey and family*

A veteran's first time working with a horse.
Photo by Horses Helping Heroes Project

A tender moment between Blue and his trusted friend. *Photo by Horses Helping Heroes Project*

Max and Jeff: best friends reunited. *Photo by Horses Helping Heroes Project*

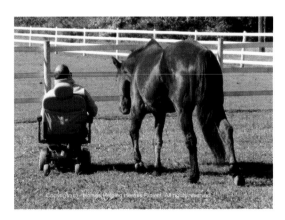

Max doing an obstacle course at liberty. *Photo by Horses Helping Heroes Project*

Mandi and Darwin share a tender moment in the yard. *Photo by Hooves Marching for Mercy*

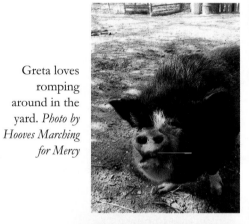

Greta loves romping around in the yard. *Photo by Hooves Marching for Mercy*

Anna Mae loves her skin treatment—and her mud bath! *Photo by Hooves Marching for Mercy*

Mandi and her husband, David. *Photo by Hooves Marching for Mercy*

Darwin, the potbelly pig that called Mandi "Mama." *Photo by Hooves Marching for Mercy*

That was close call number one.

During the forty-five-minute attack, three of Paul's fellow sailors were wounded, one a seventeen-year-old who lost part of a leg. Paul was ordered to take a stretcher up to the level where the young sailor had been hit. He was hauling that stretcher toward a hatch when the order was rescinded. As he stepped back through the door, he stumbled. He thought he had merely tripped but later found a piece of shrapnel in the heel of his boot. A rocket had exploded just on the other side of the hatch, serrating the door, with just one piece of shrapnel catching the bottom of Paul's boot.

Close call number two.

Finally, the sailors who were returning fire hit an ammo dump, and the blast sent Vietcong flying. Paul said their executive officer would earn a medal for his cool-headed leadership that day. And after they were secured from general quarters, Paul did take that stretcher up. "The gruesome sight was discovering something on the main deck and finding out it was a piece of that wounded sailor's leg," he recalled. "They evacuated him via chopper and then we got under way."

"That was almost all of the combat action that I really saw," Paul said. "There were a lot of distant things, and there were things that had happened before we arrived someplace, but that was the up-close live action I experienced. And I can say that it was enough."

Even damaged, his ship successfully made its way to Saigon, picking up about two hundred ARVN soldiers (Army of the Republic of Vietnam). It was while transporting these troops up the coast that Paul got a sense of the desperateness of South Vietnam's struggle. "The lieutenant was sixteen," Paul remembered. "That's why he was the lieutenant, because he was sixteen. The rest of them were younger than him. This is in 1968, and at that point, anyone who could grab a gun and shoot, they put him in uniform and put him in the ARVN."

They were kids from inland Vietnam, Paul and his fellow sailors would learn, hardly seaworthy. And almost all of them became desperately seasick.

"I was up on watch one evening," Paul said, "and there was a guy standing there leaning against the rail, which wasn't much more than a cable between poles, and he was just heaving over the side. Well, the ship rolled and he went over. I yelled, 'Man overboard' but most of those kids couldn't swim. It's very likely this kid just went straight down because he didn't know anything to do to stay up." The boy was among a dozen ARVN soldiers lost in that short trip.

After dropping off the young soldiers in Nha Trang, the ship was ordered to the Philippines, about nine hundred miles away across the South China Sea, for repairs. The massive hole in the side, and others above the water line, were taken care of but there were more below the water line—not critical—that would have to wait until there was time to get the ship into dry-dock for more extensive maintenance. They were loaded up with ammo and sent back to Vietnam.

Not long after some of that ammo had been off loaded, Paul had watch duty. It was nighttime, and dark, and with the ship under way, there were no lights on above deck. Paul was making his way to his post, and when he stepped around a corner, something crashed into his head, damaging his left eye. A pulley that had been used to off-load the ammunition had been left unsecured. It was swinging wildly with the motion of the ship. Paul never saw it coming. "Over the next thirty days or so, I lost two-thirds of the visual field of my left eye," he said. "I had no usable vision left."

On such a small ship, medical facilities were limited. Though Paul complained of the damage to his eye and headaches, there was little to be done. It wasn't the type of injury that merited a call for a chopper to fly him to a hospital.

"I told them I was having trouble seeing and basically they said, 'Shut up and get back to work,'" Paul said. "I told them about the headaches and the response was the same. 'Got some aspirin?' 'Yeah.' 'Well, take two and get back to work.' With the equipment they had, they couldn't see anything, they couldn't diagnose it, so therefore it was nothing."

"It" was actually glaucoma. It blinded his left eye there in Vietnam, and would, over the years, take the vision from his right eye as well. "If I had been treated right away I wouldn't have lost sight in the other eye," Paul said.

A few months later his ship was finally sent for dry-dock repairs in Guam. There, at the base hospital, the extent of his injury was finally understood, and he was admitted. By the time his repaired ship left for Japan, Paul was on his way back to the United States for further diagnosis and treatment at the navy hospital in Memphis.

Paul was medically discharged from the navy on January 10, 1969, just under two years and eight months after starting basic training in San Diego. And soon he was back on the assembly line at the Ford plant in Kansas City. "I pretty much went home and got back to work," he said. "I could still drive with one eye so I went back to my old job." But it wasn't going to be a career. The pay was still great, but Paul was bored. "It wasn't how I wanted to earn a living the rest of my life," he said.

He looked into management positions, including at fast-food restaurants, and was soon a trainee at Church's Fried Chicken. "It appealed to me because it seemed like the kind of position where you would actually have to think," he said. "You used your brain and were actually rewarded for that. I lean more toward that kind of existence." Plus, it was a chance to interact more with people, both employees and customers.

It was a good fit all around, especially for someone who was so conscious of how he dealt with others. As part of his reentry to the civilian world, Paul had started to notice that he had come home with a shorter fuse than he'd had before. "Lots of things made me angry quickly," he remembered. One flashpoint was the negative way some people talked about Vietnam veterans. "It became increasingly difficult to tamp down the anger when somebody was constantly insulting you, sometimes subtly and sometimes not so subtly," he said. "I was very proud to say, 'I'm a veteran.' I did what I was ordered to do when I was there, so I am proud of my service."

Paul didn't pick fights, and because of his size people weren't quick to start one with him. But he wouldn't back away from one either. "What makes the transition difficult is that the military pounds this attitude—kill or be killed and the survival stuff—into you during boot camp," he said. "But one thing they didn't do when we got out of Vietnam was any kind of deprogramming or resocialization. So a lot of us were wide open to having issues in certain realms of our lives and just emerging back into society with them, not knowing any better or sensing the difference."

It was a time of turmoil, the 1960s and '70s, and there was more than enough anger to go around. What Paul wasn't seeing enough of were examples of the good behavior he aspired to. "There was a lot of support for my negative behavior being just like it was, and it can pass for the norm," he said. "But for other places I wanted to be, and other things I wanted to do, it was not the norm and it wasn't acceptable. That's what motivated me to make the change."

He reached out to the VA and took a course in anger management. "It wasn't really something I wanted to do, but I took it to heart," he said. "It helped because I made it help, and I listened to what they had to say. I employed the tactics that they gave us, worked on the homework, and learned how to better curb and control myself. I'm not saying I never get angry, but I don't lash out and hurt people because of it."

And with twelve years as a manager of a fast-food restaurant, he had numerous opportunities to put his newfound skills to work. About 1983, though, a new problem arose. His right eye was afflicted with glaucoma, the same malady that had taken the vision in his left eye all those years ago in Vietnam.

"The blindness in one eye brought on the early onset of glaucoma in the other," he said. "Your body does this thing where one part of the body is para-sympathetic with another. There were other factors, obviously, but basically one eye decided to do what the other eye was doing."

Once he lost his job, fear about his future, and then depression, hopelessness, and a lack of motivation, followed. What would he do? Who would hire him? At one point he spent almost two weeks in bed. He couldn't eat. He would drink water, use the bathroom, and then go back to bed. "Why me?" he thought, when he wasn't thinking of others who "deserved" his fate more than he did.

"But then one day I sat up on the side of the bed and thought, 'Why not me?'" he said. "I've got my physicality, I've got my intelligence, I've got my motivation to do something—though I wasn't sure what to do or how to do it. But I can figure that out. I can do it. I have the support of my family. I have my faith. So why not me?"

He took a shower, gathered up $1.65, and spent almost half, eighty cents, on bus fare to the state office building. He would start to stabilize his situation by applying for food stamps, so at the very least his mom wouldn't have to help him out financially. Once downtown, he dropped a dime, which meant he was a nickel short for bus fare home. With the deterioration of the vision in his right eye, he had to get down on his hands and knees and start feeling around for that lost coin. As he did, he happened to look up and managed to make out a sign that said BUREAU FOR THE BLIND. He had never heard of them. Finally, he found the dime and went inside—carefully, as the sight he had was limited and he tried not to bump into things. He mentioned the sign to a security guard and asked for directions to the bureau. "Right over there," the man said, pointing. "I can't see where your arm went," Paul replied. The apologetic guard led him to his destination and Paul was able to talk to a counselor. Shortly thereafter he began eight months of blind rehabilitation, and the next year he was back in college.

"They and the VA Visual Impairment Services Team (VIST) coordinator helped straighten me out economically and also gave me the support I needed to return to school," he said.

Just as he'd gravitated toward a people-oriented career when he left Ford, Paul was now headed even deeper in that direction. Over the course of five years, from 1986 through 1991, he earned a bachelor's degree in sociology and a master's in social work. Not long after graduation, he was hired as a readjustment counselor at the Vet Center, a VA program in Kansas City. His only time off during those years of study was in the summer of '89, when he set aside time to acquire and train his first guide dog.

A friend of Paul's who had a guide dog started him down that path. They talked about it off and on, and one day the friend said, "Here, you grab the harness and I'm going to get on the other side and give the dog a command." Paul grabbed hold and the friend said, "Ernie, forward." And the dog did exactly that. "I just hung on," Paul said. Then the friend said, "Ernie, left," and Ernie complied. Paul's instant reaction: "Oh, gosh, I'm sold."

As his vision deteriorated, Paul was determined to remain as independent as possible. He instinctively knew from that moment with Ernie that a guide dog would provide a level of freedom he couldn't achieve on his own, or even with the use of a cane.

"I saw myself as the type of person who didn't want to just travel to the mailbox or to the store," Paul said. "I knew that, as far as traveling, I could do all the same things with a cane, but a dog would help me do the work rather than me doing all the work. That would leave me free to pay attention to other things and increase my confidence in traveling to places I hadn't been before."

His first dog, Dustin, a black Lab, came from Leader Dogs for the Blind near Detroit, a program that came with two distinct advantages. One, Michigan isn't too far from Kansas City. Two, the local Lions Club sponsored his round-trip travel. That first training was a revelation. "There were so many things I didn't know," he said. "For example, things about travel, the care of the dog, grooming, and the importance of bonding."

The freedom that came with having a guide dog exacts a considerable commitment from handlers. "When you have a cane, you get home and you put the cane in the corner and you're done with it," he said. "When you get home with your dog, you resume care of your dog. And when you get up in the morning, you resume the care of the dog. And while you're traveling with the dog, you resume care and continue training of the dog. It's ongoing. It's a give and take. You give more to the dog, and the dog in turn gives to you.

"So it brings into your life another emotional relationship, an attachment, a bond—to the point where my third dog saved my life more than once."

In one case, Paul and another of his dogs, Crawford, also a black Labrador, were crossing six lanes of traffic, with the cars on Paul's right stopped for a light. A van was in one of the middle lanes so it was difficult to tell what, if any vehicles, were in the farther lanes. And those drivers couldn't see beyond the van to determine if any pedestrians were crossing the street. So when a driver pulled out to make a right turn on red, Paul's dog pulled him back out of the way of the vehicle. "He saw the car coming and he made a left turn," Paul said. "So if I'm hanging onto the harness, it means I'm going to make a left turn too instead of going forward. In other words, he steered me out of the path of that car."

Another time, he was walking past the driveway of an auto repair business. Someone was pulling out, looking to his left and completely missing Paul and Crawford on the right. They were already in front of him as he eased out, and the dog instantly backpedaled. But he turned so quickly that he pulled the harness right out of Paul's hand. "It kind of left me with no dog right in front of this big GMC truck," Paul said. "So I figured out where I was and I started to run diagonally so I could run away from him and be in front of him all at the same time. It saved my life because he finally saw me over the hood."

It was a victory for Crawford, but there was a cost. Now the dog associated cars coming up on their left with almost getting hit. "For him, it was a situation to avoid, so he did," Paul said. "After that day, it took me months to get him to walk in front of a car that was coming up on our left."

Paul only discovered this newfound caution one day when he went to step off a curb. Crawford hit the ground. Wouldn't move. Paul had to go out of his way to always cross streets when cars were on their right. "I had to adjust my route, a lot, and practice with neighbors who would leave their cars running so that I could get him to walk in front of their car and understand that he was going to be safe," Paul said.

Finally, the lessons sank in, but a month later someone cut a right turn too close, coming up onto the curb where Paul and Crawford were standing. "It just started all over again," Paul said. "He was my best dog, in terms of the bond we formed, the traveling companionship, and the team that we made, but he couldn't get past that. After that second incident, I returned him to the school and got a replacement."

His second dog, Jasper, was a black Lab and retriever mix that liked riding on buses. A bit too much. If the dog saw a bus, he wanted to be on it and nothing—not snow bank, not utility pole—would get in the way. Once a bus came up behind them and Jasper was ready to board—right while they were by a patch of ice. He ran between a utility pole and the curb, with Paul catching himself from falling by hugging the pole and hanging on. "That's when I decided I needed to retire him," Paul said.

These incidents didn't change Paul's mind about the advantages or importance of a guide dog, but they were a good reminder of how far from the ideal things could fall.

"Even when you train them, what you've got left is a dog," he said. "And they have the varying sensibilities that we do, and you don't know what they're going to do in a situation until they've been in that situation and had a chance to react to it. Like cars coming up on your left, or seeing a bus and wanting to ride on it. Chasing squirrels is another one. I had a friend who got run into a parking meter because his dog saw a squirrel. Trainers can't anticipate everything."

Some of it is situational, and some is a matter of handler and dog testing each other. All dogs undergo a months-long rigorous training process overseen by knowledgeable and experienced trainers. But then they go home with someone who they've known for about twenty-five days, who may have very limited experience as a handler. As Paul said, "The dog might think, 'There's no more trainer around and now I've got this doofus who doesn't know anything, so I can probably do what I want.' So then it's up to you and this dog to resume its life as a travel companion, with you being the handler and them being the guide."

How the dog behaves around other dogs is one test. As working guide dogs, they are not supposed to bark at or interact with other dogs. And during training they get used to being around other dogs that behave similarly. But take them home, where they may not interact often with other dogs, and the training can wear off. "Then it's almost a new experience," Paul said. "It's a new place, with a new role, and a new handler, so you have to figure out what the dog is going to do. Will he start growling and run for the other dog or bark at it? And whatever he does that he's not supposed to do, you have to start correcting that and hope those corrections take effect."

If there are no problems, dogs and handlers can be together for six to ten years, and that can depend largely on the animal. Paul likens it to the career of a football player. "How long does a linebacker last? Same type of thing. How long can you maintain the skills and vitality to continue to do that job?" With seven years of a dog's life equal to one for humans, a nine-year-old dog is sixty-three. Like with his human counterparts, age comes with certain maladies, including arthritis, deafness, even blindness. Sometimes they are just tired.

"The dog I had before this one, he'd see me get the harness out and just come running," Paul recalled. "Eight blocks later he was huffing and puffing. I had to slow down for him. He had all the eagerness and willingness to go, but just didn't have the energy anymore."

Catherine and Paul were married for eighteen years, but their very close relationship began years before that, starting at guide dog school in 1989. Paul said, "What we did that was special, to us anyway, because we didn't get married until 1998, we had nine years that we conversed back and forth, and visited back and forth, and traveled with our dogs back and forth, and we became best friends, Catherine and I."

Like Paul, Catherine was born sighted but lost her vision later in life. But unlike him, who was legally blind for years before losing all vision in 2003, she lost hers overnight, from a complication of her diabetes. "I lost mine gradually, but she was watching TV and it just started going black," Paul said. "She woke up on her twenty-eighth birthday totally blind. She went from, 'I can see and drive' to 'I can't'—instantly. I met her when she was twenty-nine, so about a year and three months after she lost her vision she ended up getting her first dog. And so that's where we met."

She, too, had gone through blind rehabilitation, but having a friend like Paul, who had more experience at being visually impaired, was crucial to Catherine regaining a sense of independence. Take something as simple— or as challenging—as grocery shopping. Paul had a system for doing his own shopping nailed down. He would type up a shopping list on his computer, print it out, fold it, and put it in his pocket. He would put his reusable shopping bags into his backpack and walk to the store. At customer service, he would ask for help picking out the items on his list. The staff would bag it for him, or place items in his backpack, and he walked back home.

"She came to visit and I took her grocery shopping," Paul said. "So she went back home and she'd take OATS—which stands for the Old Age Transportation System. They got her a waiver to ride that, and she started calling them. So she'd take her grocery list, and her dog, and she'd go to the grocery store, and she would go to customer service just like I did. She was just beaming the first time she did that. She said that was one of the greatest things she'd ever learned up to that point.

"She felt so liberated. And she was so grateful to me—this was before we got married—for teaching her that because it gave her freedom. It gave her hope that she didn't have to be dependent on people all her life, that there were things that she could get out there and do herself. And that kind of opened her up for quite a bit."

A guide dog was crucial for that evolution.

"The dog gave her a lot of, I guess you'd say courage, confidence, and assistance in making that happen for her," Paul said. "As far as us as people, that's something the dogs give us: freedom, liberation, and a sense of self-reliance."

While Paul can travel with a white cane, and do it competently, he feels freer and, counterintuitively, more self-reliant when he travels with a dog. In part, he is less worried about stumbling over obstacles. Having a dog lets him move more quickly and confidently.

"If you're going over rocky terrain with a cane, it can get caught sixty times walking sixty feet, getting caught in holes or whatever," Paul said. "A dog will slow down and help you navigate the terrain that's uneven. If it looks really bad, the dog will take you around that if there's a way.

"So I definitely walk faster with a dog than I do with a cane," he said. "And my wife got to where she could walk pretty fast too. You can pick up the pace to where you can walk at an aerobic exercise speed and feel like the dog is going to keep you safe. So while the dog watches out for the obstacles on the ground, you can concentrate on the experience and the opportunity and the freedom of walking."

Dogs also gave the couple the freedom to travel and to thoroughly enjoy it.

"On behalf of my wife and me, I can't speak enough about how liberating it is to add that guide dog to your life when traveling," Paul said.

There are adjustments, to be sure, for both travelers and flight crew. For Paul, given his size, one consideration is whether to squeeze handler and dog into the bulkhead or take a regular seat, with the dog underneath—in three-seat rows, there is usually one middle leg after the first seat, leaving the space under the other two seats open to comfortably fit a dog. Sometimes, though, other passengers will balk at the prospect of sharing space with a dog. "I've had passengers say, 'Oh, no, I'm not sitting here. I won't do dogs,'" Paul said. "And I've told the flight attendants, 'Fine, you can put me somewhere else.' So one time they moved me and my wife up to first class. That was nice—and a lot roomier."

Catherine and Paul traveled to their time share in Cancun annually. "We would get our tickets and our passports, get to the airport, and get on the plane by ourselves," Paul said. "With assistance, we would get through customs in Cancun and to our villa, and we would walk all around that property to meals, down to the beach, to whatever everybody else was doing that we wanted to do."

Paul also travels regularly through his work with the Blinded Veterans Association, and Catherine often joined him. "I've gone to the BVA convention every year but one since 1993," he said. Catherine accompanied him until realizing that the business part of these trips kept him too busy for them to enjoy the journey as a couple. "But we made those trips together; we made the trips to Cancun together. Every year we made some kind of a long-distance trip or two, including flying up to Michigan for Christmas to be with her family."

Traveling changed after the terrorist attacks of September 11, 2001. Previously, for example, guide dogs could accompany their handlers through the metal detectors, with the understanding that the metal handle and harness would likely set off the alarm. Today, the handler goes through first and then the dog, which is also hand wanded. When these new procedures began, it wasn't always clear—to dog or the humans involved—who the dog was supposed to come to after passing through the metal detector. If the handler couldn't grab the harness until after the wanding, and the security person didn't, then the dog could run free through the terminal.

"Some of us organizations for the blind got together with the TSA and said, 'Look, if you don't want us to get the dog when they come through, then by God you need to do it,'" Paul said. "So we lobbied for that change. These things can take time, but they do listen."

Paul's constant striving for independence and the people skills that first led him from Ford to fast-food management combined to make him an effective advocate. Initially, he advocated for himself as he navigated the help available to him when the sight in his second eye was failing. Since then, that advocacy has been on behalf of others, especially in his career at the VA and his volunteer work with the Blinded Veterans Association and other groups.

"I'm one of those people who say the job I like the best was the one I had," Paul said of his assignments at the VA, "but among the most rewarding were the last two, as a computer skills instructor and as a visual impairment services coordinator. Both of those had a measure of success that you could see." Essentially, he helped people take their own steps toward independent living. "If a guy showed you the letter he just wrote to his granddaughter, in the envelope that I taught him to print so that he could mail it to her, you could tell—even though I was totally blind—that he was beaming with pride," Paul said. "There's my paycheck."

His visually impaired clients could be World War II vets or men and women just home from wars in Iraq and Afghanistan. Some had lost their sight when young, others as they aged. And he would tell them all that they could do anything they wanted—except see. Despite their skepticism, Paul and his colleagues would guide them toward developing a range of skills—walking to the mailbox, grocery shopping, cooking without burning themselves, mastering a computer (his oldest computer student was eighty-nine), even using a saw. "I had already walked the walk," Paul said, "so I was fully qualified to talk the talk and be believable."

Part of the talk is helping others keep terms like disability in perspective.

"Abilities are relative," he pointed out. "People want to focus on a glaring and definite difference that goes outside the mainstream of ability and name that a disability, which implies that you don't have any ability. That's not the case. My abilities are different from yours, but that's because your abilities are different from mine. It takes two people to be different. People forget that, and they focus on me being different because I can't see and everybody else they know can and therefore I'm different. No, that's not how that's defined for me. If there is something eight feet off the floor and you can't reach it but I can, who's got the disability?

"So, working within those parameters, I come up with different questions and challenges for people who are interacting or working with me or my different abilities."

One of those challenges he raises is helping people think about how they view themselves.

"How would you introduce yourself?" he asked. "For me, it would go, 'My name is Paul and I'm a guide dog user. I have a master's degree in social work, and I used to work for the VA, and now I'm on the board of the directors of the Blind Veterans Association. And I'm blind. As opposed to, 'I'm blind and my name is Paul.' See what I mean? It's a mind-set."

Paul's current mind-set is to enjoy the freedom that comes with having a guide dog for many years to come. "I haven't reached the point where all this daily training is more than I want to do," he said. "In a couple of years, Brook-Lyn will be nine years old. I've already had her five and a half years, so the time to retire her and get a replacement dog is approaching. Then I'll be seventy-three. At this point, I don't think that I will be so old that I don't want to do this anymore. But nine years after that, I'll be eighty-two, and I might rethink it.

"There's going to be a point where I think, 'I don't travel enough anymore, or I don't use the dog anymore.' So, yeah, then it might not be worth the work. If the handler gets to the point where he doesn't want to go through all this just to travel, then he stops traveling. He doesn't need the dog, or want the dog, and the responsibility that goes with it.

"Right now, that's not me. There are people, I guess, who don't have the burning desire—if you want to call it that—for self-reliance that I have. I don't want to be limited by who can show up to help me, and when they can show up, and so on. I want to be able to go to the grocery store when I want to go, and get my groceries, and make my way back home, whether I catch Uber or walk. But whether it's the grocery store or the drug store or going out to dinner or whatever, the dog and I can do all of that."

After all, they're family.

EIGHT

The Navy Dog Handler

"This was love at first bite."

ARON HAGLUND WILL NEVER FORGET THE DAY A FRIEND ASKED HIM TO "catch a dog."

At the time, Aaron was a sailor based in El Centro, California. His day job was an aviation electronics technician, with a specialty in the EA-6B Prowler, an electronics warfare aircraft. But much of his free time was spent with master-at-arms personnel, the men and women who make up the navy's elite law enforcement and security wing. Aaron's friend was among them, and he belonged to an even more select group: dog handlers.

Catch a dog is the expression used when someone volunteers to don a bite sleeve, meaning they will let the dog bite them—essentially catching the dog.

"I had no idea that canines were part of the military, no idea that it had working dogs," Aaron said. When his friend asked him to volunteer that day, Aaron just thought it was one more thing to broaden his military experience and perhaps enhance his service record. So he simply said, "Sure, cool, let's go do that."

They went to an abandoned barracks that had a hallway about three hundred feet long. His friend introduced him to the dog, and Aaron petted it and helped feed it. Then he was put into position, with the sleeve on, about eighty feet from the handler and the animal.

When canine handlers confront a suspect, they work their way through a series of commands.

"Sir, come to me."

If the person resists, he receives a warning. "Sir, be advised that I have a dog that is trained to attack."

The handler was working through the commands that day in the barracks, acclimating Aaron to what was about to take place—but at the same time using trigger commands to prep the dog for action.

"Sir, if you don't listen to my orders, I will send the dog after you."

About that time, the handler gave Aaron the signal to run. But he had also told him earlier, during a safety briefing for the exercise, to look over his shoulder while running so he would know when the dog was coming to him. The first time Aaron looked back, he was stunned. Normally, the friend was what Aaron describes as "one hundred pounds wet and wearing boots," not a big guy at all. Now, firmly in command of a dog that he was about to set loose, he'd been transformed.

"I remember looking back, and just for that instant, when the dog was going nuts, my friend looked like Conan the Barbarian and he was sending a hell hound after me," Aaron said. "The dog had been so docile when he first gave the command to watch me, and now it was Cujo."

Then the handler sicced the dog on his target. Aaron had grown up doing martial arts, and he'd remained in shape during his time in the service. He figured it would be an easy sprint to the end of the hallway before the dog caught up to him. Wrong.

"It was an instant, and the dog was already at me," he recalled. "It hit me, and took me right to the ground."

In that moment, downed by Cujo, his life changed.

"It was violent, it was physical, and it was a match made in heaven," he said. "I fell in love right then. People talk about love at first sight. This was love at first bite."

From that moment on, Aaron knew that he was going to be a navy military working dog handler.

The initial appeal of the service for Aaron was the thought of doing something for others. "For the first time in my life, I realized I could serve something greater than myself," he said. "And that kind of resonated with me. It was almost like a call."

It was a call that came out of the blue. He was twenty-one years old, a cook, or chef in training, for a variety of restaurants and country clubs around Great Falls, Montana. Among his peers, he was the only one with regular work that paid well. He'd started while in high school and liked the regular income so much that he'd dropped out of school in order to make more money. "I was a good student," he said, "and the knowledge part came very easy, but I was just bored with the curriculum." At age twenty-one he was enjoying life—hanging out with friends, drinking beer, having fun—but he didn't have a particular direction in mind. Then one day a buddy suggested they visit a recruiting station. Aaron shrugged and went along.

All the branches were represented at the office, but the navy's pull was strongest. "Once they showed me everything, I was ready," Aaron remembered. "I said, 'Let's go.'"

That everything included pictures of the aviation electronics school dorms along the beach in Pensacola, Florida. Not a hard sell for a young man from Montana who fondly remembered his early years growing up in the warmth of Southern California. "Where do I sign?" he asked.

He enrolled in the delayed-entry program and used the interim to get his GED—the navy wouldn't take him without it. During that time, on September 11, 2001, terrorists crashed hijacked planes into the Twin Towers and the Pentagon. A month later, Aaron was in basic training. The physical part came easily to him, and despite all the marching and seeming tediousness, he kept in mind that there was a purpose to it all, for both the military and him. "They were teaching attention to detail and discipline and helping you learn the military structure," he said, things that would prove crucial later to his work in both electronics and security. But again, there was the big picture: "It was all head games, and I understood it was temporary, but I loved the fact that I was going to become something more than I had been, that I was going to provide something for my country by doing something."

The next step was an accelerated nine-month course in aviation electronics, with make-or-break weekly tests. Fail once and they roll you back a week. Fail twice and you're out of the program. Aaron and Anthony, his identical twin brother, had always been excellent students. They'd even been offered a chance to skip middle school, jumping from sixth to ninth grade. Fortunately, Aaron said, his parents wouldn't allow it. And though he'd been bored to tears in high school, that wasn't going to happen in this school. "It was very engaging and intense and accelerated and I loved it," he said. After graduation, there was even more in-depth training waiting in Washington State, where he trained on systems for the Prowler. "More super-secret squirrel type of electronics," he calls it.

The navy put him to work back in his home state, assigning him to a maintenance unit in El Centro. The desert location was a perfect training ground for squadrons preparing for the terrain of Afghanistan and Iraq, and the maintenance crews on hand worked 'round the clock. "Jets never slept," Aaron said. "When they came in it was always go, go, go. I think for the first eight weeks at my duty station, I worked fifteen to sixteen hours a day, nearly seven days a week. Because of the runs they were constantly doing, and the tempo, we weren't even able to troubleshoot the electronics. It was pull a box, put a box. If a navigation system was faulty, we'd pull the whole unit out and put a new one in, like changing an eight-track tape."

On top of that crazed schedule, there were regular four-hour duty shifts on the quarterdeck—on a ship that would be the raised deck behind the main mast, while on land it usually referred to a building's lobby. On watch meant being the gatekeeper, greeting incoming personnel, providing directions. The shifts could be assigned for before or after Aaron's main duties, over the weekends, or even in the middle of the night. Everyone took turns. Since El Centro was a small base, with few hands on deck to share the load, Aaron often stood five or six shifts a week. Then he heard about an alternative, working security details with the elite masters-at-arms. It would mean no more quarterdeck watch and having three weekends free a month. Aaron raised his hand. "I was sold already," he said. "And you get to shoot a gun? Okay, let's do that."

The physical aspect and the weapons training appealed to him. But the mission—even if it meant twelve-hour shifts at the base gate—meant even more. "I liked the whole mentality of protection, of being on that front line," he said. "I liked knowing that I was there to protect everybody on the base. I saw a lot of honor in that. It felt very selfless."

He'd enjoyed the electronics training and his main duty but didn't feel as close to that initial calling to enlist. "That was all so rapid and technical," he said. "Protection felt more immediate and really resonated with me. I thought, 'This is why I joined the navy.'"

And then along came his friend with a volunteer opportunity. Want to catch a dog?

The master-at-arms side of the aisle welcomed Aaron's application to join them full time. Aviation electronics was not keen on the idea. The navy had invested a considerable amount of time and money in his training. Everyone agreed that he excelled at his work, and Aaron thought that earned him the right to join an elite unit. Others thought it was reason to keep him where he was. While the request was being considered, Aaron worked overtime to show his potential and his interest in canine handling. On his days off, he visited the kennels, helping wash dogs and clean up feces and urine. He would drive two hours to San Diego just to watch a thirty- or forty-minute training session. Sometimes he'd sit through eight hours of training. "I did everything I could," he recalled. "It didn't matter what time of day. The dogs eat twice a day, so I would come in at night, even when I was on leave from work, to feed them. If there was an impromptu training or other event with canines, I would go. Even though nothing was promised, I wanted to be around that so much."

Even when one of his senior chiefs said he'd never sign off on the transfer, Aaron didn't back down. "It's not up to you," Aaron responded. "This is my life."

After several months, his persistence paid off. "The military works both ways," Aaron said. "They are going to take from the service member everything they can because they are investing time. But if they have a program or opportunity, you have to be the squeaky wheel that gets the grease and eventually you will hear yes. Just keep trying. Be good at your job, first and foremost, and then do more."

Once he got the okay for master-at-arms school, the transfer to San Antonio, Texas, for Aaron and his wife Brittany came quickly. But this training wasn't like his electronics schools. This was like being back in basic, with an emphasis again on discipline and attention to detail, such as regular uniform inspections. Given the job, that focus made perfect sense.

"I learned a saying there, 'A master-at-arms has to be beyond reproach,' and I never forget that," he said. "I could never correct someone for something I was doing wrong. So I made sure I was always on point and I took pride in that. I was almost obsessive about making sure my uniform was squared away, making sure I was always early—earlier than early. I made sure I applied myself 100 percent to everything I did, and if I failed at something, then I would just try harder."

He took that approach when he learned the disappointing news that, because of a bureaucratic snafu, his next stop would not be dog handling school, as he had expected. Instead, he would be assigned as one of about six hundred masters-at-arms at Naval Air Station Sigonella in Sicily. Despite the disappointment, he was determined to excel at his job. And soon he was training other masters-at-arms in Sicily. Never, though, did he give up on his dream. "In my free time I started going to the kennel," he said, "cleaning up, watching them train, taking notes, doing everything I could, and letting them know that I wanted to be a dog handler."

Finally, his wish came true. Months later, he was back in San Antonio, this time at military working dog handler school at Lackland Air Force Base. The excitement level for Aaron and his fellow students was palpable. "We all come in there as shiny happy people, all saying, 'We're going to be dog handlers,' and thinking it's the greatest thing in the world," Aaron said. They were ready to go right to work, learning the tricks of the trade and taking on the world with their dog. Their instructors had more basic things in mind. Like learning to walk a dog—without, at first, actually using a dog. The handlers-to-be were given a collar, a leash, and metal ammo cans that were about a foot long and almost eight inches high. That's what they walked for the first week. And when they stopped they had to give the ammo can the command to sit. They put it into its proper position, petted it, even giving a scolding if it did something wrong. And when they praised it, it had to be in the high-pitched voice that dogs find so soothing and enjoyable. And much of this was usually done outdoors, in full view of more advanced classes.

"Some people had a problem doing that because they felt embarrassed," Aaron said. "I wasn't, even to this day. It was a means to an end. I'm putting everything that I am into this. I may not be the best handler in the world, but I'm going to be the best handler I can be."

The training is divided into two blocks of instruction. The first is basic obedience training and bite work, as well as the policing side of the business, like building searches. The second part is on detection for drugs and explosives, as well as force assistance—in other words, how to become a force multiplier when operating with other military units. Aaron was singled out among his classmates as best handler—top dog—for both blocks. His approach came from the hours he had spent in preparation in kennels and among handlers, at El Centro and at Sigonella. Before leaving Sicily, he had been invited by the kennel master there to interview the two dozen handlers at the base. He didn't ask the obvious questions, like how do you get a dog to do this or that. "I figured those were all tricks, things that would come to me with training," Aaron said. "What I wanted to know—and I asked every handler, every kennel master—was, 'How do you build rapport with your dog? How did you build your bond?'

"I figured that if I could get in the mind of that dog—almost like that old, really bad 1980s movie *The Beastmaster*—if I could get on the mental level with that animal, build a rapport, then we're bonded, and the dog and I will be able to work together."

Some handlers told Aaron about sitting for hours in the kennel with their dogs, next to their four-foot-by-four-foot chain-link cells. Others would read to the dog. Another technique was to be the only one who ever fed the dog. Not the kennel master, not another handler, no one else. Aaron adopted these techniques and more. "I was always there for my dog. Always," he said. "I was there from six in the morning to feed him and then again at six at night to feed him again. If my wife and I were going out, we had to make sure that I was back at the kennel at six to feed him. When I worked the night shift, I would sit in the kennel and we would just sit there all night. If I was going to be doing paperwork, I'd bring it into the kennel and sit on the concrete next to the dog and do that for two or three hours."

Aaron likes to say this about training and bonding with a dog: "You can't push a leash." In other words, the dog can't be forced to do something. But if the handler respects the animal, and it, in turn, respects its handler, the dog will obey his commands. "I tried to look at the dog as my partner, never my pet," Aaron said. "It's a very weird dynamic to explain. But on one level, I am closer to my working dog than I will ever be with my wife, and we're going on thirteen years of marriage. I will forever be closer to the dog I deployed with than with my identical twin brother, who I still talk to every day. It's an amazing bond that a man or woman can have with a working dog. The dog is there for you and you are there for it. Having that loyalty and the unconditional love and respect is second to none. And it's pure, it's not tainted."

Aaron describes three categories of people who work with dogs in the military: dog walkers, dog trainers, and dog handlers. The walker would sign up to be a handler because it seemed cool but wasn't willing to put in the time training or bonding with the dog. He would fill out the reams of required paperwork on his dog and claim hours of training time. But when tested—Aaron and his fellow handlers had to recertify every month—the dog wouldn't listen to that person's commands. "Sure you trained for 120 hours," Aaron said, sarcastically. "Your dog won't lie." Aaron describes trainers as almost dog whisperers, able to impress others by making a dog do the seemingly impossible—like fetch a beer for friends—but they are less inclined to actually work a dog. Aaron aspired to be, and became, what he calls the epitome of the profession—a working dog handler—someone who can both train and work closely with an animal as part of a dog-team unit.

"When you're good," he said, "your kennel master will say, 'Hey, you've made this dog better. It's more proficient, sharper. Now, go fix this other guy's dog.' I did that a lot. I was constantly helping new handlers and fixing the dogs they would break."

There's no room for error with animals that handlers refer to as "the only bullet you can send and have come right back to you." Something that potentially lethal has to be under control, able to obey commands in the heat of the moment. That takes thousands of hours of training. "If I send that dog to attack somebody," Aaron said, "and if a little kid jumps in the way, or an innocent civilian bystander jumps in the way, I need to be able to stop that dog—mid-jump, mid-bite—before it clamps its teeth down, and it would need to stop and come back to me. Or you send it out to bite, but then tell it to stop in front of an assailant and just bark, salving at the mouth, and never move. That's control, and that comes from training, repetition."

The repetition is crucial as handlers are dealing with an animal with the mentality of a three- or four-year-old person. So training sessions, even for the most advanced working dogs, last ten to fifteen minutes—go longer and you risk losing the animal's attention. But there can be five or six sessions per day. It's also important to break tasks into manageable steps. "People try to run before they can walk," Aaron said. "They try to teach the dog to roll over, but the dog may not know how to lie down yet. First, he has to lie down, then you have to teach him to lay on his side, and then you can teach him to roll over. There's a progression, regardless of what you're teaching it."

Aaron learned the value of an incremental approach the hard way.

After he'd received word about heading to Iraq, Aaron was approached by a senior chief, an experienced handler. He asked Aaron if he knew of anything "functional" his German shepherd Yuma could do while deployed. "My dog will bite," Aaron quickly responded. "I was all jacked up, super muscular, super testosterone. Yeah, I'm great, I thought."

"Will your dog pick up an M16 ammo magazine and bring it to you?" the senior chief asked. At first Aaron thought that was impossible, but the question punctured his sense of bravado. The senior chief wouldn't have asked if it couldn't be done. But how?

"The chiefs and the kennel masters, they would let me try and figure things out," Aaron said. "You need to. You need to be able to experiment and know what is going to work."

He started with push-ups. He would have the dog sit while he was in the up position of a push-up. When he went down, he told her, "Down." She laid down. When he pushed up, he'd command, "Sit." She obeyed. And he repeated these steps, over and over. "I got to the point where I could drop to the ground and, in her mind, I was doing push-ups, so she would instantly drop prone," he said. "I got that perfect. So every time I got to the prone position, you know laying down, my dog would follow. She'd just go down."

The next step was getting Yuma to crawl to him.

The training area in Sigonella was outdoors, surrounded by a chain-link fence and other buildings where people worked. Often they were outdoors for a smoke break, and they'd watch the dog-training sessions. Aaron had an audience, including some senior chiefs, the day he was ready to have Yuma crawl to him.

Dog and handler were practicing their push-ups, about sixty feet apart from each other. Up. "Sit." Down. "Down."

It was going perfectly. Finally, Aaron put her to the test. While down, he said, "Come." But instead of the crawl Aaron had hoped for, the excited dog sprinted toward him. With little time to react, Aaron pushed himself into the up position just as Yuma crashed into him at full force, head first. "She head-butted me as hard as she could and it rocked me," he said. "I saw stars, I rolled over. It damn near knocked me out. The chief was laughing and thought it was the funniest thing."

He was razzed about it for weeks, but that was fine. For Aaron it wasn't about the potential embarrassment. It was what he learned from the experience.

"That's one of the great moments I can think of in trying to figure something out with my dog," he said, laughing when he thinks about the incident. "I have no idea what was in her mind but she trusted me. I called and she was like, 'I'm coming.' So I realized that maybe she shouldn't be sixty feet away. I could start her at ten feet and then she can't sprint. So that was me trying to run before I could walk. It was very good for me. I was still learning the process of how dogs work, and I saw that I needed to take things in smaller increments."

They stuck with it, and the incremental approach paid off. Aaron said, "We got to the point where I could drop to the prone and point over to another handler. My dog would drop to the prone, crawl over there, grab a magazine, and then crawl back and bring it to me."

Their partnership was only a few months old at that point, but already they were tight. And they would grow even closer in Iraq.

Airplane landings in war zones are basically nose dives, from thirty thousand feet to tarmac, with the hope of presenting less of a target for enemy anti-aircraft fire.

"It was the world's worst roller coaster," Aaron said. "We were in a cargo plane, a C130, and all the lights go red, and all of a sudden we were going straight down."

Aaron was afraid of heights then, but at least he was belted into a seat. Across from him, Yuma was rolling around in her cargo kennel. "I could rationalize what was happening," he said. "Oh, we're diving. Got it. The dog? Her whole world is 'Where did gravity go?' Her eyes were as wide as silver dollars, and she was rolling around in there like she was in a washing machine."

Yuma's look of terror in that moment made Aaron more fully realize how deeply dependent they would be on each other in a war zone. "We were a team, I knew that as a dog handler," he said. "But at that point, the shock in her eyes, it hit me that she needed to rely on me, and I needed to take care of her so she would keep me safe."

That just-you-and-me feeling was enhanced by the very nature of their assignment. The military calls it individual augmentation, or force multipliers, when an individual with special skills is added to a unit to increase its capabilities. Adding a military working dog handler, for example, dramatically ups a unit's ability to detect explosives and sense the enemy's presence. Aaron and Yuma, then, were basically on call, for infantry patrols, convoys, and a myriad of other assignments. More than one canine per unit was overkill, so the dozen handler-dog teams that flew into Iraq that day soon went their separate ways. It was daunting duty but exactly what Aaron had signed up for.

"I knew that I wanted to go," he said. "It was my calling. I knew that my skill set was there to protect other US military, and for me, that was all I needed. They need me there, then that's my duty. Let's go."

However, despite all the training, he wasn't fully prepared for the reality of daily combat.

"It was terrifying really," he said. "You can simulate it all day, but until you've been to war, you really have no idea what it's going to be like."

And, of course, he wasn't just responsible for his own safety. There was Yuma to care for and worry about. The importance of that mission had never been clearer to him, as they waited on the flight line in the moments after the dive landing. "It just hit home how much I had to rely on this animal," Aaron said. "I know that I can't smell explosives. I can't walk down a street and smell them. But my dog can. If I tick her off, or ignore her, or don't feed her, she can be off or think, 'Screw you, I'm going to walk past this one today.' Then boom."

Their first assignment, in early 2006, was to Camp Cann in Fallujah, a Forward Operating Base named after Sergeant Adam Cann, a military working dog handler who lost his life trying to stop a suicide bomber from killing his fellow marines. "Fallujah was like the Wild West," Aaron recalled. "There was gunfire every day, every time we were out. We got mortared every night; you could set your clock by it." One evening, they heard a crash near the kennel compound on base, and they waited for the explosion. And waited. And waited. When they finally looked out, they saw a live but unexploded Chinese-made mortar round.

"When that's your every day, everything changes," Aaron said. "Every day that I went outside the wire, every day that I woke up, I thought it was my last day on Earth. Every. Single. Day. That's your reality—seeing people dying all over the place, running toward gunfire all the time. You just know that every day you wake up could be your last day."

He vividly recalls his first convoy along a stretch of highway that was regularly implanted with improvised explosive devices (IEDs). For three hundred yards, the road was pockmarked with dozens of "scabs," asphalt patches that combat engineers had poured into craters created by IEDs to keep the road usable and the convoys moving. But those patches could also provide a false sense of security. The enemy soon learned to plant IEDs under the scabs too. So before a convoy could travel that stretch of road, Aaron and Yuma had to walk ahead and check for explosives.

Aaron stepped out of the Humvee with Yuma, got his gear together, and started walking. He began to talk to his spotters, not on the personal role radio (PRR) attached to his neck but over his shoulder, assuming the marines scanning the area for enemy activity and covering him were in earshot. But when he turned around, he saw that he was alone, about twenty feet ahead of everyone else. Over the radio, one marine said, "Don't worry, you're covered"—but from a distance. It was a way to minimize casualties should Aaron and his dog set off an IED.

"That was the first time I really felt like it was just me, just me and a dog, walking in the road in the middle of the sand in fucking Iraq," he said.

The spotters kept an eye out for people in the distance. Sometimes if a dog sensed explosives, it would sit. And an enemy keeping watch might choose that moment to set off the IED, knowing it had been discovered. Or they might just shoot the dog or the handler—there was a price on their heads because of their effectiveness in thwarting enemy attacks.

"It was like a movie, hearing all these voices in my head as I walked that four hundred yards," Aaron said of that first patrol. "It was insane and incredible and partly a rush. Just a plethora of emotions, and the convoy kept up with me as I was walking, but I really felt like that was my green mile."

Whatever he was feeling on that long, lonely stretch of road—excited, nervous, and scared—he had to keep in check. He had to focus on looking for bombs, so the dog would too. "It's like taking your child to war," Aaron said. "If he's spooked, you can't control him, and then you're going to be exposed while you're trying to get your dog together and become an easier target. If a kid falls off a bike and people make a big deal of it, the kid will pick up on that and start crying. It's similar with a dog team. You learn to shut off your emotions in order to function. There is still a mission. You do whatever you can to make sure the dog can perform. Is it thirsty? Is it hot? Is it agitated? Are its paws blistered? There's a lot going on, constantly, including gunfire, explosions, and debris falling."

That shutting down of the emotions in combat, Aaron believes, contributes to post-traumatic stress later. "You have to learn how to turn off your emotions, every day," he said. "You train yourself so you can worry about what's in front of you. But then those emotions stay turned off."

On another mission, with the Marine's Third Recon Battalion, Aaron was having a terrible time controlling Yuma. They were enroute to an observation post at dusk, the five-foot-eleven navy handler accompanying what looked to him like a special forces unit full of massive professional wrestlers. Testosterone city. And Yuma was not cooperating. "She's pulling every which way, she's not listening to commands, and it's embarrassing me because I can't control my dog," he recalled. "She won't sit, she won't stay, and I can hear these guys laughing and making jokes, 'I'm glad we brought this fucking guy along.' I remember looking down and telling her, 'I'm gonna break your neck.'"

It didn't matter. She wouldn't settle down, wouldn't listen, like a fish out of water bouncing all over the place. In his frustration, Aaron started to reach for her—at least partly thinking he just might wring her neck—when Yuma bit him on the leg. She didn't draw blood. She just grabbed him.

The marines loved it, and they started laughing and joking about the bite, the dog, and clueless sailors.

And then Aaron saw it. A land mine, partially sticking out of the ground. They had walked right into a mine field.

"Here I was worried about my feelings, superficial embarrassment, and my dog was trying to save my life the entire time," Aaron said. "That was her only goal, trying to tell me, 'Stop, do not go in there.' And I ignored it. And that was the first and last time."

After many painstaking hours of retracing their steps, not easy to do in the desert, they all made it out. No casualties.

"We live to see another day—great, awesome, we go on—but I ignored that dog, selfishly," Aaron said. "It made me much more in tune to what was going on with that animal because it showed me that she really knows. This dog has a purpose, and I need to make sure that I'm picking up on everything that's going on with it."

That was on the professional side. But there was always more to this relationship.

"It really showed me the unconditional love and loyalty an animal can have with its handler," Aaron said. "Even in the world's worst place, truly hell on Earth, something that pure can still be there. It's a very . . ." He pauses, to get just the right words: "I will have a dog with me until the day I die. Always."

Sending navy dog handlers to augment marine units was an experiment, and Aaron was among the first sailors assigned to that duty. The dogs quickly proved their worth, whether it was sniffing explosives or being sent in first to clear buildings of bad guys. Units that once dismissed the thought of using dog teams soon clamored for them. But Yuma proved popular in down times too. If Aaron walked into a medical clinic for supplies, for example, people made a fuss. They asked if Yuma was thirsty—"Never once in my entire deployment did anyone ever ask if I wanted water," Aaron said—and would clean a bowl for her or even offer her ice water.

"The morale boost that a dog would give people was powerful," he said. "Anything that could distract from what was going on in Iraq or provide a feeling of normalcy."

And that reaction was a reminder for him of the specialness of his assignment.

"There were days when I was having a really hard time," he recalled. "Maybe I was outside the wire for twenty or thirty days at a time. I was just exhausted. Completely filthy but too tired to shower, too tired to eat. I just want to sleep and my dog is like, 'Hey, let's go play' or 'I need to go out.' One time I actually pushed her away, 'Leave me alone,' and I thought, 'There are people who would kill for a minute with my dog just to make them feel at home.' So I couldn't take that for granted. It put a lot of stuff into perspective."

Aaron spent much of his deployment along the Syria-Iraq border, a five- to ten-mile stretch of no man's land that neither country could—nor wanted to—control. One night a squad was sent out to fill up the base's water tank. The troops came under attack and about three in the morning called for help. Aaron and Yuma were part of the team sent to assist. It was a chaotic scene.

"It was night, dark, no streetlights, just whatever lights or night-vision goggles we had, and everyone had their corner as we set up a perimeter," Aaron said. On the way, the gunnery sergeant turned to Aaron and asked, "Will your dog go bite somebody?"

"Absolutely."

Aaron had never set a dog on someone before. Most trainers never do. During training, sure. Training while deployed? Constantly. And always with intensity, understanding that, if it happens for real, it's likely to be in an amped-up situation. Like a firefight, with marines yelling, jumping, and shooting, and civilians and combatants intermingled.

Still, Aaron didn't hesitate. "Absolutely," he responded.

Their Humvee skidded to a halt in the mist of the melee, dust everywhere, and immediately a man ran past them. "Let the dog go," the gunnery sergeant ordered.

"I jump out and run past the front of the Humvee and I let my dog go and she gets him," Aaron said. "She took him down, and I just remember a puff of smoke. There was dust and dirt everywhere, and we can't really see anything. But everybody stopped. They were just staring. They were getting yelled at over the communications system because they'd stopped paying attention to the firefight to watch the dog take this guy down. They were all cheering, 'Cool' and 'Awesome.' It was exhilarating and a rush, but at the same time I'm scared to death for my dog."

His mind flashed to worries of the man having a knife or Yuma being hurt. So he immediately called her back—to the disappointment of his audience.

"The mission was: guy is running away. Check, that's what I'm here for. Done. And once we did that, it was, I hope she's okay. But it was incredible."

Aaron was in the Iraq-Syria border region when his orders to go home came through: after eleven months of being the guy out front, on point, always on alert, his deployment was over. He packed, woke up early, and he and Yuma were ready to board the chopper out. But when they arrived at the landing site, the load master didn't have Aaron's name on his list.

"No, I have my orders," he said. "I'm going home."

"Not today you're not."

The rejection was devastating.

"I was just worn out," Aaron recalled. "It's very hard on the human psyche, knowing that every time you go out you might not come back. It's even worse for dog handlers. When I find a bomb, I am only a dog leash away from it. That's about six feet, and I'm not in a protective suit. And when the dog sits, everybody within eye distance, or with binoculars, knows what I just found. So I'm a huge target. And no one else is around you."

A recent close call with an exploded IED had been a grim reminder of the danger. So the orders to finally leave were a godsend—and being turned away at the helicopter was a cruel blow. That night, back on base, was the only time during his deployment that Aaron thought about taking his own life. He remembers cleaning his weapons—a constant with the endless firing and the sandstorms. He remembers thinking about the marines he'd seen killed. He remembers wondering, despairing really, if he would ever get out of there. And that's when Yuma caught his eye.

"I remember my dog looking up at me," he said, "and I could not leave her alone. I could not."

Yuma is back in the States, retired from active duty. She lives on a ranch in California with Aaron's dad. That wasn't the original plan, though, when Aaron set about to adopt his deployment partner.

There was, as expected, an excessively long bureaucratic process to adopt the animal that had so often saved his life. So Aaron and Brittany were in the States long before Yuma. And when she finally arrived, they assumed she'd fit into their family, along with their American bulldog Pandora. But the bonds that she had formed with Aaron in Iraq were as strong as ever. Yuma was still fiercely protective of her handler. When the dog was around, no one got close to him—not even Brittany. The ranch, then, seemed a good compromise.

That was just one aspect of a difficult transition for the couple. First, Aaron was medically discharged from the navy because of a diagnosis of post-traumatic stress disorder.

"I fought it every step of the way," Aaron said. "But with PTSD, you're no longer deployable, and if you're not deployable that is grounds for a medical discharge. Ultimately, though, I realized I wasn't married to the military. I was married to my wife, and that had to be the priority."

Brittany had done her homework before Aaron came home from Iraq, studying the information available on post-deployment transitions and the difficulties such times posed for married couples. "Honestly, she did a lot of research," Aaron said. "She is by far the more intelligent of the two of us."

Still, he adds, "That first year back, 2007 to 2008, was really bad for us. My wife says I'm not the same person she married, and I'm not. I don't know that I ever will be."

The hypervigilance and survival instincts that were necessary to operate effectively in a war zone can't be turned off. Aaron still doesn't sleep well. He'll get up in the night, unnecessarily, to once again make sure the house is secure. While not afraid of being around people, he finds it hard to trust them. If he goes to a restaurant and is seated with his back to everyone else, he'll leave—yes, even if they've just driven an hour to get there. If he and his wife go out, he is almost mission oriented: we eat, we're done, we leave. Sitting around and chit-chatting only invites risks. Don't even think about adding something to the itinerary like a stop at a book shop or antique store. He can't sit still long for anything, on a bench in a park or even at home watching a sitcom. Normal everyday life can seem trivial. He often has to feign interest in things, and while it might not show, he's impatient with people who complain about a tough day in the office—a safe, secure office where no one is trying to kill them.

He's gotten angry with doctors who challenge him, asking what are the odds that someone will throw a bomb through the window of the room they're in. "I guess they do that to make me agree with them, but my brain has rewired itself," he said, "It knows I lived in the worst place on Earth. It's telling me, why would you let your guard down knowing what people are capable of? I don't know how to not think in a secure or hypervigilant manner. It's not possible for me."

One doctor, after learning about his skills as a handler, suggested he try a service dog. This is when Echo, a German shepherd who looks suspiciously like Aaron's deployment partner, entered his life. Just as Yuma had his back in Iraq, Echo, his service dog at home, helps keep him safe and even somewhat relaxed.

"When the dog is around, I don't have to be 110 percent," he said. "It's soothing because I know what a dog is capable of. A service dog is always on, it's always alert, and that helps me. I don't have to worry about looking behind me all the time or worry about people in the distance. No one will sneak up on me. It's not going to happen."

He doesn't even mind when people ask to pet Echo. "That's part of it and that's okay," he said. "One good thing is that it forces me to have human interaction. I could be a hermit. If I had to, I could live in the middle of nowhere with dogs."

He'll still pace at home and make sure all is secure, but the dog will follow, making him feel that much safer. It's the same with going out. "Just having the dog there makes me feel better," Aaron said. "It's a huge security blanket."

While he credits Echo with keeping him functional, it is Brittany who keeps him focused.

"When I was medically discharged, I was furious and angry," he said. "I just didn't know what I wanted to do in the world or with my life. It was really hard."

Brittany, who earned her law degree while he was finishing up in the navy, pushed, and pushed, and pushed some more. He's since earned both a bachelor's and master's degree in cyber security. "My God, when you've got an attorney for a wife, with eighteen million degrees on the wall," he said. "But she's kept me moving forward. She makes me go out and do things. She is so super supportive. I wouldn't be where I am without her."

She even understands his need to always have a dog—though it is not something she shares. The couple is currently based in the United Kingdom, where Brittany is stationed. Since his discharge, she joined the air force and currently serves as a lawyer with the Judge Advocate General's Corps. When their bulldog Pandora passed away there, she was heartbroken and in no hurry to find a replacement. But Aaron was lost.

"I was miserable," he said of life without a dog. "There were days I didn't even bother getting out of bed, I didn't do anything. The longer time goes on, the harder it is to understand the need to process the combat stress, but she knew I needed a dog. She could see it."

He gave her two months to mourn Pandora, and then suggested a trip to a local breeder to look at puppies—"What woman doesn't want to look at puppies?" he asks. They didn't bring one home that day, but Aaron was soon back to talk to the breeder, who thought he was interviewing a potential dog owner. Aaron turned the tables. "I'm probably the best person on the planet to get a dog, so I was there to see how he took care of his dogs, how they interacted with him," he said. "That would tell me everything I needed to know."

When they brought in Echo, he knew she was the one. She was alert, attentive, inquisitive. And when she kept going both to the breeder and his wife, Aaron knew this was a couple that took care of their dogs. Brittany, of course, knew that this would be more his dog than a family dog. So, a year later, they returned for another German shepherd, Atlas, Brittany's almost hundred-pound-and-still-growing lap dog.

Now, when the family of four is out for a walk in their neighborhood, the ever vigilant Aaron has noticed something. If they start talking to a neighbor—even someone who has been in their home, someone the dogs know well—or that person approaches them, Echo steps forward. "She will put herself in front of us, between the person and the family," Aaron said. "She's half the size of Atlas, but puts herself in front of anything and the family, which is . . ." He stops, and sighs, thinking about the devotion—and security—that Echo's move brings. "If I could put that sigh into words. It's just incredible. It's perfect. That's what I want. It makes me feel even easier around her—and happy.

"I didn't have to train her for that. And there is nothing threatening about these interactions. But she will put herself—and other service dogs will do the same—in danger to protect their handler. And it's thankless. They're not doing it for recognition—most people don't even notice it. But that's what they're doing. A dog is willing to give its life to protect its handler."

That's no small thing for a veteran who needs a sense of security, someone who has talked to much older veterans and knows that PTSD is something he will likely always live with. And he's willing to talk about what he's seen, in the service and with service dogs, if it will help other vets.

"If I can share my experiences and help someone else, then it would be wrong for me not to," he said. "I'm not ashamed of having PTSD, I'm not ashamed of being scared to death in combat, and I'm not ashamed of not feeling sorry for me coming home when my enemy did not. I'm not ashamed of anything that I've done. It made me who I am. So if sharing that will help someone and make them think, 'Let me try a service dog,' or give them some perspective about their own lives, then awesome."

Aaron will be the first to admit that it isn't always easy to share his experiences. Brittany knows this too. After one recent phone interview about his deployment, he left his office and went downstairs, and there she was, waiting with Echo on a leash ready to be walked.

"She knew," he said. "It was like, 'Here you go,' and I felt better thirty minutes into my walk. Then the whole day was easier. It's better than any pill I've ever gotten, and I've had my share of those."

PART II

MORE CREATURES, GREAT AND SMALL

NINE

The Vietnam Infantryman

"Grab a bird, put on a glove, and go for a walk."

THEY ARE STRONG, FOCUSED, POWERFUL, FIERCELY INDEPENDENT, AND AT the top of the food chain. Birds of prey and warfighters share other traits as well, including their willingness to fight to survive. They are birds of a feather—with the ability to help each other heal in the most unexpected way. They peacefully hike together along forty-one acres of tall palm trees and walking trails in a wildlife habitat in Largo, Florida. Some are missing legs, arms, and parts of their brains, others an eye, a talon, or a broken wing. These special birds and veterans have found each other just in the nick of time. While they both share visible and invisible wounds and have suffered through war, abandonment, or accident, they are tethered for life thanks to a sixty-six-year-old Vietnam veteran who knows what it feels like to hit rock bottom. His name is Patrick Bradley. One wounded bird and one wounded warrior at a time, he is bringing them back to life and giving them a reason to live.

Patrick Bradley was born in Italy to a career US Army officer and lived all around the world as a typical army brat. "I was raised in the service, and my dad ran an army base at the time," Patrick said. "He was also a Korean War veteran, and you might say we didn't live a normal life; the military was all I really ever knew." In addition to his father, many of Patrick's uncles were also service members, and for him, it was an honor to serve his country in Vietnam.

"When I was eighteen and in my first year of college, I joined the ROTC," Patrick said. "I lived in Arkansas at the time, and decided in 1967 to enlist in the army so I could fight in the Vietnam conflict."

Many other young men were drafted to go to Vietnam in the turbulent 1960s and '70s. It was a costly war where fifty-eight thousand Americans were killed in support of South Vietnam's fight against the Communist North. At the height of US involvement, there were more than five hundred thousand American troops there. But US military involvement ended in 1973, with South Vietnam falling to the North two years later. Patrick was an excellent soldier, and even though he had heard that people back home were protesting against the war, he was steadfast in his conviction that serving the nation was his duty. Then, only two years after he joined the US Army, the unthinkable happened.

It was a dark day that is now etched in Patrick's memory forever. As he and his fellow soldiers were walking through the thick brush and mucky earth to return from their mission, he felt tired and just wanted to get some shut eye. As he was relaxing in his bunk, he was violently thrown from it by the force of a Vietcong mortar. His base had been attacked, and he and his platoon mates were now among the dead and injured.

"I was blown up at our base camp by a mortar attack that was devastating," Patrick said. "I had shrapnel all over my body, massive wounds, and many other injuries as well. I was eventually flown to Walter Reed to get fixed up. I was there for almost a year, and even to this day I have a wrist problem and others wounds that still haven't completely healed." Patrick explained that his physical wounds eventually did heal, but like so many other Vietnam veterans, he returned broken emotionally. "They took care of my visible wounds, but I wasn't prepared for returning to civilian life; I had wounds that people didn't see. Plus I was angry and mad at the world," said Patrick.

To complicate matters, Patrick and his fellow veterans were not welcomed home with great fanfare or gratitude for their service in the way that veterans are today. "A lot of us vets are still angry about how we were treated when we got back. It's not like now where this generation is welcoming vets with open arms and wanting to help them," Patrick added.

Patrick and many other Vietnam veterans suffered too long in silence. When they did seek help, those cries went virtually unnoticed. Friends and family didn't understand what the veterans needed emotionally, and so it seemed to the returning warriors that the American people just didn't care.

"To say I was a mess was an understatement," Patrick said. "When we got back from Vietnam, we felt like we were vilified and that was a horrible feeling. It was the worst time in my life. I literally hit rock bottom, had no direction, and I was mad at the world. I knew I had to do something with my life to help me get rid of the nightmares that were consuming me." Luckily for Patrick, help came in the form of an unusual suspect—an American icon in its own right—a giant American bald eagle.

"One of my doctors at Walter Reed wanted to help me, and he happened to come across a unique program sponsored by the Canadian government that was looking for people to study bald eagles. I was always fascinated by birds of prey, and as it turned out, my doctor was also a falconer. So he pulled some strings, and the next thing I knew I was off to Canada for an adventure of a lifetime."

Patrick arrived alone, wandering around two and a half million acres of the Canadian wilderness with only his backpack and a few months' supply of food. That didn't frighten him because he was a trained survivalist who could fend for himself. There he was, alone, with only the sound of his voice and the screeches, chirps, and calls of Mother Nature all around him. It was a secluded place where there were no distractions, no one to talk to, and only his thoughts to keep him busy. But he had a rigorous schedule to follow and a lot of data to record. He would soon learn a lot about American bald eagles and, in the process, some valuable lessons about himself. Being all alone for such a long time forced Patrick to face his own demons. And coming face to face with the avian world's fiercest predator helped him overcome the trauma of battle and the visible and invisible wounds that were the tragic byproducts of being a soldier.

"I had no direction before I left for Canada, and I didn't know what to expect either," said Patrick. "In 1970, I took this opportunity to escape the world; it was as if I were dropped off in the middle of nowhere." For the next three years, Patrick was immersed in nature and captivated by the majestic birds he was studying. Floyd Scholz, one of the world's most celebrated artists, avian authors, and bird carvers, said of the American bald eagle in his book *Birds of Prey*: "The American Bald Eagle is the most recognizable, most often portrayed and, sadly, the most caricatured of all the bird species. Despite all of this exposure, very few people know what Bald Eagles really look like." Scholz said that they range between twenty-eight and thirty-eight inches high and have a wing span averaging seventy-five to eighty inches. They are normally found near open waters or rivers and eat fish and waterfowl, many times pilfering food from other raptors' kills.

"What a thrill it was for me to observe these majestic birds in the solitude of the Canadian woods," Patrick said. "It took only about a year for me to begin to realize that my problems were all fixable. I found what I was doing with the birds helped me open up again. And when I left the woods in 1973, I was in love with all birds, period!"

With Patrick's renewed sense of well-being and hope, he went back to college at Arkansas State University and graduated in 1975 with a bachelor of science degree in zoology. He was excited to begin his new life and even more thrilled to get his first job out of college as the education director of a reptile theme park and wildlife preserve in Maryland only one year later. But that park was not finished yet, so the owners sent Patrick to another of their facilities in Silver Springs, Florida, called Ross Allen.

His new assignment was to teach the public about three of the animal kingdom's most feared predators. He had an alligator show, one with boa constrictors, and a third with rattlesnakes. "I discovered the short road to hell when I went to work with rattlesnakes," said Patrick. "A nurse on staff that I was dating at the time left some venom from my milking glass in a large jar on the table. By mistake I put my arm in there, with my open wound, and didn't know what was in it. After about ten minutes or so, I passed out, was rushed to the hospital, and luckily after about three days I was able to go back to work."

Patrick had had enough and asked one of his colleagues, who was working with birds of prey at the time, to trade places with him. "I cut a deal with the guy. He knew how much he liked alligators and how much I liked birds, so we decided to swap jobs. After about a year or so, the company I was working for at the time gave me a new title—director of educational services—and it was in a wildlife rehabilitation center too."

Patrick designed an education program for elementary and middle school students and was booked five days a week for nine months of the year. He took the most feared and unlovable species to classrooms all around the country on the "Animals Nobody Loves" tour. He would bring birds of prey, such as vultures, as well as weasels, scorpions, tarantulas, and other off-putting species, up close and personal for the kids. Every year, to keep things lively, Patrick would add other animals to his lineup. "It was a wonderful experience, and I wouldn't trade it for the world," Patrick said. "We were so successful that we even had a booking company arrange for all of our visits to schools. That's how popular they were with the students. I would always tell them—when they would snicker or run away in fear of my animals—the motto I've always lived by: 'Don't forbid yourself to do what you want to do.'"

Sometimes, he would tell the students about his unusual experiences with birds that didn't go quite as planned. Like the time he was working for the US government banding birds, most notably vultures. He and his partner, Marty, targeted birds near Dulles Airport, outside Washington, DC. It soon became obvious to Patrick and Marty why no one else attempted to band vultures in the wild. "We did our research and learned that vultures gorge to the point where they have trouble flying," Patrick explained. "So we asked around to see if we could find a stillborn calf and use it to attract the birds to the food. Then, when they would overeat, they couldn't fly and that made it easier for us to grab one and band it." What Patrick and Marty didn't know was that a vulture's defense mechanism is to projectile vomit. With the bountiful meal, so came about two dozen vultures. When the guys attempted to grab a bird for banding, the others, outraged, vomited all over the two young scientists. "It was totally disgusting," said Patrick. "We couldn't believe what they did to us and how much it smelled. We had no other choice but to strip down naked, jump in our car with the window open and head back home for a shower. We never went out with vultures again." The pair also subsequently learned that banding vultures can literally kill them because they tend to urinate on their legs to cool them down. That urine reacts with the metal in the band, effectively acting like a tourniquet. "The last thing we wanted to do is band a bird and then have to send it tumbling to its death. Trial and error is all part of the scientific process," said Patrick.

Patrick left the job in 1985 for a much-needed mental and physical break. He continued to live by his motto, still enjoying his life, experiencing only a few flashbacks and traumatic memories from his time in Vietnam. He had no regrets; he was living the good life. Then, after a few years of doing interesting but odd jobs, Patrick was feeling the urge to return to his beloved animals. He went back to his old employer, Silver Springs Park, where he was named the head of a new attraction called the Lost River Ride, which incorporated a part of the river where an old Tarzan movie had been filmed. As park visitors traveled downstream, they stopped at Patrick's site, and he would lecture them on a wide variety of animal species. He did that job for a year, and then he and his wife, Carol, moved to St. Petersburg, Florida, her hometown.

Then the unthinkable happened. In 2008, Patrick had a severe stroke. At the time he was working at a kayak and fishing company as a guide, and he refused to stop doing what he loved during his recovery. "I couldn't paddle my kayak anymore and I even had to use a motorized kayak just to get by," said Patrick. "It was a tough recovery for sure, but I'm not one to give up on a fight. So one weekend my wife and I decided to visit a nature park, and we saw a bird of prey display. I noticed something was off in the display and decided to ask the person in charge about it. After I told her my concern she said, 'How come you knew to ask that question? Can I get your number?' The next day the director called me, said he knew my references, and asked me to come back to the park to observe their operation for rough spots."

The next thing Patrick knew, he was named the volunteer head of the Boyd Hill Nature Preserve's "Birds of Prey" education program in St. Petersburg. This new position required Patrick to go in every day and revamp the program, using his knowledge of raptors to help engage the public and learn even more about these majestic creatures. That was in 2010. The director of the program at the time, Dr. Gabe Vargo, was in his seventies. He had been there for twenty-six years and wanted to retire. He began giving Patrick more responsibility, and after four years, Patrick helped to turn this 245-acre nature preserve into a destination park and, surprisingly, a haven for veterans with physical injuries and PTSD.

However, soon Patrick was ready for another challenge, and it came in the form of a phone call and an unlikely road trip. "It happened quite by accident," Patrick said. "While I was still at Boyd, I received a call from Pat Edmond, who was the president of the Friends of Largo Nature Parks in Largo, Florida. She was interested in perhaps having me bring the company who initially trained me in the finer points of birds of prey, called Earth Quest, to set up a program there. As it turned out, when my son and I were taking a road trip to visit another park in Honeymoon Island, Florida, we happened to drive by the George. C. McGough Nature Park and decided to stop in. That was just sheer luck that we did that. Apparently, the funding fell through anyway for the Earth Quest deal to be located at Boyd, and Pat asked if I would want to take over their existing birds of prey educational program at their operation."

Clearly, Patrick knew firsthand the healing power of birds of prey and was excited to be able to share those remarkable qualities with the world. After all, he got over his own persistent demons thanks to spending time studying American bald eagles in the Canadian wilderness and getting to know wounded birds of prey from his volunteer work.

After a few months in the new job, Patrick began to develop the Birds of Prey education program in Largo. He started with approximately ten birds, all of which were injured, abandoned, or otherwise disabled. At the same time, his son, Skyler, who had just retired after spending seventeen years in the army, was having serious problems. "My son just got out of the service and became a patient at the local VA hospital as part of their PTSD program," said Patrick. "He was a wreck. After nine deployments, I could see he was doing things that were odd, and he couldn't talk about what was bothering him. He was really a mess. Skyler also had a concealed carry gun permit, and always had his .45-caliber pistol in his pocket. That was really worrying me."

Skyler, like his dad, always had a passion for birds. He had grown up around them and soon became a regular at the Birds of Prey Center where Patrick volunteered as the director. "One day when Skyler was here I said to him, 'Son, why don't you just grab a bird, put on a glove, and go for a walk?' Sure enough he did that, and the next thing I knew he was going for long walks almost every day with his favorite bird—a bald eagle named Abiaka."

Patrick said that big birds have to be handled every day and taken out of their habitats. Like humans, they get bored and need a change in scenery, especially because their eyesight is seventy times more powerful than humans. Every day Patrick saw that his son was coming out of his shell, even leaving his gun at home and seeming to calm down every time he put on his glove and took his bird for a walk. In some strange and mysterious way, veterans were being rehabilitated in the same place where the wounded birds were, and Patrick was beginning to see a pattern of healing emerge that was breathtaking.

Word was beginning to spread that Patrick was having great success with veterans who came to the park to walk with the birds. After about three months, a recreation therapist from the outpatient unit of the Bay Pines VA Healthcare System paid Patrick a visit. She heard about his work at Boyd and tried to find him there. They told her he had moved on to a new nature park and so she tracked him down. "Elizabeth came out and talked to me about our program, and I said to her, 'All you need to do is take a bird and go for a walk.'" As with everyone who has experienced this emotional connection, she was hooked too.

Soon, doctors from the VA hospital were calling Patrick and asking him, "What are you doing over there to make such a difference in our vets with PTSD?" Patrick knew in his heart what was happening. "These birds are deep and fierce and they don't often reveal their feelings like dogs. But when they sit on a wounded veteran's arm and spend time with him, they learn to trust again. So does the warrior." Patrick explains it this way: "I always tell people when they ask me the difference between a dog, a horse, or a raptor and how they affect veterans with PTSD that, with a dog, it knows when you are feeling down. It is a tactile experience for both the animal and the human; the dog soothes you and you soothe the dog. Birds of prey also know when you are stressed and show that by trying to fly away, fidgeting on the glove, or appearing nervous themselves. The birds react that way to a veteran's stress level, but they can't be calmed down just by someone petting them. So if veterans who have issues and flashbacks see the bird reacting to their stress, they have to consciously work on themselves to calm the bird down. It ultimately motivates veterans to look inside themselves to solve their problems."

While his work is being vetted in order to make it an established therapy program, Patrick knows that is it making a tremendous difference in veterans' lives. "I've seen so many broken people become whole again through the power of our birds," said Patrick. "We start them out with our small birds like a one-quarter-pound screech owl, then move them up in steps to walk with bigger, stronger, and more dangerous birds like the barred owl, the red-tailed hawk, the great horned owl, and—at the top of the food chain—the bald eagle."

As the program gained regional and national attention, Patrick had many people from all walks of life wanting to volunteer. One young woman was a kidnapping victim in the Bahamas and had PTSD. Another was a rape victim. Some are professionals and others outdoors enthusiasts. All Patrick has to say to his new volunteers is, "Grab a bird and go for a walk."

It was clear to Patrick that something was working, so he decided to formalize the program and focus on pairing birds of prey with veterans. "I called Bay Pines and talked to the rec therapy folks," said Patrick. "They agreed to talk with us, and during their site visit, they each put on a glove and took a screech owl for a walk. When they came back, they were convinced that we had a viable idea, and it was something that they saw firsthand that worked. So they decided to make it a regular thing."

Over time, therapists at the VA hospital began sending large groups of their PTSD patients to the park for therapy sessions. Soon, Patrick had eighteen wounded birds and eighteen wounded warriors taking part in the program. The birds were all rescue birds. The wounded warriors were in need of rescue themselves.

Patrick believes that working with birds of prey benefits everyone. The birds get a chance to settle in and feel secure; they also love being in the spotlight and that helps limit their boredom. The wounded warrior can also be at peace, knowing that his companion, one of the fiercest warriors in the bird species world, is a wounded warrior too. As more and more veterans began coming to the park on a regular basis, Patrick just let them do their own thing and get lost in the moment. "I always tell our vets, 'My hope is that you will come out here enough, grab a bird, and mentally and physically get lost in the moment and in the park.'"

And get lost they did, so much so that Patrick, Skyler, his employee, Kaleigh, and his key volunteers decided to come up with a new name: the Avian Veteran Alliance. Over the four years that the Alliance has been in operation, Patrick estimates that more than two thousand veterans—all from the Bay Pines PTSD/TBI program—have come to the park. "Anyone can come here, and I feel strongly that if you face combat, you suffer from PTSD," Patrick said.

"I know for sure that veterans can see what the birds face, and because of the fact that they are predatory birds at the top of the food chain, the warriors can relate to that because they are also," Patrick said. "These incredibly magnificent birds are damaged and they are less than what they should be. They can't do what they are supposed to do, and they are struggling, just like our vets."

Of the twenty-one birds now living permanently at the park, most have wing or eye injuries. "This is their new forever home," Patrick is fond of saying. One bird was hit by a vehicle, a second was attacked by another bird, and a third was found in the engine compartment of a car. A great horned owl was injured on a golf course. Another bird was discovered as a baby, just fourteen days old, and it imprinted to its human parents. That bird, and others, don't know how to be birds in the wild.

One of Patrick's most remarkable rehabilitation stories is about a bald eagle named Sarge, who has a bizarre feather disorder. Patrick had a reason for choosing that name, firmly believing that noncommissioned officers are the backbone of the military. "I named her Sarge because most of the bald eagles are named for American iconic themes such as Liberty or Freedom. I wanted her to have a blue-collar name, and Sarge to me was just the ticket."

Patrick said Sarge can't grow all of her feathers properly. She was found in Tennessee by a group of hikers, severely dehydrated and with all of her main feathers broken. The hikers took her to the theme park Dollywood, which had a veterinarian on site. They did triage and helped her survive. But they had no rehab center, so Patrick put in an application for the eagle to come to Florida. It took a year, but now this beautiful bird is coming along well. In fact, in a few months Patrick will introduce her to the other bald eagles and soon get her on a glove and take her for a walk.

Patrick is humbled by the success of the Avian Veteran Alliance and the impact it has had on the veterans who have come to the park and walked with his birds.

"I can't tell you how many success stories we have had over the years. One veteran who was in hospice has dramatically improved, and a year later he still visits us almost every week. Another has come out of his shell after being holed up in his apartment for eight years. My son, I'm happy to say, is now in college pursuing a business degree, and he is back to his old self. And even though it is hard to see changes in our raptors, the one thing that is accomplished for sure is gaining their trust. They know that when the veteran puts on the glove, they are safe and won't be harmed. Also, the vets have no pressure to tell their feelings at all. The only thing I ask is to take the birds for a walk."

Patrick has also seen visible changes in the veterans' faces. "When they first come here from the hospital, they have that hangdog look," Patrick said. "But then when I put a bird on their arm, they can go out on their own and do whatever they want to do with no questions asked. Their faces are happy and animated, and that is special." Patrick said that, even when the veterans leave the program and move to other cities, they still keep in touch.

"It's wonderful that we are spreading our wings all over the country. Other programs call me all the time and want to know how they can incorporate our system into their own rehabilitation efforts," said Patrick. "I even got a call from a program that certifies vets for scuba diving to use the same concept we use to introduce peace and serenity in veterans' lives through nature. What better payback than that?"

Patrick hopes this work will keep him busy and engaged as long as he is able to volunteer. His birds and veterans will always be close to his heart. Some closer than others though. He proudly sports tattoos of his favorite animals throughout his body. His bald eagle, Liberty, is on his left shoulder;

his golden eagle, Sundance, is on his right shoulder; his beloved black bear, Mandy, is on his left calf; and Tawny, his Florida cougar, is on his right calf. They are constant reminders of the love and healing power of animals—not just dogs and cats but also some of the fiercest avian predators in nature. They are his motivation to wake up each and every day to share his life's work with his fellow veterans, who, like Patrick, have given so much in service to their country.

TEN

THE ARMY RESERVIST

"My God, no one is going to adopt her."

S HE LOOKED KIND OF SILLY. HER FUR WAS DARKISH GREY WITH ORANGE spots throughout, and if you looked closely you could see her one white paw. Not the best photo of Tessa, for sure. After all, she had been living in the Tampa, Florida Humane Society shelter longer than any other cat, and this was not the time for a professional glamour shot. This girl was ready to go home, somewhere.

Little did she realize that her quirky photo would melt the heart of a tough US Army veteran, who, like Tessa, was lost and alone.

Like many young men his age, Jonathan Hedrick wanted to make a difference. Right after the terror attacks on September 11, Jonathan decided to join the US Army. He was twenty years old and working in a Publix Supermarket in Tampa. "I was born in Cape Canaveral, Florida, the place we used to call the 'Space Coast,'" Jonathan said. "Over time it became a tourist trap, though, and there wasn't that much to do there after the space program fizzled. So I decided to enroll in school at Hillsboro Community College full time and started my career in retail at the Publix in Tampa. But working in retail never sat well for me. I had no passion to bleed green."

Jonathan had big dreams; he wanted to make something of himself. "It was becoming obvious to me that I needed to expedite my career," he said. "Then, right after September 11, I decided I wanted to do something to support my country and, at the same time, learn a skill that I could use for the rest of my life."

The military seemed like the perfect choice. Jonathan had come from a family of patriots. Grandparents, uncles, and an aunt served in the US Army and the US Air Force. He saw firsthand their sacrifice and love of country, and he wanted to do the same. "I decided to enlist in the army with the eventual goal of going to X-ray school," Jonathan said. "I joined the US Army Reserves in February, 2005, and was on my way to becoming a licensed X-ray technologist. I guess that most guys my age weren't knocking down the door to get into that field after they joined the army, but I guess you could say that I was never a typical guy anyway."

Jonathan lived with his mother as a child, and he never knew much about his biological father. The couple had never married, and he was out of the picture before Jonathan was born. Throughout his youth, Jonathan often questioned his mom about his dad, but his pleas fell on deaf ears. Nevertheless, he was fortunate to grow up with the love and support of his stepfather. "Considering what I found out about my father later in life, I could see why my mom never wanted me to know that much about him," Jonathan said.

Before Jonathan moved to Tampa to begin his career in the US Army Reserves, he adopted Ziggy from a person giving away kittens. This adorable and animated feline was Jonathan's great love and constant companion. Next to his girlfriend at the time, this adopted cat meant the world to him. They would go on trips together and snuggle at night, and Ziggy was a ball of fur with attitude! When Jonathan was ready to leave for basic training in Fort Knox, Kentucky, he asked his mother to keep Ziggy until he returned. It was hard for him to be separated from Ziggy, but boot camp is no place for a cat.

"As anyone who is in the military knows, basic training is super tough," said Jonathan. "I always said it's just one step above prison; they throw away your individuality. When they say, 'wake up' you do it; when it's time to sleep, you do. You have to wear the right clothes and show up for formation on time. Your freedom is basically gone, but that's how the military builds teamwork and teaches you to obey orders."

Jonathan did extremely well in basic training, excelling in leadership and team building, and he received a number of awards. "I was among the top soldiers in my cycle, and I even got to give a speech at graduation, but I was really proud of the fact that I just made it through," Jonathan said.

After completing basic training, Jonathan was transferred to Ft. Sam Houston in Texas, and then Ft. Stewart in Georgia, where he formally enrolled in X-ray school. He took classes while continuing his advanced individual training, which would prepare him for deployment overseas to fight in the War on Terror.

"I loved my life at that time, and believe it or not, I even liked the hard physical work that went along with combat training," he said.

But what Jonathan could not have predicted was the tragic turn of events that would end his dream of going to Iraq or Afghanistan to fight the bad guys.

"When I was still an active reservist, we were going over a complicated training exercise that I was sure I could handle," said Jonathan. "It was a hot afternoon and I was moving quickly up and down some steps with a forty-pound pack on my back. The next thing I knew, I fell down the flight of stairs. The pain was excruciating! When I tried to get up I couldn't. Then when I looked down at my foot, it was turned completely around and my knee was pointing straight to the sky. It was pretty nasty!"

Jonathan was taken to surgery right away. The doctors told him that not only did he break his leg, but he would also need additional surgeries on his foot to repair the extensive soft tissue damage and other injuries he sustained in the fall. He was placed on convalescent leave, giving him a break from training and time to heal. Jonathan stayed with his grandparents during recovery, which took about two months. When he was finally medically cleared by the army doctors to return to active duty, he finished his degree in X-ray technology. He was thrilled to have met his goal and eager to return to military life full time. Finally, Jonathan moved back to Tampa and was reunited with Ziggy.

Jonathan was also thrilled that his unit was gearing up for deployment, where he could put his skills to the test. But, before he could go, he was required to have a medical exam. "One doctor saw all my surgeries and told me in no uncertain terms, 'You can't go overseas with an injury like that.' I was crushed. They gave me the option for an honorable discharge, which for some soldiers means a get-out-of-jail-for-free card. But for me, it wasn't. I wanted to serve more than anything. But eventually I realized it was a blessing in disguise, because I had a very tough injury. Even with all the physical therapy I had, my leg still wasn't the way it was before.

"Sometimes I feel so petty complaining about my own injuries when men and women in the military are missing their arms and legs," Jonathan said, "What happened to me doesn't even compare." Despite his reservations about leaving the army, in 2008 Jonathan was honorably discharged.

Adjusting to civilian life for most veterans is a challenge, and that certainly was the case for Jonathan. His dream had been to make a career out of the military, like his family members before him, and he was depressed that his injury prevented him from fulfilling that wish. Plus, soldiers who are injured in training exercises, unlike those wounded in combat, receive no Purple Heart or other recognition. Many feel like their sacrifices were in vain.

"Most people have no idea how many men and women in the military have had injuries training right here at home," said Jonathan. "It's not like a Matt Damon movie where soldiers are only injured on the battlefield. I wanted to make a career out of the military and fulfill my contract to serve. But I broke my leg on their terms. I didn't get an injury riding my motorcycle but rather training hard to fight the bad guys overseas. I am proud of the time I did serve, and the experience for sure made me more mature. I was there to learn and improve myself. I needed this career and thought long and hard about it before I signed up."

After leaving the army, Jonathan's civilian career really blossomed. He worked in a hospital as an X-ray technologist for five years and then moved into the education field, teaching X-ray classes at a variety of schools. By the age of thirty-five he was specializing in the billing aspect of health care, working at home for the Parallon Company, an organization owned by the health-care behemoth HCA Corporation. Jonathan reviews medical records and matches them up with bills before sending them to the insurance companies or Medicare. His main mission is to assure that there are no fraudulent claims or charges.

You might say Jonathan's life was going pretty well. That was until February, 2015, when his best friend, Ziggy, died after a battle with cancer. "He was my constant for twelve years," said Jonathan. "When I was away in basic training, every time I talked with my mom, and even when I wrote her letters, I always asked, 'How's Ziggy?' I called him my 'little gentleman,' and he was an extension of my being."

Losing Ziggy was devastating, an emotional trauma Jonathan had never experienced before. "Animals are always there for you, no matter what," he said. "Ziggy was my world, and now he will only be a memory." Jonathan smiles at those memories of his cat's quirky personality. "Ziggy used to greet me at my door when I would come home from going anywhere, and he would be so excited," said Jonathan. "He would do this thing where he'd tuck his head so far between his front legs that he'd actually roll onto his back with his belly exposed. He played more like a dog than a cat. Then I would use my foot to pet and shake him. He also loved looking at squirrels through the windows, and God help a lizard if it ever made it inside the house. And if I didn't keep an eye on him, he would slide a piece of pizza right off of the table. He was one heck of a character."

After Ziggy's death, Jonathan donated some of his things to the Humane Society of Tampa, including his cat carrier, which he always hated. There also were cans of food and some toys that Ziggy never responded to. It was Jonathan's way to continue Ziggy's legacy and help another shelter cat as well.

A few days later, though feeling good about his donation, Jonathan couldn't help but still feel heartbroken. He visited the Humane Society website, which had a real-time, up-to-date list of all the pets available for adoption. "I started looking at the cats to see what was there. I give them props for keeping videos of them," said Jonathan. "The very first one I saw was a picture of a cat named Tessa, who was living at the shelter the longest. She had a unique thumbnail photo that was silly but cute. Each photo came with a first-person description of the cat in their own words. Hers read: 'I am an older girl but I have lots of love to give.' I learned that she was a senior cat and was surrendered by her owners because they couldn't take care of her health issues. I thought to myself, 'My God, no one is going to adopt her. Everyone wants kittens and puppies only.'"

Jonathan was in love and felt a duty to adopt her. He kept visiting the website, hoping she would still be there and soon filed the adoption paperwork. In the meantime, Jonathan went to the pet store and bought bags of the same food that Ziggy used to eat. He combed the store aisles for anything and everything that he knew Ziggy loved and Tessa might too. "You are so in the habit of cleaning up their litterbox, picking up their toys—even after they're gone," Jonathan said. "Not having a ritual was tearing away at my soul. While I was waiting for the paperwork to come through I kept going to the Humane Society to look at all the cats, just in case. During one of those visits they told me that Tessa had her own room away from the other cats. They said she needed more human interaction than the others, and she became depressed after she was surrendered. They called it 'failure to thrive.'"

Jonathan would soon discover that when Tessa was dropped off by her owners, she stopped eating and cleaning herself. Luckily, the staff came up with the perfect intervention. They moved her into their office, where she would watch them answer phones and do paperwork. They made room for her despite her difficulties.

After about three weeks, Jonathan officially adopted Tessa, and the shelter told him that he was the first person ever to adopt a cat through the Pets for Patriots program! It was only one month after Ziggy passed, but Jonathan's grief soon turned into joy. "When I came to pick Tessa up, the girl behind the counter looked shocked! She said, 'Someone is finally going to take Tessa.' Tessa made an impression with everyone," said Jonathan. "One girl even cried."

Jonathan brought a carrier to take Tessa to her new home and inside had a collection of new toys and some older ones that had been Ziggy's. When Jonathan opened the door of the carrier and let her out, she sniffed everything, looking all around the house and checking things out. "In about an hour Tessa was sitting on my lap," said Jonathan. "Later that night she hopped in bed with me and laid on my chest, and she has been there ever since."

"I don't mean to make it sound too huge a thing, but she gave me a purpose again," he said. "Not to say I didn't have one before, but she's my reason to work in life. If I don't go to work, then I can't pay the bills and she won't have a place to stay. I try to be a better person for her. She is my responsibility, and she didn't ask for the life she got. They could have put her down, and I am grateful to her first owners for not doing that."

Over the past year, Tessa and Jonathan became a team. She is now a whopping twenty pounds and prefers to lay around a lot, which is probably the reason for her girth. "She doesn't bounce around and run all over the place," Jonathan said. "She's a very docile cat and just loves to cuddle. She does like her toys, though, especially her scratching post. She has a good life and is not wanting for anything. But she is very different than Ziggy. She'll eat anything, where Ziggy was picky and set in his ways. Tessa just goes with the flow; she's very content. Plus she is very friendly and doesn't run away and hide when she meets new people. All she wants is to be scratched."

Jonathan never wanted a trophy pet. He wanted a cat with style and personality. Like Ziggy, Tessa needed a permanent home—and an owner who would not abandon her at the slightest provocation. Jonathan was Tessa's salvation. Tessa was Jonathan's key to love lost and found.

Maybe that's one of the reasons that Jonathan decided to use Twitter to memorialize Ziggy and give Tessa a legacy for the eight years in her life that he missed. He created "Tessa Tuesday," posting new pictures of her each week that are often retweeted by his many followers.

"I have no pictures of Tessa as a kitten and she deserves to be put in the spotlight," said Jonathan. "A Tampa television station aired a story about me and Tessa and Ziggy, and I was told that, after my story ran, someone donated $5,000 to the shelter! Ziggy's story still continues to help other animals even though he's gone."

Jonathan said that he believes that pet adoption can help anyone, especially veterans as they cope with depression. He often tells people who are looking for a pet, "Don't go shopping; go adopting." He is convinced that no matter how little or great someone's depression is, adopting a pet gives him purpose. "In my case, having Ziggy and now Tessa helped make me a responsible adult. They taught me to not be selfish and forced me to take responsibility for my actions. They also taught me compassion for others; I'm not living just for myself anymore."

Sometimes Jonathan feels uncomfortable when, as a veteran, people give him and others in the military standing ovations at ball games or shower them with other attention. "I wish I could have done more in the military, but my injury prevented that," he said. "Now, I have arthritis setting in, my ankle makes this clicking sound, and I can't do a twelve-minute, two-mile run anymore. But I am blessed to be healthy and hope to one day get married and have a family. Now with Tessa, I'm able to feel love again, and even though she is a cat, still, she brings joy into my life and that is wonderful."

Jonathan's mother, like many moms of vets, is very proud of him. She lives in the same county, about a twenty-minute drive from his house. One day after he and his mom talked, Jonathan decided it was time to learn more about his biological father. He did a Google search and learned that his dad was in jail for attempted murder. He shot two people in a bar brawl, which he claimed was in self-defense. After years of phone calls and letters back and forth, which he never told his mom about, Jonathan decided it was time to meet his father in person.

He traveled to the Colorado prison and was nervous about what he would find. The first time he laid eyes on his dad, he felt a sense of relief. "It was a watershed moment for me for sure," Jonathan said. "I believe there are three sides to every story, so I listened to what he had to say. I told him about my life too. It was an interesting visit for sure. When I was in Colorado, I stayed with a friend of my dad who told me this: 'It was a good thing that he wasn't in your life for all those years; he was hell on wheels.' That was a good point. But I used this experience with my father to make me a better person." Jonathan didn't tell his mother about the trip to Colorado until months after he returned. "I try to keep the relationship with my biological father just between us," he said.

With photos of Ziggy all around Jonathan's house and Tessa snuggled in his arms, Jonathan is at peace. He knows firsthand what it feels like to be abandoned. That's why his cats mean so much to him. Ziggy and Tessa were also left alone but, thanks to Jonathan, were given a second chance at living a happy, secure, and fulfilling existence. As Albert Schweitzer once said: "There are two means of refuge from the misery of life—music and cats."

ELEVEN

THE COWBOY MARINE

"Here's how you saddle a horse."

COLONEL JOHN MAYER, COMMANDER OF THE US MARINE CORPS WOUNDED Warrior Regiment, was disturbed by something he was seeing among his charges.

The regiment, based in Quantico, Virginia, is tasked with helping wounded, sick, and injured marines in all aspects of their recovery as they prepare to return to duty or transition to civilian life. The goal is to strengthen them in mind, body, and spirit. Their families, too, are brought into the process, supported through their current challenges, and made ready for the ones to come.

One of the many programs associated with the regiment when Mayer was in command from 2010 to 2012 involved therapeutic horseback riding. Mayer loves horses and has several of his own at his ranch in Texas. With that background, he just assumed that the men and women he aided through their recovery process would adore these animals too. So he expected a certain level of enthusiasm from those who saddled up. Instead, he was finding that his marines were . . . bored. With trail riding. With riding around in circles in an arena.

In response, the mission-oriented Mayer did what marines always do when a roadblock appears. He improvised. He adapted. He overcame.

"At first, I couldn't understand why none of them wanted to ride or why they were getting bored," he said. "But I said, 'Fine. You guys don't want to do therapeutic riding? Then we need something more challenging. We need to do cowboy work.'"

Mayer partnered the Wounded Warrior Regiment's riding program with the Semper Fi Fund. Thus, the Jinx McCain Horsemanship Program was born, one of the many life-saving opportunities offered to post-9/11 veterans by this nonprofit organization that supports wounded, critically ill, and injured service members and their families.

The inspiration for this innovative program is Colonel Jinx McCain, a four-time Purple Heart recipient whose service spanned World War II, Korea, and Vietnam. In the 1960s, while stationed at Camp Pendleton, California, he would take amputees out on trail rides to boost their morale. Like the legendary colonel, the program named for him emphasizes the connection between marine and horse and the benefits for each that results. But forget riding for pleasure. Sign up for the Jinx McCain Horsemanship Program, and you'll be put to work. Hard work. Dirty, dusty, dawn-to-dusk work. Cowboy work.

John Mayer took the concerns of those bored wounded warriors to heart when he and Karen Guenther, the chief executive officer of the Semper Fi Fund, co-created the program in 2011.

They don't ride in arenas, and trail riding is a rarity. Instead they travel to ranches in places such as Arizona, Wyoming, and Montana for roughly two weeks at a stretch. They help the ranchers with herding or branding cattle or whatever other work needs to be done. Jinx McCain pays for airfare and any lodging. The ranchers supply the horses, tack—and the cows.

"Remember we're talking about the one percenters here," Mayer said. "One percent of Americans join the service, and after September 11, 2001, the people who joined knew they were going to go fight in a war, that they were likely to experience combat. And once those guys and gals have had that experience, it's hard to ask them to get excited about riding a horse in circles around an arena. I mean, they'll do it once, they might go back a time or two, but they are going to get bored very quickly."

Mayer doesn't allow his Jinx McCain riders, no matter what their experience level, time to be bored. "Here's what's neat about this is," Mayer said. "Say you have a guy who's never touched a horse before. I will have him working a cow on day two. Most riding places will say I'm absolutely insane for doing that, it's hugely dangerous and all that. But I say it's the best way to get these military veterans the challenge they need and to bring their confidence back."

Mayer was invited to be director of the program in September 2014, when he retired from the Marine Corps after thirty-three years. He's on the go running what he calls large clinics, about seven a year, from spring through fall. Each session will put ten to sixteen vets to work on horseback, in spectacular settings that they might have only seen before in the movies or on television. "Listen to this," Mayer said excitedly. "In March we were on a big ranch in Texas; April we were down in Mississippi; June we were on a ranch in New Mexico; July a ranch in Wyoming; August we were packing mules into the Rocky Mountains in Montana; September we were packing mules into the San Juan Mountains of Colorado; and October we were in Arizona on a big ranch. So if you have a choice between riding in circles in an arena or on a big ranch in Wyoming, which one are you going to pick? You're going to pick the big ranch—and you're going to keep coming back."

They return for the work and the challenge—and some of the things that are gone from their lives since they've left the military.

"Think about this," Mayer said. "Marines and other service members are recruited from across the country. They train together, they deploy together, they fight together, and many times they get wounded together. And then they recover together. Now the military takes great care of the wounded, but once they're recovered, we send them home. Alone. And they have lost that brotherhood that they've grown accustomed to—that's why I stayed in for thirty-three years, the brotherhood."

Some adapt to that newfound life, while others do not.

"Many of them joined the service right out of high school, and they've been told what to do every moment of their life," Mayer said. "Then we send them home, sometimes with a $5,000-a-month disability check, and if they're not self-starters to begin with, they don't know what to do with themselves. At first they might think, 'Hey, no work, steady pay, this is the greatest thing in the world.' But many become trapped, and bored, and some turn to drugs or alcohol. They don't really have a meaningful purpose."

Mayer wants Jinx McCain to be step one on the road to that purpose. First, he wants to rekindle part of the service experience that once gave them meaning and direction.

"Think about the military," Mayer said, "where first you have to be an individual and you have to be good at your job, and then you have to take those skills and work as part of a team to accomplish a mission. So that's what we do at Jinx. First, you have to become a rider, so we teach them how to ride. But then we say, 'Now you have to work as part of a team to move five hundred cows through the Bighorn Mountains of Wyoming.' I tell you, it's magical. They just eat it up. There's nothing out there like it that I know of."

Mayer believes his formula works in part because he is not a certified instructor. Instead, he says, "I'm just a guy who loves horses and being a cowboy." And while he won't call what they do therapy, he gets the therapeutic aspect. "What I say is, 'We're gonna go out and go cowboying.' We get them out there where they can do a hard day's work and accomplish something," he said. "Of course, there are great benefits in that for your spirit. You're breathing fresh air, and we try to go places that cell phones don't work so they are not tied to any of their troubles at home. We sleep around a campfire, we cook around the fire. We never stay in hotels. We stay where you have to rough it up—the rougher, the better."

He had eight veterans with him on the New Mexico trip, on a 120,000-acre ranch with 466 pairs—mothers and calves. They rode out at dawn each day, gathering different portions of the herd. They spent the afternoons separating mother and calf—cowboys call it cutting—then roped the calves and dragged them to the fire to be branded. "We did that for five straight days, 466 calves," Mayer said. "And I'm telling you it was hard work. It was hot work, it was dusty work, up in the New Mexico desert, and the guys loved every minute of it."

And here's the unspoken therapy part: "Because it was a demanding mission," Mayer said, "they had to work as a team to develop the brotherhood that those guys will remember for the rest of their lives."

As important as the trips themselves are, even more critical for the vets is what comes next in their lives. And while it was gratifying that Jinx inspired return visits, there were worries among the staff about the vets having too much spare time—and perhaps not enough meaningful purpose. That concern led, in June 2015, to the creation of the Semper Fi Fund's Apprenticeship Program, which Mayer also directs.

"This is for guys who are 70 percent or greater disabled or who can't find a meaningful job or won't because of their PTSD or traumatic brain injury," Mayer said. "We help them start home businesses or find employment. What I always tell them is 'If you can dream it, and we can find a way to train you to the professional level, then we will sponsor you.'"

In fall 2016, there were thirty-one apprentices, most of whom were Jinx McCain alums. They included bakers, a saddle maker, an organic farmer, a taxidermist, leather workers, a hat maker, a cowboy boot maker, a blade-smith, a wood worker, a commercial drone pilot, a horse trainer, a photographer, and dog trainers. "These are the kind of businesses that you can train for in a relatively short period of time," Mayer said, "and we hook them up with a mentor who brings them up to a professional level."

For Mayer, it's a natural evolution from working cows to a new and more purposeful life.

"We really use the horses and going out and doing cowboy activities to bring the confidence back and to remind them of the abilities they already have," he said. "If you can move a herd of five hundred cows through the mountains of Wyoming, you surely can start a business making leather belts and holsters and that kind of stuff. So what we do is get them excited about life again, give them a purpose, and then we provide the apprenticeship program to help them achieve that purpose or get them focused on going back to school or finding a job. The two work hand in hand, and it's been quite successful."

Stefanie Mason has been in love with horses since she was a little girl. Her uncles raised and raced horses, and Stefanie would often join her mom and grandmother at the race track. Wanting to be a jockey came naturally— though the tall, lanky Stefanie would, quite literally, outgrow that career goal—and she has always had a passion for fast horses. She took lessons for many years, not far from her family's Wilmington, Delaware home, in the precision-driven world of dressage and had even worked up to jumping before her lessons came to an end. She would move on to many other interests, but the embers of that first love remained, awaiting rekindling.

Her next most memorable time on a horse came many years later, in Richmond, Virginia. Stefanie was then an army reservist, recovering at the Veterans Affairs' polytrauma center from injuries sustained in a vehicle accident during her third overseas deployment, this one in Kabul, Afghanistan. In April 2010, the up-armor SUV she was riding in crashed, and Stefanie's head smashed into the thick bulletproof windshield. She suffered a traumatic brain injury; nine facial fractures, including a broken jaw; a tibia plateau fracture from her leg crashing into the dashboard; and a degenerated disc in her back. Though she received life-saving treatment immediately, her condition was grave. When her mom, Paulette, received word of the crash in Delaware, she asked, "Is she going to make it through the night?" All the doctor on the other end of the line could say was, "We're going to have to wait and see."

She did make it, through years of often agonizing physical therapy, as she and her medical team fought to ensure that she could walk again. They, and the always present and ever supportive Paulette, did their jobs well. Stefanie not only walked but while still in recovery began to swim competitively in the Warrior Games, an annual all-forces competition for wounded veterans held at the US Olympic Training Center and Air Force Academy in Colorado Springs, Colorado. She was a gold and bronze medalist her first year and collected more medals in subsequent years. She even pushed herself back into running, in which she had excelled before the accident. That, however, came with a price. "I tried doing a 5K at the hospital a year before I left," she remembered, "but I was in so much pain I started crying."

Early on in her recovery, only about two months after being brought out of a medically induced coma, she was asked to join a horse therapy session for wounded warriors at the Richmond VA. Though still pretty banged up, she exclaimed, "Yes, sign me up." Her damaged leg was still immobilized, but they got her up on the horse, a person walking along on either side to ensure she wouldn't fall. Almost immediately, she asked, "Can I start trotting?" The nurse that had accompanied the vets to the session reminded Stefanie—in no uncertain terms—that she couldn't put weight on her damaged leg, which meant she couldn't put her feet in the stirrups if she worked up from a walk to a trot. No problem, said Stefanie, and trot she did, still with a person on either side, hustling to keep up. "Oh, this is so much fun," she thought at the end of the outing. "I have to do it again."

It took longer than expected, but Stefanie is riding regularly again, thanks to America's Fund, which is, like the Jinx McCain program, an arm of the Semper Fi Fund. America's Fund pays for weekly lessons for veterans interested in honing their horsemanship skills close to home. (Jinx actually does the same, supporting many of its alums who take lessons in between clinics with John Mayer.) The lessons, and the reconnection with that first love, couldn't have come at a better time for Stefanie, who had recently lost her job with the Delaware court system.

"Something about the horses is really nice," Stefanie said. "You can talk to them—and they don't argue back. Sometimes they can be stubborn, but mostly it's just so enjoyable to be around them. There is a calmness about them that can be so relaxing."

Stefanie isn't there just to ride; she wants to show again and expects to be able to start in spring 2017. In the meantime, she is back to enhancing the skills she was perfecting almost twenty years ago: walking, trotting, cantering, and—she hopes by December 2016—jumping. "It's all coming back pretty easily," she said. "I just need to get back to the level where I'm competitive, and then I can start showing again."

She's at the stable once a week, a half hour before her lesson starts. She finds her partner Bo, a tall, tan thoroughbred—she still likes fast horses—and brushes him down before saddling him and preparing for the lesson. "When you ride, taking care of the horse is part of the deal," she said. "I can't just go over there and ride. You and your horse are part of a team, two athletes, working together as one. So you have to work together as a team, and that means doing a lot of things for your partner to help him out. It teaches discipline, plus you learn a lot about your horse while you're taking care of him."

She compares working with Bo to the time people spend getting to know a dog. "At first, if you're a stranger, the dog will bark or be intimidated by you," she said. "But if you spend time with it, the dog gets used to you and starts to trust you and will obey you when you give it a command. Same with a horse. The longer you work with him, the more you get to know each other, and the stronger the bond you will have with each other."

That learning process helps when one part of the team has to push the other. Stefanie said Bo can sense when it's almost time for the lesson to be over, and he lets her know that he's ready to head back to the barn. "Sometimes he gets lazy," she said. "I have to tell him, 'We're having our lesson now. We have to work hard, and then you can enjoy yourself.'"

Just like during the Richmond outing, she didn't hesitate because of her injuries when it was time to begin lessons. "Oh, I was loving it," she said. "I was ready to take him for a run as soon as I got back on a horse." Her one concession to the serious head injury she suffered was to ensure she had a high-quality helmet. "Falling off a horse is expected when you're riding," she stated matter of factly. "Just like it's normal to be stepped on or bucked. But it's nothing life threatening. Hey, I was in the Middle East for three deployments and suffered a car accident, so I don't really think much about getting hurt on a horse."

The stable also takes safety seriously, guiding Stefanie, as with other students, through proper procedures and making sure she can handle each step—walking, trotting, cantering—before moving on to the next one. "Like any sport, you can always get injured," she said. "But safety is the main part. And while emphasizing safety, you can also enjoy riding, too."

She thinks of her lessons as therapy, as she looks for another job and works on her master's degree in international relations at American University in Washington, DC. "Mentally, I'm loving it. I'm so happy right now," she said. "Riding really cheers me up, and when the hour is over and I'm getting off the horse, I'm already looking forward to the next week. When I get a new job, I'm going to start taking lessons twice a week because I love it so much."

Ask her to describe the best moment since her return to riding and Stefanie laughs. "I have liked every moment I've had so far," she said. "We are so funny here, and even though I'm the oldest one taking lessons—most are high school age or younger—we all love hanging around horses. Even the smell of them is so enjoyable. One little girl's dad said she loves horses so much that she can't wait to get over there and it's almost impossible to get her off her horse. I thought, 'That is so me.'"

Tom McRae didn't respond to his friend's initial calls about the Jinx McCain Horsemanship Program. She left messages, sent him information. It's not that Tom wasn't interested. He was just busy, fixing up his new home and ten-acre property in North Carolina—and being a single dad to his daughter, Aidan, who turned nine in April 2017.

The friend—a case worker for the Semper Fi Fund—met Tom during his years-long recovery at Walter Reed. He had been a marine NCO specializing in the extremely hazardous but mission-essential field of Explosive Ordnance Disposal in Afghanistan—his sixth deployment since 9/11—when he was blown up by an improvised explosive device on January 16, 2012. The blast took both of his legs above the knee and his left arm, destroyed his right eye and severely damaged the left, and resulted in a severe penetrating brain injury. Saving him was a miracle—and a good bit of the credit goes to his mom, Carolee Ryan, who was by his side from the moment he was returned to the States. (She's still not far. Tom's parents moved from Alaska to a place near him in North Carolina. Since his limited sight keeps him from driving, it's Carolee who takes Aidan back and forth to school every day.) But even once it was clear that he would live, it was weeks before anyone could determine the extent of his brain injuries and consider the kind of life he might be able to lead. Carolee wouldn't let Tom—or his medical team—give up. "It's extremely important to have family around them for them to succeed," she said. "Yes, they are going to have challenges, and, yes, everybody is going to be frustrated. But whatever we have to get through, we can get through it."

Case workers at the Semper Fi Fund share that same don't-give-up spirit. The one who knew Tom also knew how much he loved horses. Heck, he already had a couple with him at the new place. As he has said, "I had horses for eight years before I got blown up. And that's one thing I won't give up. I just really enjoy it. It makes me feel normal when I'm up on a horse."

So the case worker went over Tom's head. She contacted John Mayer and asked him to reach out to Tom.

When the two finally connected, it wasn't clear that Tom was a good candidate for the program after all. Start with the logistics. He hadn't traveled on an airplane without his primary caregiver—his mom—since he'd been blown up. So unlike the other participants, he wouldn't be able to just show up at a ranch solo and get right to work. And, of course, there was the larger question. Could he handle cowboying, fully participating along with the other vets? He had ridden since the explosion, at his home and while at Walter Reed. But all the horses he'd been on had been trained for a rider who was missing legs. Even then he'd never spurred his horse into anything faster than a walk, and he'd only been on flat terrain. Jinx McCain would present much greater challenges. Would he be able to ride a normal horse once he got out to a ranch and actually get it to respond to his commands? And could he keep up with his fellow cowboys, riding at a trot, often over hilly terrain?

The first part was easy, in part because Tom and Carolee have become such an adept team at overcoming any and all obstacles. She would travel with him for the upcoming session in Arizona, and while he cowboyed she could kick back, enjoy the weather, and read. Not such tough duty.

The other questions Tom couldn't answer as readily. But Mayer had a suggestion. His second-in-command at Jinx McCain, Mo Smith, had a place not far from Tom in North Carolina—complete with horses and cattle. Go on up there, Mayer said, and see what you can do. "The idea was to prove that I can stay on a horse," Tom said. "John didn't seem too thrilled that I hadn't done a lot of things on a horse since being blown up. But after riding for a few days, there were no issues."

When he arrived for his visit, Tom quickly learned that Mo wasn't big on ceremony. "When I got up to his house, he just picked me up and threw me on the horse," Tom recalled. "So I rode his horse for three days and played with his cattle. And I was able to stay on, going up and down hills, trotting, doing a lot more than just flat-ground walking, which is what I was used to at that point."

Mo supplied the saddle for Tom's trip to Arizona, a normal saddle with only one alteration to accommodate a triple amputee: a leather strap that goes around the back of the saddle and over Tom's stumps. "That's the only thing holding me down in the saddle," Tom said. "But it was enough to keep me on, even when I was going fast."

His previous horsemanship experience was a huge help. Having spent time before his injury riding bareback, he knew how to balance himself on a horse, even without a saddle. He has to call on those skills now, riding without legs. "I have to balance a little more, but it's not too bad, although there were a couple of times I had to say, 'Whoa,'" he said with a laugh.

The fear of what could happen, and the possibility of getting hurt, doesn't deter him. "I'm not afraid to fall off a horse," he said, "and every day that I pushed a little harder, going up and down those hills and stuff like that, I thought, 'Okay, I didn't fall off so I can try to do a little bit more next time.'"

He sums up the trip to Arizona in two words: "incredibly satisfying."

He remembers maybe one trail ride, through a bit of desert. The rest of the time they worked, herding cattle. "It could take four hours to work a pasture," he said of the ground they covered daily. "It's a lot of riding over a pretty rugged and varied terrain, going through washes and things like that. There are a lot of hills, and some of it was a little bit in the mountains. It was all above and beyond what I've done for years and years."

The vets were given time to get used to the horse they were assigned, at first riding in a pen at a walk or trot. Some cattle were even put into that mix, to test their skills a little further. "It was a good chance to get used to working on a horse around that kind of stuff," Tom said.

If they passed that test, it was time to hit the trail. "We spent most of the day in the saddle," Tom said. "Some of the days you ride from breakfast to lunch. Then you go down to the mess hall, and right after that you're back on the horse and back out there until dinner."

Except for those three days with Mo in North Carolina, working with cattle was a new experience. "We had to separate them and push them into different pens," he said. "And then on the final day they were doing branding and castrating. So we got to partake in that, though I was in my wheelchair that day."

Even before this trip, Tom didn't usually use his prosthetic arm to ride. He holds both reins in his good arm. "Most people use one rein per hand," he said, "but I need a horse with a neck rein. So instead of pulling on one rein or the other to make the horse turn, you lay them across the horse's neck." It was fortunate that he was used to that style, as his prosthetic arm broke the first day on the ranch. "It wasn't anything major, just a snapped cable," he said. The break did give him an excuse to rib John Mayer a little. The program director likes to point out that he's never had any of his veterans injured during the clinics. "But wait a minute, John," Tom would say, "I broke my arm today."

This will not be Tom's last clinic with Jinx McCain. In fact, on his way home, he and Mo stopped off in Ohio to have a saddle custom made for Tom. He'll also be honing his skills with an instructor in North Carolina that will help him with riding and working cattle—courtesy of Semper Fi Fund. "Mo is helping me look for someone now," he said. "My place is flat, so I need somewhere with different terrain and with horses and cattle."

After just one trip out west, Tom is more than happy to recommend the program to fellow veterans. "Oh, I really would," he said. "And not necessarily just for people who have been on a horse before, but for people who want to try it out and learn how to do something like that. It's a really good program."

That advice, and the philosophy of Jinx McCain to encourage veterans to prepare for the next phases of their lives, fits well with Tom's own beliefs about looking ahead.

"I won't dwell a single day on what happened to me," he said. "If I look back, I think more about what happened to my friends, but not to me. The people who dwell on what happened, it stifles what they can do. It can lead to long-term problems and depression, and then they can wind up self-medicating with alcohol and other things instead of getting over it and saying, 'I'm going to do this and I'm going to do that.'"

Tom—and the people at the Semper Fi Fund—rightfully see the Jinx McCain Horsemanship Program as an important step in moving forward.

"That's our goal, to get them excited about doing something and finding a meaningful purpose," Mayer said. "So they can be better parents, better spouses, and better citizens. It's not just about raising their spirits for a short time, but about raising their spirits for the rest of their lives.

"There are veterans who will tell you that, because of the Jinx McCain Horsemanship Program and just getting involved, they are alive today and not another statistic, not one of the twenty-two veteran suicides a day that you hear so much about. Instead, they are alive and doing quite well. And it all started with, 'Here's how you saddle a horse.'"

TWELVE

THE AIR FORCE VET AND VETERINARIAN

"Our house is a pet menagerie."

"*I WAS ONLY A BABY. I HAD MY ENTIRE LIFE AHEAD OF ME. MY MOTHER thought I was pretty cute, and she always fussed over me. They said I had big brown eyes and a very expressive face, which was no surprise to me because my parents were quite good-looking too. I vaguely remember living with my mom in a dirty alley in what I thought was a big city. Or maybe it wasn't so big? I was young, so my memories are kind of fuzzy. Anyway, one bright sunny morning when I was playing outside, I felt a sharp pain in my back. Then, when I tried to see what it was, another pain hit me and it was even worse. The next thing I knew I couldn't move, and I wasn't in my back alley home anymore. There were cars and trucks everywhere; I was lying motionless in the middle of the street. I guess my mom had to get my brothers and sisters to safety. She must have been sad to have to leave me behind. I heard people screaming, but I wasn't sure what they were saying. I was really scared. They say someone came to rescue me, but I don't remember much after that. When I woke up, I wasn't home anymore. And what was worse, my back leg was missing. When I opened my eyes to see what was going on, I couldn't see a thing.*"

Meet Crixus, a defiant German shepard pit bull–mix puppy named after the Gallic gladiator and military hero in the War of Spartacus, and his rescuer, Shawn Dunn, a US Army captain and Air Force sergeant and veterinarian.

Shawn herself was an unwitting victim of abuse and abandonment, and she has overcome almost insurmountable obstacles in her life. She first heard about Crixus—whose name back then was Forrest—when the Michigan Humane Society in Detroit advertised that an abused puppy with special needs was available for adoption.

Crixus was about six weeks old when he was violently shot by someone wielding a BB gun and left to die on an inner-city street in Detroit. One BB was lodged next to his spine, which left his rear leg paralyzed, and he had a host of other serious injuries. Veterinarians at the Michigan Humane Society determined that they had to amputate the paralyzed leg to save Crixus. While his emergency surgery went well, he had serious postoperative problems. At one point he stopped breathing and had to be resuscitated. While he did survive, the loss of oxygen to his brain, and other complications, left him almost totally blind.

The story made headlines in Michigan and around the country. Everyone was outraged at such a heinous act against an innocent young puppy. The Humane Society of the United States has worked to help law enforcement agencies stop animal cruelty, and it is considered a felony in all fifty states. Unfortunately, that doesn't stop the practice.

Clearly, too, animal homelessness is a national tragedy. The Humane Society reports that there are approximately 3,500 animal shelters in the United States; ten thousand rescue groups and sanctuaries; and six to eight million cats and dogs entering shelters each year. Of the three million cats and dogs euthanized in shelters annually, 80 percent are healthy and treatable and could have been placed into adoptive homes. Exotic animals, too, are similarly abandoned as they grow into adults and their owners realize they can no longer care for them.

Once Crixus's story hit the media, the Michigan Humane Society received more than three hundred requests to adopt him. One of those was from Shawn, who initially didn't want another pet. "I certainly didn't need another pet, but I believe that the animals we rescue really rescue us," she said. "I was worried someone else would adopt him, and because of his condition, he would be too overwhelming for them. I knew that if I didn't adopt him myself that I would worry about him for the rest of my life, and I couldn't let that happen. I sent in an application and had faith that if it was meant to be, it would. I just held my breath, waited, and hoped for the best."

You might say that it was destiny or just sheer luck that this physically broken puppy would find a loving home with an army and air force veteran who just happened to be a veterinarian. Their unlikely journey together has its roots in Shawn's own remarkable story of faith, determination, and resilience.

Shawn Dunn was born in Detroit in 1966. Her childhood wasn't the easiest. Her parents were divorced when she was just seven. Shawn learned of the divorce by accident, when she came home from school one day and didn't hear her dog Baron's collar jingling on the other side of the door. Her parents had, unbeknownst to Shawn, given her beloved Doberman and best friend away. After the divorce, Shawn and her mom moved from one family member's home to another. Her sister was sent to live with their grandmother. "It was a rough time, and I went to dozens of different schools as a kid," said Shawn. Six years later, her mother remarried. "My dad was not very nice to me and my sister, or Baron, and so we were happier to not be with him anymore. I was hoping things would be better when my mom married my stepfather, but that sure wasn't the case for very long," she said.

Shawn's stepfather was a retired long-haul truck driver. She was happy at first for stability in her home life. Plus, her stepfather allowed her to have a dog. It was that little dog, Snoopy, that helped her deal with the chaos that was to come. "Things got worse at home and I didn't get along with my stepfather at all, so at fourteen I ran away from home. My mom was threatening to send me to live with my dad in Florida or send me to juvie. After being caught by the police, my mother did put me in juvie, where the counselors said I didn't belong, and then I ended up in a halfway house. After that, when I was fifteen, I was sent to live with my dad in Florida," Shawn said.

While there, she received a telephone call from her mother that would rock her world.

It was Christmas Day, 1981, and her mother told Shawn that they had put her beloved Snoopy down. Why? Apparently her mother and stepfather simply didn't want to take the dog to the vet to treat a rash from fleas. "I couldn't stop crying," Shawn said. Her father, with little emotion or concern for her feelings, told her, "Shawn, stop it, it's just a dog." But she was inconsolable.

After a few months living in Florida, Shawn ran away to Detroit. Her mother and stepfather said they wouldn't allow her near their house. She went anyway, only to find two of her suitcases, with all of her clothing, thrown from a window onto the driveway. Abandoned again, with no place to live, she was forced to drop out of high school. Shawn was afraid and alone. She lived on her own, mostly on city streets, sleeping anywhere she could find shelter—in school playgrounds, stairwells of office buildings, or secluded places where she thought she wouldn't be seen. "I really never forgave my mother for killing my dog. I could forgive almost anything—her nervous breakdowns, her neglect, anything. But how could I forgive someone for taking away something I loved so much? Even to this day, when I go to confession, the killing of Snoopy keeps coming up. Maybe that's one of the reasons I became such an advocate for animals," said Shawn. Fifteen, and still homeless, Shawn started dating a guy who was thirteen years her senior. "I didn't realize at the time that my boyfriend was abusive and a gang member," said Shawn. "He would beat me up. I guess he joined the biker gang because he was messed up from having a metal plate in his head after serving in Korea. I finally escaped from that abusive relationship when I was seventeen."

Lost and confused, it was time to make some important adult decisions. "As a kid I felt worthless, though I was always smart in school. My teachers used my papers to show the other students what was possible. But I was always that weird kid who loved horses and guns, so the other kids tended to make fun of me." Shawn decided that the best way to get her life back together was to join the military. After visiting army, navy, and marine recruiters, she finally landed in the air force office. Why? It was the only branch of the military that would allow Shawn to keep her long blonde hair!

By that time, Shawn had only completed her education through the eighth grade. But the air force accepted her because she scored high enough on her electronics tests and in the ninetieth percentile overall on the Armed Services Vocational Aptitude Battery tests. She received her GED and, on April 1, 1985, officially joined the air force, where she would train to become an avionics specialist. She was just eighteen years old and, at five foot three, only eighty-five pounds when she arrived in Lackland Air Force Base in Texas for her basic training. She was so skinny, in fact, that her drill instructors made her eat a few pieces of pizza and two ice cream sandwiches at every meal to help her gain weight and pass the mandatory weigh-ins. Looking back, Shawn credits her grandmother with helping her make it through that time. She had been a huge advocate of Shawn's and encouraged her throughout her young life. "I was blessed to join the air force," said Shawn. "My grandmother instilled in me a love of country and great pride and patriotism. I felt so lucky to be in the air force and able to work on planes. It was the best thing to have structure and discipline in my life."

Despite all of the chaos in her young life, somehow Shawn weathered the storm. She traded in her instability for a chance to have a stable and fulfilling career. "I went from being a street kid with no home to having a meal card, a permanent roof over my head, and money in my pocket and becoming a proud member of the US Air Force," said Shawn.

Shawn was an excellent student and took many of her undergraduate courses in the air force. She loved her time in the military, but five years into her service, when she was stationed in England, she married another airman who was deployed constantly. And with a child on the way, Shawn decided to leave the military to raise her daughter. On February, 1, 1990, Jessica was born, and the young family packed up their belongings and moved to Oklahoma.

Once the family was settled there, Shawn sought to fulfill her lifelong dream of working with the animals she loved by becoming a veterinarian. She was still in the reserves, though, and was almost called up for active duty during Desert Shield. Two days before she was to report, she was told to stand down, and her eight-year military commitment ended in November, 1992.

Shawn's dream finally came true in 1995, when she was accepted to Oklahoma State University College of Veterinary Medicine (CVM). There she met her best friend, Ronald Powell, whom she remained in touch with after graduation. Ever the overachiever, Shawn graduated with a 4.0 GPA in all veterinary school prerequisites. She became a doctor of veterinary medicine in 1999 and, after graduation, started working in a small animal private practice in Ft. Myers, Florida. She was happy in her new role, but after a few years, she was missing the camaraderie and connection she had had with her fellow airmen.

"I loved working in private practice," Shawn said. "While I never loved the politics in the military, still, I missed it every day of my life. I missed my soldiers and friends so much. We were always like one big family and we had no barriers of any kind. I wanted to be hands on with the animals, not just do public health, so I was commissioned into the army. Most people don't realize that army veterinary officers care for animals for all the branches of service. My first assignment was at the Air Force Research Lab at Brooks Air Force Base in Texas. It is so important for the survival and health of the human species to work with lab animals like monkeys and pigs. Our protocols always insured that no animals suffered; we were dedicated 100 percent to their enrichment. Many warfighters' lives were saved because of this vital research. But for me and many of my colleagues, we always faced the moral dilemma of doing this type of research. It wasn't done to test makeup products or other frivolous pursuits; it was to save warfighters' lives."

After two years of lab work, Shawn accepted an assignment at Port Hueneme in California, where she would run a clinic that took care of military working dogs and the pets of military members and retirees. "The military dogs I cared for were some of the most remarkable dogs I have ever known and had the privilege to treat," she said. "They are special animals, and I miss seeing them day in and day out; they are just as much heroes as any human serving our nation." One of them, Shawn explained, was a sixty-five pound Belgian Malinois that could take down a 250-pound man, standing on top of a car, from a sitting position! "They are amazing athletes with hearts of gold," Shawn added.

Shawn said her other duties included food inspection at all military bases she was assigned to cover and establishments that sold food products to the military. "We would inspect everything from Coke bottling plants to Krispy Kreme doughnuts, and we also inspected all of the commissaries to make sure there were no biosecurity threats or food vulnerabilities."

After a few years there, Shawn's daughter, now a teen, was eager to enter junior high school. Shawn decided to leave the army and move back to Michigan so Jessica could complete her remaining school years in a safe environment. Shawn got a government job with the US Department of Agriculture and bought a farm in Gaylord, Michigan. Life was going great. Her new job, to test cattle for tuberculosis and other illnesses, offered her stability. "I was happy to be going north and even happier when I walked into my daughter's new junior high school and saw the words on the sign in the entrance, IN GOD WE TRUST." Things worked out well for Shawn and her family in Michigan. Her daughter graduated in 2008, and she enrolled in the University of Oklahoma, eventually earning her bachelor of science degree in zoology.

Shawn was feeling the empty nest syndrome and again missing her time in the military. She decided to go back into the army and, in 2009, arrived at Warner Barracks in Bamberg, Germany. "What an adventure," said Shawn. "I was thrilled to be working with military working dogs again and running clinics at several army garrisons and also inspecting food establishments throughout Europe."

In 2012, after twelve years' active duty in the army and air force, and almost six years of government service, Shawn thought she had her life just where she wanted it. She went back to federal service and took a job at the Ambassador Bridge, the crossing point into Canada from Detroit.

Shawn was thrilled that she was back in Detroit after her thirty-year adventure. Now divorced, she began dating her best friend and veterinary school partner—fellow army veterinarian Ron. What she didn't know at the time was that Ron was suffering from PTSD—or that she would soon undergo treatments for cancer.

Despite those challenges, they teamed up to run the farm in Gaylord—complete with six horses, three dogs, four cats, and a Starling bird that now claims Shawn as her own. "Our house is a pet menagerie, and except for the horses, they are all rescue animals," said Shawn. "I love them all; yet I was still heartbroken over my German shepherd, Ian, who died back in 2009. When I heard about Crixus's story, I just cried and cried. I believe that we don't choose our pets; they choose us. Crix filled that hole in my heart that was left when Ian died."

At the time Shawn learned about Crixus, she was dealing with Ron's PTSD and her own bout with cancer, not to mention suffering from a traumatic brain injury from being kicked in the face by a cow she was treating. Her level of patience was razor thin. Still, the urge to adopt Crixus was overwhelming. "I was just devastated by Crixus's situation and all animal cruelty in general. I wanted him to have a happy ending—not to be chained up in someone's backyard," Shawn said. "I knew Crixus would have medical problems for the rest of his life, like having little control over his bladder and other nerve deficits. How could a layperson deal with that? So I asked Ron if I could apply for him to live with us, and Ron was all for it."

Shawn is still angry at what she assumes were the kids who shot Crixus and left him on a cold Detroit street. "These hoodlums ruined his life. His remaining rear leg is not fully functional and he can't stand up straight. Mostly he scoots around like a seal," Shawn said. "But being a half pit bull and half German shepherd, Crixus has a will of steel. Nothing stops him from guarding the horses, playing with one of our other dogs, Teeny, and turning into a lion when he wants to show off his tough side. But Crixus is a pussy cat at heart, and now that I've had him nearly two years, I've been able to help him recover, cope with his anxieties, and live a happy and normal life. He really has no idea whatsoever that he has a disability."

Shawn believes that Crixus is her savior and an angel sent by God, and she is grateful to Pets for Patriots for helping her with many of Crixus's expenses. "God sent him to me when I needed him the most. He even has a cross on his chest that you can see in a certain light," she said. "It is truly amazing to me how much Crixus calms me down. When I am upset, I hold Crixus in my arms, and my blood pressure literally goes down. We fall asleep always touching each other, and I rush home from work as fast as possible to make sure Crixus is the first to get kisses. The analogy I would give about the love between us is that, before I had a baby I felt all alone, but when Jessi was born no one else mattered. I had her. Crixus helped me avoid a mental breakdown while Ron was dealing with PTSD and I was recovering from cancer treatment. We were there for each other. No one else mattered. Crixus is nothing but pure love and will never know anything but love."

As a veterinarian and a veteran, Shawn knows firsthand the power of the animal-human bond. "As someone who grew up homeless and had so much abuse and neglect in my life, I had to be armed mentally," she said. "Crixus taught me to be patient; he would not let anything happen to me and I have to be there for him. I've seen countless examples in my practice of the love and bonds between people and their pets, and there is nothing more rewarding than to help an animal who is abused or alone. I think Crixus and I were simply meant to be. And as my daughter and I are fond of saying, 'Evil did not prevail!'"

Shawn said that there is an old Irish tradition that on a Leap Day—February 29—a woman is allowed to propose marriage to a man. "I decided that instead of proposing to Ron, I would propose to Crixus. I said to him: 'Crixus, I love you more than life itself, and I promise to always take care of you until death and the life beyond. Will you marry me?'

"I heard an old saying once that goes something like this: 'With over five million dogs in the world, why would I need you?' Well, once you meet my Crixus, it's obvious the reason why!"

THIRTEEN

THE NAVY BOATSWAIN'S MATE

"I just had to have him."

WHO SAYS YOU CAN'T TEACH OLD DOGS NEW TRICKS? JUST ASK NAVY veteran Molly Taskey, who fell in love with a six-year-old pit-bull mix named Cossack. In 2013, she adopted Cossack from an animal shelter in Virginia Beach, Virginia. It partners with the nationwide nonprofit Pets for Patriots, which places abandoned dogs and cats with veterans in need of love and companionship. Since then, Molly's senior adopted dog, with big, bright-yellow eyes and an even bigger heart, has helped her battle depression and readjust to civilian life. He's become her emotional lifeline and her one-dog support system.

Older dogs living in shelters are some of the most difficult to adopt, often waiting years for a permanent home. Many people fear adopting an older dog because of losing them too soon or the potential costs of medical care. One program, Sanctuary for Senior Dogs in Cleveland, Ohio, strongly believes that "the privilege of loving a senior dog makes every single day special, as you and your companion share love, friendship, and a special relationship that grows stronger with the knowledge that you have given a fine old dog a second chance at life."

While puppies demand much in training and care from new owners, senior dogs are in relatively "move in" condition. They reward their owners with extra gratitude and love, make excellent companions, know to do their "business" outside of the home, have learned many of life's lessons, and, as a result, are more relatable and obedient.

It was love at first sight for Molly and Cossack. There was an instant connection between the young woman, who was suffering with depression after leaving the navy, and Cossack, who was abandoned by his owner and had to overcome the stigma that pit bulls are vicious and unadoptable. Loneliness and fear brought them together. Love and devotion kept them together.

On July 25, 2007, Molly Taskey, a bright, young twenty-year-old from Indiana, decided to enlist in the US Navy. It was her dream to serve her country and travel around the world and the navy offered a chance to make that dream come true.

This five-foot-nine, hazel-eyed beauty briefly attended a private college in Northern Indiana but soon she realized it wasn't for her. "I wanted to do something in forensic science, but microbiology kicked my butt," she said. "I ended up going for just one semester, and my parents finally told me, 'Molly, you need to figure out something else to do instead of college.' So I took their advice and enrolled in a community college where I took general classes, but what I really wanted to do was take some classes in occupational therapy. I've always loved helping people, and I thought that degree would be perfect for me. I remember I felt that way even when I was a teenager. I even worked every summer in a camp that helped underprivileged and disabled kids; that was where my heart was."

But community college didn't seem to be the right fit either. Then another idea dawned on her. Her sister, Shelly, was in the ROTC program in high school. If her sister could be part of the navy, why couldn't she? "It was funny," Molly said. "I thought to myself, 'Well, my sister was never the athletic type. But I am. I'm the swimmer. If Shelly can do it, why can't I?'"

The very next day, Molly marched into the navy recruiting office in Lafayette, Indiana. "I said to the recruiter, 'Sign me up!'"

With those three simple words, Molly's life would take a very different path than she had ever imagined. "Before I signed on the dotted line, I asked the recruiter what types of positions I could have if I joined the navy," Molly said. "I told him that I wanted a job that would be fun and exciting. Then he offered me a desk job. 'Sir, I don't know if I can handle a job where I'm not outside and can talk a lot.'" The recruiter came up with a career that he thought Molly would be perfect for and would match her skill set and interests. She was going to be trained as an aviation boatswain's mate

(AB) and eventually would be stationed on the USS *Dwight D. Eisenhower*, out of Norfolk, Virginia. Molly was over the moon.

The rural Indiana farm girl was going to be a sailor. Molly excelled in boot camp and graduated from aviation school with a wide range of skills. The aviation boatswain's mate position was established in 1944, and the main duties are to fuel, maintain, launch, and recover naval aircraft safely from ships. ABs are also trained to handle firefighting, rescue, and salvage operations. Clearly, this high-pressure job takes someone with knowledge and precision to perform at their best day in and day out. "I worked mostly launching and recovering aircraft but was never really that keen on all the grease and the hydraulic fluids everywhere," Molly said. "Over time, though, it was exciting to hook up aircraft to catapult for launch. I was raised on a farm, so it didn't take long for me to get the hang of the job; I was never afraid of getting my adrenaline pumping."

Any mistakes aboard an aircraft carrier could be very serious. "We would have to declare a 'hang fire' if the aircraft wasn't hooked up right," said Molly. "Sometimes if the winds were not correct, we would have to alter course, but making a mistake in my job is not acceptable. Luckily, there are a lot of people involved in the process, so it would be rare to lose an aircraft."

Despite the pressures of the job, Molly spent five years and two deployments on the USS *Dwight D. Eisenhower*, traveling to France, Dubai, Bahrain, Portugal, Turkey, and Italy. "I tried to always explore the places we traveled to and take advantage of as many tours as possible. It was fun learning about the different cultures and feeling like we were part of the scene."

During her time in the navy, Molly saw how tough military life was, especially for women. Many of her friends and fellow women sailors had young children at home. She witnessed how their long deployments kept them away from their families. "I was determined that I didn't want to be away from my kids for that long," Molly said. "I wanted to be a working mom, someday, but not a military mom who wouldn't see her kids for six or nine months. I could also see the strain it put on the family in general, and coming from a home where my parents were divorced, I didn't want to make that same mistake."

Molly decided she would change direction and attempt to pursue a career back in the civilian world.

Of course, she had reservations about leaving the military. "It was tough trying to decide if I wanted to leave a life where I didn't have to worry about paying my bills," Molly said. "In the military, all of our medical bills are covered, and I never had to worry about losing my job unless I made the decision to lose my job. Plus, I thought that if I went out into the real world, I would have more bills to pay, and how would I pay for an emergency situation? Plus, there would be no more free vacations for me either. I mean, how many people can say they traveled the world?"

Molly was also concerned that she might lose the self-satisfaction and respect for others that come with serving in the military. As she weighed the pros and cons, she realized she was losing the get up and go to perform her job the way she was accustomed. That really bothered her. "I started to think realistically that I really wanted to be in the medical field, and I didn't want to wake up every morning and have to press the snooze button on my alarm clock because I didn't want to go to work. That's just not me."

Molly said she was totally drained after five years on active duty and another three in the US Navy Reserves. "I thought to myself, 'Oh my, look at all this grease and steam. Look at how my friends who are in their thirties look like they are in their sixties. This life is just too stressful.'"

Molly made her final decision to leave the navy after being turned down for a transfer. She was too qualified for the job, she was told, and the navy couldn't cover her AB slot if she moved. She was honorably discharged in 2010, and a few days after she walked off the ship for the last time, her fellow sailors and friends left for another deployment. She had no time to say goodbye.

Molly thought she was ready to return to college, but she hadn't realized how leaving the military would negatively affect her. She was feeling depressed and overwhelmed about starting school all over again. "I hadn't hit a classroom in years and I felt so out of place. I started feeling sad, and within about six months or so I got lazy and had no motivation to even get out of the house," said Molly. "I made up a million excuses about why I didn't want to go to school. I stopped enjoying my life and was antsy even looking at my homework. Life became too overwhelming, and when I got my grades back for the first semester they were terrible! My dad came to visit me, and he would call me when he got on the road and say things like, 'Molly, I'm proud of you.' My mom would do the same thing, telling me things like, 'Molly, I don't see that twinkle in your eye anymore. I want to swoop you up and bring you back home.'"

Molly attributed her depression to a number of factors. Aside from feeling a bit lost after returning to the uncertainty of civilian life, she also lost the security of having a regular paycheck and being around people who were there for her and had her back. As a child of divorced parents, Molly longed for some much-needed steadiness in her life. To make matters worse, she and her new boyfriend were having problems.

She eventually had to look back at her years in the service for strength. "Being in the military made me a stronger woman," she said. "Growing up in small town with only three thousand people, everyone knew you, and I had no idea that in the real world people are going to hurt you. I couldn't be the social butterfly I was back home or think that there was no stranger I didn't like. In the navy there were so many diverse people. I had to learn to say 'no.' I gained so much more character and grew up so much in my first two years in the navy. I will forever be grateful for that."

The one bright spot in this dark time came with the adoption of Cossack, who had originally been named Cujo after the vicious St. Bernard in Stephen King's thriller novel, which later became a feature film. In the movie, Cujo famously terrorizes a mother and her child while they sit in their car. The shelter staff wisely decided to change Cujo's name, fearing it would make the loving pit bull that much harder to adopt.

Meeting Cossack was the beginning of the end of Molly's depression, helping her find her true and "happy" self while she began a new life apart from the military.

Molly always loved pets and had grown up with them all of her life. So when it came time for a companion after the navy, she visited the Virginia Beach SPCA to see what they had available. As she was walking around the shelter, she saw a sign for the Pets for Patriots program. She asked a volunteer about it, mentioning that she was on a very strict budget and wasn't sure if she had enough money to buy a dog. Plus, as a student, she wouldn't be guaranteed a check on the first and fifteenth of every month like she had in the navy. She was thrilled to learn that Pets for Patriots would offer her a discount on her adoption and, once the process was completed, would send her a welcome home basket with pet food and other goodies, plus discounts on a wide variety of services for veterans.

"I was hesitant at first about getting Cossack because of all the negative pit bull stories I've heard in the past," Molly said. "But then on his application there was nothing about aggression at all. It just said that Cossack liked to throw tennis balls back and forth and had a very loving personality. That was good enough for me." The next day, Molly returned to the SPCA to see if she felt the same connection as the day before. "I went back and visited with him again and this time all he wanted was a rub down. I was taken with him; I just had to have him!"

"I guess I always knew that I wanted to adopt Cossack the first moment our eyes met," said Molly, "but I first wanted to make sure he got along with my three-year-old nephew, Mason, before I made a final decision. I couldn't believe it when Mason jumped all over Cossack and Cossack just sat there almost saying to himself, 'Whatever.'" Mason was far from in danger.

The more Molly interacted with the sixty-pound Cossack, the more she realized that he had a far different personality from the negative perception of pit bulls.

He was a lover, not a fighter, at heart.

Eventually, Molly decided to move back home to Monticello, Indiana. Cossack loved the road trip. After all, he was a city dog and was used to being in a car and seeing all the sights and sounds of the city from his perch in the back seat. When they finally arrived, it was getting colder, and Molly had to find a new apartment that would allow dogs, especially pit bulls. Molly was thrilled to find a place but was flummoxed by a sign on the door that read, No Poodles, or Beagles. "Wow," she told her mom, "Well, what do they accept?" The next day Molly and her mom went to the VA Center for Molly's appointment and they spotted a beagle. "Mom, watch out," Molly said, "it's going to eat you!" They both cracked up.

Over time, Molly came to realize that Cossack was actually quite prissy; he had the heart of a Poodle. She noticed this one night when they were visiting her dad's house for a barbecue. He had a campfire cement pad, and the family was sitting around enjoying the fire. They heard owls screeching and crickets and frogs chirping. Molly noticed that Cossack had to go potty, but he seemed afraid to move off of the pad to find a suitable place to go. "I think he was kind of spooked because we were in the country, and Cossack had never heard these kinds of noises before. I swear he looked at me and I knew what he was thinking. 'Please, Mom, I got to go okay? I can't walk in this weird grass and in the dark all by myself.'" Molly just laughed.

Winter was just around the corner, and Molly's new apartment was on the third floor of her building. As the first snow fell, Cossack freaked. It was likely the first time this Virginia dog had seen snow. "I took Cossack outside to see the snow and he gave me that look. It was as if he were saying, 'Mom, so you think I can walk on this stuff? Are you serious?' So, I would go first, he would follow me, and then we would throw a few snowballs at each other. Yes, Cossack could throw a snowball. Then, I could see he was walking ever so lightly on the snow, and I could tell it was weirding him out. 'No worries,' I told Cossack. I picked him up and carried him up the three flights of stairs up to our apartment; he was relieved."

As Molly and Cossack got to know each other better, she had to learn his idiosyncrasies and he had to recognize hers as well. "We both decided that we were not going to harm each other, and that made us both tougher," said Molly. "It was like he was saying to me, 'Mom, are you going to play with me? Do you want to pet me? What do you want me to do now?'"

Molly believes that Cossack is almost human and too smart for his own good. "My dog is a bag of fun. In all honesty, I feel like when Cossack and I were still in Virginia, he always knew what I was going to do even before I did. He could sense, for example, when I was going to take him outside. And he knew just what I wanted him to do. If it were for a walk, he would be right by my side. If I wanted him to do his business, he would. I could see in his face that he was asking me, 'Mom what I can I do to please you?'" Molly said Cossack even knows when he gets under her skin. "It's like we have unspoken words," she said. "If he feels I'm annoyed he does everything in his power to please me. If I'm down, he knows it. If I don't feel well, he knows that too. He comes right up under me and gives my face a nudge. And when I sometimes have to take him to the sitter when I have to travel, he gives me a look as if to say, 'Hey, Mom. What are you doing to me? Come on, you don't have to go away on that trip, do you? Hey, which comes first—a pit bull or a paycheck? Mom, get your priorities straight.' Then, when I came back after a few days, I knew by his wide pit bull smile what he was saying. 'Thank God you rescued me from that other woman! Don't leave me again, Mom, okay?'"

Molly says that Cossack even reads her emotions outside of the apartment. Like the time she took him out for a walk and he could sense she was tired. "Mom, why did you take me out if you are sleepy? Why aren't you walking like you usually do?" And sometimes when Cossack is out of sorts, Molly can tell. Like when he had a belly ache and refused to chase the ducks around the pond as he normally did. "I said to him, 'Cossack, stay focused, you love to chase ducks. Come on, man, do it.'" But the look on his face told her, "Mom, you are not going to yell at me, are you? I'm just having a bad day. It's me; not *you*."

Cossack even played a role in helping heal Molly's breakup with a boyfriend back in Virginia. Molly believes the guy was jealous that Cossack was getting so much of her attention. Cossack knew that, too. "One day I could tell Cossack had enough. It's like he was telling me, 'Mom, ditch that animal hater. It's plain like the fur on my ears that he's against all of us, so why would he like you?'" Soon, Molly broke up with that guy.

Cossack is quite beloved by family and friends now, so much so that when Molly's mom and dad call, the first thing they ask is, "How's Cossack doing?" And her new boyfriend, also a former sailor, loves her adorable pit bull.

Life for Molly has dramatically changed for the better since Cossack came into her life. She graduated college with an associate's degree, and now she works in an outpatient surgical center, where she is a certified surgical assistant. Cossack continues to chase ducks, catch tennis balls, and be there for his beloved Molly. Together they are a team. They are by each other's side in good times and bad, and they are defying the odds. Old dogs and sailors are something special.

"I'm so proud of Molly for all that she has accomplished and her dedication to adopting an older companion dog," said Beth Zimmerman. "Pets for Patriots made a commitment to the most overlooked dogs and cats—those who are older or have special needs, like Cossack, and the larger breed dogs. Nearly every pet adopted through our charity has a story of its own. Many have endured abandonment or abuse or have never had a stable home. Veterans come to our program with stories, too, and seem to relate to the pet's struggles with their own. Molly and Cossack are living proof of that."

FOURTEEN

MAX, THE HORSE
THAT HELPS HEROES

"We have all fallen in love with him."

MAX WAS ONE IN A MILLION! WHEN HE STRUTTED OUT OF HIS STALL AND onto the field, everyone stopped and stared. He was as graceful as a ballerina yet as powerful as a heavyweight boxer. His big, brown, soulful eyes could transfix even the toughest warrior. Among the tallest Morgans Debi Demick has ever owned, Max was lean and sleek, and at 1,100 pounds, he cut quite an impressive frame. He was a Morgan, after all. He lived the latter part of his life with one purpose only—to give everything in his power to make others happy. Max didn't have a perfect beginning either, and his striking good looks couldn't shield him from being abused and shuttled between too many owners. Nevertheless, once he moved to a beautiful farm in Virginia and met up with a rare group of wounded warriors, Max became a therapist that others of his kind could only hope to emulate.

Meet Max. The Morgan, the healer, the muse, and the best friend of Jeff, Leo, Tom, Spike, Leila, and countless other veterans lucky enough to share his life.

Debi, who has owned and taken care of horses most of her life, is the founder of the nonprofit organization Horses Helping Heroes Project. She said that her Morgans were one of her main inspirations for wanting to start an equine therapy program for veterans, especially those with brain injuries.

"These Morgans are very people oriented, but Max, because of his own traumatic background, seemed able to relate to veterans who had their own issues to deal with. His reaction was very special and life altering, according to some of the veterans."

This is Max's story.

As anyone who is familiar with the Morgan breed of horse knows, they are among the best for tractability, intelligence, temperament, and curiosity. They are the equestrian example of people pleasers, versatile, able to ride beautifully, and at the same time display their intelligence and grace on and off the field. "I already had two Morgans, so why would I need another?" Debi explained. "The reason for me was pretty simple. When I would ride one of my horses off-site, the other would always get anxious. I needed a companion horse, and Max sure fit the bill. He never broke to ride and wasn't particularly interested in people, so he was an easy horse to have at the farm."

Max was born and bred in rural Maryland, and he comes from quite an impressive lineage. Max was the son of Twin Pond Disco Kid, the multiyear, world nonpro reigning champion. Although Max inherited his sire's amazing athleticism, he was never put under a saddle, meaning he wasn't trained to carry a rider. This was a tragedy, especially for an incredible athlete like Max, according to Debi. "As the story goes, Max was abused at a very early age, which resulted in an intense mistrust of people, and that led him to being shuttled from one frustrated owner to another," said Debi. "We had heard that the abuse was pretty significant and life altering for Max." As a result, Debi said, Max was very wary of people and, when he felt stressed, would totally shut down or run away.

All horses are flight animals, according to Debi. "They don't analyze, they leave; that is part of their natural response as prey. It is a survival instinct. So, for Max, not only did he not trust humans, but his nature and tentative personality also made him a difficult horse to train," Debi added. As a result, he lived the first half of his life as basically a pasture horse with minimal human handling. Max did get to experience some semblance of human love and attention during his stay with the person from whom Debi bought him.

"Actually, Max's previous owner just loved him to death, but all he would literally do was sleep and eat," Debi said. "Fortunately, I found out about Max from another Morgan enthusiast, and I decided to buy him. It turns out he was the half brother of my very first Morgan."

Max's luck would change when he finally found a permanent, loving home with Debi. For the first few months after he arrived at her farm, he lived with his halter on all the time. He would only come into his stall and private paddock area through a back gate; that's how shy and nervous he was. Although Debi says that Max doesn't have a mean bone in his body, he was the quintessential flight animal who stressed when he was exposed to crowds. He would stand at the far end of his paddock even when there was hay in his stall. Max always had to have an exit strategy for when his stress and fear won out.

Over time, and with much patience on the part of his handlers, plus Debi's devotion and attention, Max gradually came to trust people—but only a chosen few. He was taught that a single cluck meant he had to move a foot forward, and this became the signal he was given whenever he became overwhelmed by a situation. Max was a quick study. As a result, he was finally able to control his fear of people and take a step toward them rather than run away. Debi considered this a huge milestone.

It was soon obvious to Debi that Max's beauty on the outside was matched by an equally big heart on the inside. "The key to unlocking Max's heart was to build trust with him, and once he trusted you, there really wasn't much you couldn't do," Debi added.

Debi clearly adored Max, and he returned the adoration. Thanks to Debi, Max learned to trust humans and seek their attention and companionship. Unlike many of his previous owners, Debi took the time and had the insight to work with him to unlock his potential. She saw something special in him, a sparkle in his pleading brown eyes that she knew was worth the effort. What Debi could have never dreamed, however, was Max's ability to relate and respond to wounded veterans. After all, he was wounded as well.

"Over the fifteen years that I've had the privilege of having Max in my life, I have asked him to extend beyond his level of comfort so many times, and he has generously accommodated me," Debi said. "But nothing compares to what he's done since I free-leased him to the Horses Helping Heroes Project." For example, and without missing a beat, Max has done some amazing things, like letting a veteran lead from the offside, allowing the veteran to use the only hand that still functions normally. "I've seen Max slow to a crawl for a veteran who drags his limp leg yet speed up for the able-bodied veteran as they both move through the obstacles. Max has followed veterans in their wheelchairs, even if they use the same hand to drive as to lead, sometimes with too tight a lead rope. It is so heartwarming to see

Max actually close his eyes when a veteran strokes his neck. Somehow, Max instinctively knows that he is creating total peace for that individual. I'm convinced we are all better people because of Max's generosity and sensitivity," Debi added.

These unique qualities are just some of the reasons why Max and the other Morgans are Debi's breed of choice for her growing nonprofit organization. Her ultimate goal was to help wounded veterans with physical, emotional, and mental challenges heal through an equestrian experience—an idea that was very new for the veteran population. There are equestrian programs across the country that help children with autism and young adults with disabilities, but working with veterans was a relatively new concept in 2010 when Debi launched her project. While she originally paired wounded veterans with horses strictly for riding, she soon shifted focus, and now she uses an eye-to-eye approach, where the veteran and the horse face challenges together on the ground. That means the veteran works with the horse in a variety of ways, including grooming and feeding, stall cleaning, taking it out to graze, participating in obstacle-course training, or just spending the all-important quality time together. Every activity is tailored to meet veterans' needs while challenging them to continually move forward.

"I've been a horse person most of my life, working in a therapeutic setting with children with disabilities," Debi said. "It occurred to me that our disabled vets would greatly benefit from this type of therapy, and that was my motivation for changing my focus."

As the program developed, the space they were using at a local boarding facility was clearly not the right setting. Debi soon realized that she would need privacy for the veterans and horses to work together effectively. In the spring of 2011, Debi found the perfect new home, and with her six Morgan horses, including Max, she set up shop. Debi and her team laid the foundation for what is today considered the emerging field of equine therapy.

It takes a special horse to become a therapy horse, and Debi said Max was a superstar from the start. "Max has positively impacted every veteran he has come in contact with since the program began," Debi said. "He has that special star quality that you can't help but notice. But what is so amazing about Max is his ability to relate to people, his compassion and anticipation in meeting their needs. He knew just when to put his head on a veteran's shoulder or look her right in the eye when she needed comfort."

Debi said that through working with Max and her other Morgans, the veterans have learned to build trust and have improved their communication skills, as well as their overall physical and emotional well-being. Through their relationship with the horses, the veterans have become more self-confident and have improved self-esteem. Their family and friends have noticed this remarkable progress. And Max blossomed too, the high-strung and cautious horse coming out of his shell more and more. "I always say that Max was one of a kind," said Debi. "Everyone who has ever been touched by Max was overwhelmed by the love they felt when they were with him. He and I had a special bond, and I can say that Max was one of the most amazing therapy horses that I have had the privilege to know and love."

As time went on, word of Debi's program began to spread, and she was more than happy to expand her services to accommodate a diverse veteran population. "When our program first started, we weren't set up to safely mount large adults who used wheelchairs, so we required that our participants all be ambulatory," said Debi. "But, over the next two years, some of our participants worked around the horses using Canadian crutches or canes. Then, in the fall of 2012, we got three calls asking us if we had room for their family members who all needed to use wheelchairs. We had virtually no time to expose the horses to a wheelchair; we didn't even have one on-site. But we were more than happy to give it a try."

On the first day of class, they introduced all the horses to their newest participants and their wheelchairs. Debi said Max didn't even snort or spook, and it only took a few moments for him to acclimate to the new people in the barn and their strange equipment. "Max I'm sure had no idea what these contraptions were, but he was as cool as a cucumber," said Debi. "He not only was the first horse in the barn to be led by someone in a wheelchair, he was the first horse to follow alongside without a halter or a lead rope. It turned out to be an incredibly empowering experience for every one of the veterans."

Debi said that at the start of each new session, the trainers spend time trying to match the participants to the right horse—with the goal of maximizing the therapeutic benefit for the veteran while minimizing the stress on the animal.

With Max still new to his role in therapy, Debi and the staff assumed that his first session would be extremely stressful. Max was paired with a tall, muscular former marine who was experiencing difficulty assimilating into his new civilian life. He had very high stress levels, and Debi could see he needed a special experience.

Max to the rescue!

Within only an hour of meeting each other, Debi knew Max and the marine were a perfect match. The marine would talk to Max softly, and you could see that his gentle voice soothed Max's nerves. Max's eyes were fixed on him, and he seemed to focus on what the marine was asking. "Max's responses to the marine throughout the session were empowering for him, and I could see their bond was immediate and strong," said Debi. "After he left the program, whenever the marine felt overwhelmed, he would email us saying, 'I wish I had an hour with Max' or 'I sure miss Max. I haven't been able to spend any time with him, but I really miss him. Max has made me a better person.' This is the magic of equine therapy and our special therapy horse, Max."

One of Debi's board members said Max steals the hearts of everyone he comes in contact with. "Max seems to identify with our veterans as they face difficulties in their lives," said Lisa. "And the veterans identify with him, too, some even sharing similar experiences and ailments. Max has become the horse for our most nervous first-timers. As Max overcomes his uneasiness, so does the veteran. Whether he's being groomed by a veteran in a wheelchair or taking his turn through an obstacle course, Max performs with grace and dignity; he transfers that approach to his veteran partner and the veteran's confidence grows. While I think Max would walk through fire for his owner, he has shown that same faith with his veteran handlers. His heart is huge, and we have all fallen in love with him. He has stolen our hearts."

Tom, a navy veteran, adores Max. He said, "I call him Maximillian the Great. Max is extraordinary. When I became a participant with Horses Helping Heroes Project, I didn't know what I was getting into. Standing in the presence of such a majestic animal and never having been that close to one was nerve wracking. Max made it easy, to a point. He was just as nervous about me as I was of him. Learning about the herd mentality and that Max, being eldest, was the leader and had to see and take care of the rest of the herd hit home with me. When I was active duty, I was in charge. Even with all the responsibility he had, he went out of his way to ensure that I was at ease. Such an act of humbleness and respect is a quality that is lacking in most humans today. When I was having a bad day, Max would comfort me and let me know that everything was okay. Once we learned to know each other, Max made it easy, be it grooming, ground work, or liberty work. The bond between Max and me is strong. I don't see Max as a horse. I see Max as a comrade, as a friend."

Max, according to Debi, knew that what he was doing was important and was turning wounded veterans' lives around. "Max had a sixth sense about people who have issues," said Debi. "I've seen him so many times stay close to a veteran who he feels needs him and overcompensate to make sure that veteran doesn't feel frustrated or go to a dark place. Max was a healer in the truest sense of the word."

All of the project's classes are based on letting veterans learn to read the horse's body language and understand the sensitivities that they can take with them when they are relating to the outside world. The participants' identities are also protected to assure complete confidentiality. "We only have ten veterans at a time in our matriculating program, and that is because we want them to feel comfortable and get the one-on-one attention they need," Debi said. "When we teach them about horse behavior—and most of them have never been with a horse in a setting like ours—they have an instant connection. These guys have been through a lot and are on hyperalert, just like Max and horses in general. So we encourage them to think for themselves and anticipate what the horse needs and what they are telling the veteran by their behavior and body language."

Debi said the program works so well because it complements what a military experience stresses—independent thinking and problem solving. "These guys in the military are trained to know everything about what they are expected to do and how to get the job done regardless of the challenges they may face. We try to emulate that experience by giving them the background they need to make independent decisions. The end goal is for them to learn what the horse is telling them and to create a strong bond. The power of that relationship is astounding," Debi said.

For US Army Specialist Jeff, Max was a godsend. He said: "After being released from the army, I dealt with a lot of issues from post-traumatic stress disorder—from a lot of the things I dealt with throughout my time serving and confrontations I was exposed to. In April 2010, I received a traumatic brain injury, which only caused more problems with dealing with my PTSD. I started attending a Brain Injury Association facility, which doctors said would help me to possibly release some of the issues. I was also seeing neurologists, psychologists, etc., but the techniques they were using were not able to help to the extent that I needed. I kept going from one to another until I got tired of hearing, 'I know what you mean.' It would just upset me more, and I found no more reason to keep attending."

Then he found Max. "I was informed about the Horses Helping Heroes Project, where I met everyone and was invited with open arms. We started our classes with the horses, and I kept asking for more time to spend with Max," Jeff said. "I just felt something inside of me. Mr. Max and I had such a good bond that once we just had a carrot and a few peaceful times together, we would understand that we could be good friends. We would talk as we were in the arena figuring out the other obstacles to overcome together. He showed everyone else that he is the one that would stand by your side."

Jeff said that, like many of the veterans who have had no direct exposure to horses, he was at first skeptical. "One thing with Max is that he stayed away until I approached him," Jeff said. "When I first met him, I knew that both of us were the same. Max was shy and I could see he was uncomfortable, just like me. But when I was with Max I felt calm, and it was like I had no problems. All I would do is concentrate and talk to Max. He gave me the opportunity to be me because he wouldn't question or judge me."

That was important to Jeff, who suffered a life-threatening head injury and had to relearn almost everything—speaking, reading, understanding commands, even holding a knife and fork—after he finally came out of a coma. Unlike having a visible physical injury, veterans who suffer from invisible injuries, like Jeff, often appear physically normal, but feel far from that on the inside. Horses for Jeff became a lifeline, and his experience with Max in particular was what kept him motivated to keep pushing forward, despite at times feeling like the life he knew before was over. "Horses don't question you, they accept you for who you are," Jeff said. "I could be having a tough day and Max would understand that. When I would walk in to see him in the morning, he would lay his head on my shoulder and give me a hug. Max could feel me too, and he pulled me out of it when I was down and showed me the way."

Soon, Jeff found himself wanting to be around the horses more and more, and he would come in early to help Debi. "I would spend time with Max before class and help Debi clean him up and the other horses, too," Jeff added. "But I really wanted to spend extra time with Max and I always hated to leave. My good world was right there." Soon, Jeff was encouraging other veterans who had the same trepidation about the horses that he did at first. He wanted to let them know that there was light at the end of the tunnel. He wanted to share his positive experiences in hopes that they too could turn their lives around. "I tell other veterans that I can't explain it to them—you know, the power of horses—but I just say to them, 'I hope you'll try it and then enjoy it because it will make a difference in your life.' Then I say that 'Max brought me back and he can do the same for you.'"

Jeff recalls another special experience he had with Max. "The thing that made me the proudest was when Max made me look like the good guy when a British film crew (FEI Equestrian World) came to our program and I heard them asking about how to get Max on film. Max let me give him our little 'let's show them' speech in his ear and went on and did everything like the pro he is. Everyone tried to give me the credit for that, but it was my big buddy Max willing to be the best and showing everyone that he was the best. In my eyes, Max is the warrior because warriors lead the way! He has proven ever since that day that he is the man of the year," Jeff said.

Leo, a Marine Corps veteran, wrote about his experience with Max in an award application Debi submitted to recognize Max for his achievements. "About four years ago, I found the memories of war becoming too burdensome to carry and sought help in healing. My search brought me to the barn of an organization called Horses Helping Heroes Project. They had a number of therapy horses specially selected to help wounded and injured troops, as well as caring volunteers to work with the wounded. As I worked with the therapy horses, I found each one had traits that assisted us in healing, but one in particular, Max, had a personality that displayed intellect and perhaps a bit of mistrust of people. When approached, he was a little nervous and showed caution. Upon inquiring, I discovered Max, in his early years, was abused and was selective as to whom he would trust. I thought to myself, 'This sounds like the PTSD the troops deal with.' On many occasions, I had the pleasure of grooming Max. At his advanced age, it took a soft touch and soft voice. The day I really recall as special, I took Max out with a slow walk and soft words and he seemed especially at ease. His head was down and his ears at attention. As I gently brushed him, he nuzzled my cheek. I choked up and felt as if a weight had been lifted off me. It seemed like Max needed me, and I was able to help him as he helped heal me," said Leo.

On January 26, 2016, sad news spread like wildfire among the staff and veterans of the Horses Helping Heroes Project. Just two months shy of Max's thirty-first birthday, he passed away from colic, a gastrointestinal disorder. "I was so upset that I couldn't tell the veterans in person, so I sent them all the terrible news in an email," Debi said. "I was so touched that many of them wrote me back and also posted such beautiful memories about Max on Facebook. As for me, it was so emotional. I kept remembering the love we had for each other and his sweet gestures like nuzzling his head next to me or doing almost anything I asked him to do. That's what a horse does for you. Max worked the magic like the Morgan he was."

The sad reality for Debi, her staff, and the veterans was that Max, the beautiful, strong, caring Morgan, was gone. No one could believe it at first. Just the thought of him or the mention of his name would bring tears to everyone's eyes. Looking at his empty stall made the pain even worse. At times, it was almost too much to bear.

Debi and everyone at the farm would mourn Max's passing for months. Then, one day, someone heard about a couple of national awards and they decided to nominate Max. It would help alleviate the pain of his loss and focus their energy on solidifying his legacy.

Debi asked some of her veterans, in their own words, to memorialize Max on the application form for the award. Jeff, who had made tremendous progress and now was in Pennsylvania, was happy to contribute: "After spending a long two years away from Max, I came back thinking my buddy would have forgotten me. After all, he had been busy helping all the other veterans overcome personal issues from the military. But as soon as we met again, Max put his head against my shoulder and this time he was the 'whisperer.' He let me know, once again, that he was by my side and never forgot or gave up on me. We got back to it again and drove on because *surrender* is not a soldier's word." Jeff had an image of Max tattooed on the inside of his right arm to always remind him of his best friend.

Debi, Jeff, Leo, Leila, Tom, Spike, and everyone who was ever touched by Max were blessed to have him in their lives. The poet Maya Angelou once said, "People will forget what you said, people will forget what you did, but people will never forget how you made them feel." This intractable and transformational kind of love was experienced through the special bond between horse and veterans. Max was one of a kind. He will be walking alongside the veterans, never forgotten, nuzzling gently into their memories forever.

FIFTEEN

THE ARMY VETERAN

"Together, they heal and grow."

PIGS GET A BAD RAP. FROM PORKY THE PIG TO PORK CHOPS, WHEN MOST Americans think about pigs, they either imagine a cartoon character or dinner. They've been portrayed as dirty, smelly, or just plain disgusting. But this is far from the truth. Pigs are intelligent, sensitive, clean, and very sociable, and they make excellent pets. And one surprise about potbelly pigs: they help veterans heal. One grunt, squeal, and pant at a time, potbelly pigs are endearing themselves to our nation's bravest. And thanks to army veteran Mandi Tidwell, the sanctuary she created in Douglassville, Georgia, called Hooves Marching for Mercy, is giving pigs and veterans a safe and nurturing place to reclaim their lives together.

If that isn't remarkable enough, Mandi does all this, working day in and day out with her precious pigs, knowing that she doesn't have long to live.

On Memorial Day, 2015, Mandi had a brainstorm. As she and her husband, David, were hiking on Stone Mountain in Georgia, she started thinking about how she could help homeless veterans and also do something to better the lives of abandoned and abused animals. Mandi has always been an animal advocate and has been involved with animal rescue for more than a decade. She also was an admirer of our nation's warfighters. Her grandfathers both served in the military, and Mandi enlisted in the US Army herself, though her career was cut short when she dislocated her hip in basic training. While that injury prevented her from serving, she never lost her love for service.

That passion for animals and her commitment to veterans was so strong that she and David decided to transform an eight-acre farm into an animal rescue and sanctuary. "I especially feel for homeless veterans and have always wanted to do something to help them," Mandi said. "One day it hit me. Why don't I combine my love of abandoned animals with my concern for homeless vets? I decided to expand my sanctuary in hopes that I could eventually have a place where the two could live together in a peaceful and nurturing setting."

Why focus on potbelly pigs? Mandi has a compelling answer to that question. "The sad part about working with abandoned animals, like the pigs, is that their owners fail to research how to train and care for them. They're so cute when they're babies, and people often forget that one day they'll grow into larger animals. Potbelly pigs fall into that category, for sure. But the truly amazing thing about them is their intelligence, long-term memory, and compassion. Believe it or not, pigs also suffer from PTSD. To me, that is the perfect combination—pigs and veterans helping each other," said Mandi.

In addition, pigs have a relatively long lifespan—from twelve to twenty years—are fairly low maintenance, don't shed, can be litter box trained, and relate very well to humans as long as they know that you are the boss. That makes them great pets for responsible owners and loyal companions for wounded warriors taking part in Mandi's sanctuary.

The website, PotbellyPigs.com, says of these amazing animals: "Pigs have very advanced communication skills. They are the fifth most intelligent animal, with man ranking first, followed by monkeys, dolphins, whales and pigs. They function by instinct, intuition, and memory. . . . They learn quickly and don't forget what they master. You can indeed nurture a very rewarding and interactive relationship with a pig, as a pig will treat you as an equal if given the opportunity."

According to Mandi, pigs are also sentient beings that have a conscience and can learn right from wrong. They can even deceive you if they have the mind. Being very emotional creatures, they also cry real tears and feel very deeply.

"Sadly, for the potbelly pigs that end up at our sanctuary, most if not all of them have been abandoned by their owners or abused in some other way," Mandi said. "The twenty-three pigs we have here at our farm are all rescue animals. They've suffered emotional and physical trauma from neglect, abandonment, and abuse. But the beautiful thing is that when we pair them up with veterans who are also suffering from trauma themselves, something remarkable happens. Together they heal and grow, through mutual love and respect."

That was just what happened to Mandi when she was diagnosed with lupus in 2010. The Mayo Clinic describes the disease as, "A chronic inflammatory disease that occurs when your body's immune system attacks your own tissues and organs. Inflammation caused by Lupus can affect many different systems—including your skin and joints, kidneys, blood cells, brain, heart and lungs." For some, like Mandi, the disease is fatal.

"My pigs are the reason I get out of bed in the morning," said Mandi. "I grab my bottle of Skin So Soft and give them all a rub down; they just love it, and they dive in head first into the mud hole as soon as I put the Skin So Soft inside. Wilber, my big pig, can't wait until I feed him his favorite frozen fruit snack of the day. Even though I sometimes feel awful, it feels wonderful to be with Wilber and the rest of my babies; it gives me what I need."

Soon after Mandi joined the army through the delayed-entry program in 1993, she learned she was pregnant. "The army recruiters were wonderful and gave me the time I needed even before I joined to take care of my son. They worked with me all the way, and they were the best bunch of guys I have ever known," Mandi said. "They used to tell me that Aaron was 'their baby,' and I couldn't wait for his health to stabilize so I could officially become a member of the US Army."

She finally enlisted in January 1996. But after waiting all that time to serve, she developed a devastating hip injury during her fourth week of basic training. "I was so upset that my dreams were shattered, and my hip too," Mandi said. "I got an honorable discharge, and even though I couldn't stay in the military, it was the best experience. It taught me what I was made of and what I wasn't. I learned to say, 'Yes I can.'"

After her discharge Mandi moved back with her in-laws, along with her son Aaron, and worked as a certified nurse's aide in hospice. She was part of a hospice flex team, traveling to different places where she was needed. "When I got out of the army, I have to say I was lost and injured," said Mandi. "I was dealing with a sick child who was born prematurely and also with a failing marriage. We were both so young that, looking back, it was no surprise that my marriage didn't last."

Those two great losses—leaving the army and her failed marriage—led Mandi to make some poor life decisions. "I made some reckless and naive choices," said Mandi. "I lost my way for a bit." To help pay for her son's medical care, Mandi became a prostitute for two years. "I stopped believing in me for a while," Mandi said, "and at some point after being in that world, which also included working in a bar as a dancer, I realized I deserved to treat myself better. It was the beginning of my new life."

Her love of animals and her desire to create a new life for her and her son soon had Mandi answering an ad in the local paper for a vet tech position. "I had no idea what I was thinking or doing, but I was going for a dream of working with animals despite my lack of knowledge or training," Mandi said. "And even though the job called for an experienced vet tech, I thought, 'What the hell, I can do this.' That really paid off, too, because the doctor liked my confidence. That was the beginning of me learning to like myself and view life differently—to believe in myself instead of being someone's victim from so long ago. I took ownership from that moment on in my life, and I haven't looked back. It's been a struggle but well worth the ride."

Mandi's life began to turn around, though she still faced some challenges. She remarried and desperately tried to have another child so that Aaron could have a brother or a sister. Eventually, Mandi became pregnant, but the baby girl died after four days. Mandi was pregnant ten times between 1994 and 2001, but each resulted in a miscarriage. But Mandi is a strong woman who transferred her energy into studies, enrolling in a formal veterinary technician program. It would give her the educational credentials she needed to expand her new career. She had finally found her passion, something that spoke to her soul.

After her second divorce, Mandi was sure she would never be able to have any other children safely. Then, to her surprise, she met the man of her dreams, David, someone who is so well liked that his ex-wife is now close to Mandi. "No one can believe it, but David's former wife and I are the best of friends," Mandi said. "We all need each other in a different way, and we have been there for each other through thick and thin. David is my rock and support, and we both share a love and passion for animals."

But pigs? Mandi's friends weren't that surprised by her sudden fondness for them. "It was around 2012, and David and I were talking about trying to have a child, this time through adoption," said Mandi. "He asked me, 'Honey, do you want to have a baby?' I said, 'No, David I want a pig!' He just said, 'Honey, if you want a pig, you can have a pig.' I knew he was the man for me." Mandi's adventure began that day. She had a friend who had run a pig rescue for twenty years and decided she would research how to successfully operate her own. "I knew nothing about pigs until someone came to me with a week-old pig. I thought to myself, 'I'm a vet tech. How hard can it be? I can raise this pig, sure, why not? He's just a baby!'"

Reality soon set in.

"Oh good God, it was like having a newborn child," said Mandi. "It's not like having a kitten or a puppy. They don't scream, 'It's time to wake up,' like pigs do."

They named their adorable baby pig Darwin. He came into Mandi's life with many health problems, primarily from inbreeding, a common problem with pigs bred as pets. But, despite Darwin's maladies, he touched Mandi's heart in a profound way. "He was my spirit leader and showed us the power of love," Mandi said. Not long after Darwin arrived, Mandi got him a friend named Greta. Soon she began getting calls about other pigs in need of rescue. Word was spreading about Mandi's sanctuary, and her frequent trips with her pigs to PetSmart gave her even more visibility. She also began opening up the sanctuary to the public, veterans, and even local schools. Mandi was becoming the go-to source for anything pig. Georgia Animal Control learned about Mandi in 2013 and began bringing abandoned and abused potbelly pigs to her in numbers she could hardly imagine. "I never thought about it in depth, but having pigs is just like having three- and five-year-old kids in your home," Mandi said. And her home was quickly filling with more pig babies than she could ever have dreamed!

After Darwin and Greta, her next pig was Sir Gaddy. She built him his own a pen, which she uses now to isolate all new pigs before they are neutered. "He was a chewer," said Mandi. "He even chewed through a metal fence one time. Sir Gaddy was my baby too, and there is something to this pig thing that I always tell people. They can destroy anything in seconds. They can open doors, get in drawers, so you have to baby-proof your entire house. The question I often get is, 'Why would you want pigs in your life if they are so destructive?' I tell them, 'They cry real tears. They feel and give love, more so than any other animal.'"

Mandi said that she wasn't initially prepared for the emotional aspect or the intensity of the pigs' ability to love. "Pigs have a strong desire to be with you 24/7. Wherever I am, they are trying to get to me. My Darwin used to literally scream my name and yell, 'Mama, Mama' when he needed me. They also have an innate need to bond and are curious about everything. I've learned so much from my babies," Mandi added.

So how strong is a pig? Mandi said a one-hundred-pound pig's strength is comparable to the combined strength of four grown men. Mandi saw that strength in action during a trip to the veterinarian with Greta for an X-ray. "It was quite a sight to see. We had to literally have eight people lay on top of her to keep her still enough to take the X-ray," Mandi said. That is one of the reasons that Mandi provides information, counseling, and training to people who want to buy a potbelly pig as a pet. She also tries to help pig owners who are having problems so their animals don't end up in a rescue. Though she is glad to have them, keeping pigs with their families is always her preferred outcome.

But, a pig, is a pig, is a pig, is far from the truth in Mandi's eyes. There are domestic farm pigs, feral wild pigs, and potbelly pigs that originally came from Vietnam, as well the kune-kune pigs. They have been domesticated for more than six thousand years, she notes, adding that there are distinct physical differences between farm pigs and potbelly pigs. Farm pigs have longer faces, longer bodies and ears, no bellies, and curly tails. The potbelly big, by contrast, has straight ears and tail and has a distinct little belly. Pigs, just like humans, come in all shapes and sizes. They will grow to their ideal body size and weight if they are fed properly. (Eating like a pig is probably the one truism about this intelligent animal.) Any others, including the mini pigs and tea cups, according to Mandi, are frauds. "There is no such thing as a mini pig. It is becoming a legal issue because unscrupulous breeders are actually starving their pigs and telling new owners that they must follow a strict diet. They recommend feeding them a quarter of a cup of food twice a day, which is less than you would feed a Chihuahua," Mandi said, "This is an outrageous practice. It is a fraud in the breeding industry."

As time went on, Mandi made changes in her personal life based on her budding relationships with her pigs. Like the time she and her husband were out for dinner with friends at a steakhouse and Mandi ordered a baked potato and a steak. "Our best friend, who was with us at dinner that night, looked at me and for some reason called me 'Mama.' Just like Darwin used to do. That scream curdled my blood when I first heard it from an animal; that was it for me. I called the waiter back to the table and said, 'Can I change my order? No steak, just a baked potato for me.' A week and a half later, I threw pork out the window completely. And in four months, all meat was gone from my life too!" It wasn't the easiest thing for Mandi and her husband to give up all red meat, but, as Mandi often says, "Life is process."

By mid-2013, Mandi named her nonprofit rescue and sanctuary Pigs are People Too. She was beginning to get five calls a week, not just about rescuing pigs but other farm animals as well, even chickens. "It always makes me sad when people don't do their research and are not prepared," she said. "It took me three years of research before I totally understood what to expect with pigs, and even then I was a bit overwhelmed. You should never buy an animal on impulse. You're buying a life!"

One of the main issues that owners have with their pigs is not understanding what to expect. "What they are saying to you is, 'I need to be in charge,' but what you need to say to them is, 'I am in charge.' When a pig runs and charges at you, the intrinsic response is to run away. On the contrary, you come right back at them and let them know that you are the dominant one," Mandi said. "That's one of the reasons that we make house calls and try to help people work with their pigs. But if they can't, we want to help them have a happy and safe life. Often times, a person buys a cute little pig and thinks they will get along well with their dogs. But pigs and dogs are not great together. Dogs are predators. Pigs don't understand the dog's look to back away, and they don't know how to react to them. Plus pigs are stubborn. Why put an animal in a situation where it is going to fail?"

The joy and hard work of creating a sanctuary for abandoned and abused pigs came crashing down for Mandi in 2014. Darwin, at only eighteen months old, had to be put down. Her constant companion, the pig that slept in her bed and called her "Mama," was gone. "He did everything with me, but he had so many inbred health problems he couldn't be saved," Mandi said. One sunny afternoon, Mandi had been rubbing Greta's belly and she saw Darwin from the corner of her eye coming toward her. It was very unusual for him, but with his spine and brain injuries, he just wasn't himself anymore, and she had seen signs of his growing emotional instability. And now her beloved companion was coming for her, the person he loved the most. Mandi continued to rub Greta, but in an instant Darwin began to charge. She rolled on her stomach and took cover, but her 275-pound boy charged her, got her on the ground, and was biting her arms and back. He wanted Mandi dead.

People often have asked Mandi why in the world she would love an animal that was ready to kill her. The answer is simple. "Darwin showed me the capacity of what pigs have to give," Mandi said. "All they want is to be loved and love you back. Darwin had brain damage and that's not who he was. But he loved me so much and I felt the same way. I was able to give him a quality of life he would have never had. The stitches and kicks and bites were more than worth it to me." As Winston S. Churchill said: "I am fond of pigs. Dogs look up to us. Cats look down on us. Pigs treat us as equals."

As Mandi recovered from her injuries, she knew that she wanted to devote her life to the animals she loved. She continued to take her pigs to the local PetSmart, where children and adults could see them up close and personal. "My pigs just love to pose," she said. "When they see a camera it's like they are saying to themselves, 'I am the star here, and so let me get into position. Aren't I just too cute?' That's how much these babies need somebody to be there for them; they have so much to give."

Over the next year, Mandi tried to manage the sanctuary's growth but had concerns about the future and keeping the operation as a nonprofit. She worried that her health would deteriorate, and then who would run the operation? "I thought to myself, 'Do we shut it down, stay private; what do we do?' I needed an exit strategy so my babies could be taken care of," Mandi said. She also felt that her mission wasn't totally complete and that she was missing a key part of her ultimate vision for the sanctuary. She remembered her dad's friend, a wounded veteran from Vietnam, and she was troubled by how that generation of vets was treated when they came home. "I started thinking, what about rescuing homeless vets, breaking the cycle of homelessness for both the animals and the veterans? I wanted all of them to have a purpose and allow that purpose to grow and bloom. That's when I came up with our new name, registered it as a business in 2015, and called it Hooves Marching for Mercy." Like everything Mandi touches, she does it with full force and a soldier's determination and resolve.

As time went on, Mandi created a new board of directors and brought in other advisors. She also decided to raise more money in order to grow the property to thirty acres. In addition to having veterans and military families come to the sanctuary, she wanted homeless veterans to have a permanent home. "I want them to have a place that is theirs—a cabin or small house, whatever. That is my dream."

Mandi was encouraged by the veterans who visited—first to pet and feed the pigs, then even to adopt them. One of those veterans was Bryan Hodkins, a soldier who suffered from multiple emotional traumas. Pigs, Mandi believes, can one day be used as therapy animals, especially for veterans suffering from PTSD like Bryan. "Pigs could be wonderful for working with veterans as long as their owners provide enrichment," she said. "As long as they can be in the mud and dig, they are happy. Since pigs also have long memories and also experience PTSD themselves, they would be excellent at alerting someone if the veteran they love is having a seizure, heart attack, or other problem where she is unresponsive. The pig would squeal like you have never heard if its person had passed out or otherwise became unresponsive to it. That God-awful scream cannot be ignored!"

The relationship with Mandi's pigs certainly made a big difference for Bryan. He got along well with the animals right from the start, especially two very colorful ones named Lucy and Ethel—so called because their antics together are like those of their namesakes from the hit TV show *I Love Lucy*. Bryan, Lucy, and Ethel just clicked, and over time Bryan decided he was ready to adopt the girls and give them a permanent home. "It was awesome to see," said Mandi. "Bryan made a quick house for the pigs and even fenced in a special area for the girls. But Lucy and Ethel were a handful, and we all got a kick out of how funny there were together, especially when they were with Bryan." Even with all of their hysterical escapades, Bryan was never once dissuaded from loving them—first as a foster parent and then when he permanently adopted them.

An example of their mischievous nature was revealed while Lucy and Ethel still were residents of Mandi's garage at the sanctuary. It didn't take them long to realize that Mandi kept their food in that building. And one Saturday afternoon, Mandi mistakenly left a big bag of food on the table in plain sight. Lucy and Ethel couldn't be denied. They jumped up on the table in tandem, and helped themselves to the bounty at hand. It didn't matter that it was a twenty-five-pound bag, way more food than their daily diet allowed. Needless to say their stomachs weren't happy, and Mandi describes the aftermath of their gluttony as truly disgusting.

The next day, Lucy and Ethel spotted a large bag of flour in the garage and knocked it off the shelf. They were clearly delighted with themselves and ran defiantly into the yard, oh so very proud of their efforts. The girls were completely covered in flour—even the black pig was pure white. It was hysterical. Lucy and Ethel would continue their antics, taking the hinges off most of the doors in the house and knocking over anything that was upright. But soon, thanks to Bryan's steady hand, the girls calmed down. Though not perfect angels today, they at least know what *not* to do.

Mandi's rescue pig population continued to grow, and some of their harrowing stories of abuse and abandonment were heartbreaking. Like the little pig who was brought to the sanctuary after being found wandering around with her ears torn or cut off—Mandi still doesn't know what really happened. "When they brought Anna Mae to us, she had no ears, and we were told it took three hours to catch her and bring her to her rescuer's home," said Mandi. "We said that this is her place for life; no adopting, just loving her. I want her to be whoever she wants to be. I want to see her with a veteran, too, because she has so much to give." When Mandi first picked Anna Mae up in Tennessee, she was scared to be touched by a human. She had some skin problems as well. "We put her in a small area and noticed she would never sleep in her house or any other structures either," Mandi said. "She was clearly traumatized. One day she burst into our bigger yard to be with the other pigs, but she still wouldn't let us come near her. We talked to her every day and let her play in the mud when she wanted, but we didn't push her to let us touch her." Every day Mandi and her team would show Anna Mae how much they loved the other pigs, hoping she would see that and know she was in good hands. "She saw us love on them and watched as they would go to sleep in their houses," Mandi said. "It was like she said to herself, 'If they can go in there to sleep, maybe I could too?'" In just three months, this frightened and abused pig allowed Mandi to touch her, and soon she had her first belly rub. "It was amazing," Mandi said. "I could see she trusted us, but she did have her eyes on me that first time. Those are the things that make my heart melt."

Mandi said that pigs are simply big goofballs. One of her other pigs, Wilber, likes to take the hose and play tug of war. He also delights in grabbing her skirt and following her around the yard, just for attention. "Willie is my best performer too," she said. "He likes posing for the customers at PetSmart. He's my ambassador pig, but when he comes home, he acts like a four-year-old boy. He loves to flip things. He comes inside just to flip things. Nothing can stay upright when Willie is around."

"These pigs are so intelligent, and their intimacy and long-term memory are beyond compare," said Mandi. "There is so much grief when you lose one, and there is no way to prepare for the loss. It was like the grief I felt when I lost my children. Pigs bond for life with humans, and they also feel depression when they lose you or another pig they love. We had one pig, Alyek, who we had to put on suicide watch because he stopped eating and drinking. He would rock in the corner and call for his mama when they first brought him here. He was very angry and he just wanted his mom. Then we brought in another rescue pig that came to us from animal control and a court case. The two met accidentally, and from that day on Tina couldn't let go of him. I could hear her saying to Alyek in pig talk, 'Hey, dude, you may be sad but you need to get over this.'" Today, they are bonded for life, with each wounded pig helping the other one heal. Mandi has a front-row seat to all of this and is an eyewitness to love in its purest and most transformational form.

That love is what keeps Mandi going, despite her doctors giving her only weeks to live. "My pigs are the only reason that I'm not in the hospital," said Mandi, who wasn't sure if she would make it until the end of 2016. "God always promised me that I would have children. My son, Aaron, who is now twenty-two, is the light of my life, and having children opened my eyes for sure. But I can honestly say God kept his promise, though many of my children come with four legs. I have to be there to make sure they stay safe."

Mandi is touched that, despite the harsh reality of her disease, her staff and board members are willing to keep her dream alive. Anna Watson, one of her board members, is a practicing and well-regarded animal trainer. She believes in Mandi's vision for a place where veterans and pigs can come to heal and live in peace and safety for perpetuity. Mandi met Anna at PetSmart one day when she was visiting with Darwin. "I knew it was meant to be and I have to thank Darwin for bringing us together," Mandi said. "When Anna went over to Darwin to meet him, he gave her a love bite, and from then on she has been a big part of my life. Now Anna will take over for me, when I'm not around anymore. I'm so happy that the board stood up and said, 'We will keep this running. Your dream will never die.'" Mandi said she even has a life insurance policy in place with half of the money designated to keeping the sanctuary up and running for many years to come.

"These wonderful animals have healed our lives," Mandi said. "Over the years I've observed their behaviors and tried to be more like them. I know it sounds silly, but more people should just do what they do—and that means eating healthy by going for colorful fruits and vegetables first, relating to each other with love, and never going to bed with animosity. Those are just some of what makes them special. It was eye-opening because, in my opinion, no other animal species is like that."

Though she is a fighter and hopes to beat the odds, she has also put safeguards in place so that her pigs are not devastated if she passes. "I want my pigs to feel secure since they don't handle change very well," Mandi said. "I want them to be able to accept someone else taking care of them."

In the meantime, Mandi is living her life to the fullest. This tough army recruit doesn't know the meaning of giving up. "As long as my babies see me, and I see them, I'm happy," she said. "Sometimes I get a little depressed and I'll have a cry about them. But, knowing I have to wake up every day and keep them regimented, well, this is what I need right now and I can't be distracted."

"My dream is to have my pigs and homeless veterans living together in a peaceful and nurturing setting," she adds. "To live in harmony, with love, respect, and the belief that all lives have value and deserve a second chance."

SIXTEEN

SECRETS FOR AN ENDURING BOND

"Until one has loved an animal, a part of one's soul remains unawakened."
—Anatole France

L IKE ALL HUMAN BEINGS, ANIMALS NEED THE BASICS IN LIFE—FOOD, water, shelter, love, and connection. It is a scientific fact that people who have animals in their lives are happier and more fulfilled. Animals enhance the quality of our lives. They improve our health, increase our sense of well-being, combat loneliness and depression, help us manage our daily chores, and guide us through the inevitable challenges of being human. This is just as true for veterans and their service and companion animals. But these relationships don't just happen. Proper training is critical to enjoying a long and happy life together.

Thankfully, many animal experts dedicate their lives to training service and therapy dogs for veterans; their unwavering commitment to people in need is indeed admirable. Training for service or therapy animals can be lengthy and expensive. The training for companion animals can be less costly and involved, but all these efforts make a profound difference in veterans' lives.

Professional animal trainers such as Andrea Arden, Patrick Bradley, and Dr. Shawn Dunn know the power of the animal-human bond and have studied the many species that have proved beneficial to healing our nation's brave warfighters. Regardless of the training regimens, there are commonalities that they agree will work to train all animals successfully: a special treat and positive reinforcement.

"In my experience, once you get an animal calm, the main thing is to find something it loves. I call it a 'super treat,'" Patrick Bradley said. "For me and my birds, I try to see what they will eat first. They love sunflowers seeds, so when I'm training them, I withhold their favorite treat and won't give it to them unless they do what I am asking. When you feed them that super treat, they will do anything to get it.

"Of course, a wildlife situation is very different than a pet situation," he added. "Basically, in a wildlife situation, all you can do is reinforce an existing behavior; you can't create a new behavior. I'm happy to know that there are more and more wildlife groups popping up and helping veterans through walking with birds of prey or getting to know wolves."

Of course, dogs are the most common and widely trained animals. Andrea Arden has been training them professionally for more than twenty years and knows a thing or two about what makes them tick. She's seen a rise in her business among people who seek training even before their puppies arrive. Older dogs can be successfully trained as well, though it may be a bit harder to undo years of deeply ingrained behaviors. She believes that preventive training can give dogs a happy life and ensure that they won't be abandoned because their owners can't handle their bad behaviors.

"One of the many great things about teaching people to teach their dogs is seeing the pride and enthusiasm in their eyes when they bring their pup in for the first lesson," Andrea said. "One of the tough parts of this profession is watching people go through the very typical cycle of puppy parenting, the next stage of which has a lot to do with being frustrated when a pup makes housetraining mistakes, chews inappropriate items, and barks and whines at all hours of the day and night. While even the best doggie time management won't prevent mistakes 100 percent of the time, it will certainly help keep things under control and keep their pup on the path to ultimate success."

Andrea added, "A lack of puppy management is surely going to put a strain on the canine/human relationship. Puppy parents play a huge part in their dog's lifelong behavior. In addition, each dog is an individual whose genetics also play a part in its behavior. But I always try to encourage people to go into raising a pup under the assumption that their pup may suffer from any number of behavior issues. It is better to err on the side of caution, to do everything you can to prevent potential issues, rather than to have a wait-and-see attitude."

Andrea said most dogs are inhibited when they first come to their new home. "There is a first time for everything, and most young pups start displaying behaviors that may seem new, but are usually just more exaggerated and frequent after the first week or two in their home, once they feel more comfortable and come out of their shell," Andrea said.

Andrea wrote a case study on her website's advice section that gives an example of how to handle a pup with attitude. About one terrible terrier she writes: "Marta from Long Island sent me an email today asking how to stop her five-year-old West Highland white terrier from sabotaging her social life by barking up a storm whenever she holds a phone to her ear. Connor had been crowned with the title of Sir Barksalot by the time he was a year old, and since that time Marta had reluctantly focused on texts to make contact with people. I explained that it was likely that when Connor was a puppy he barked at her for attention while she was occupied on the phone. Marta had inadvertently reinforced this behavior by giving him attention as a result. Her attention may very well have been in the form of pleadings to shush, but for most dogs, attention is attention, regardless of whether we deem it as negative or positive," Andrea wrote.

"I suggested she keep Connor on leash when she was there to supervise as a way of having a gentle but effective means of controlling him. In addition to ignoring Connor when he barks (because if a behavior gets no reward it will eventually become extinct), I suggested she plan some set-up phone calls during Connor's meal times and use her cell phone to call her land line and vice versa. Each time the phone rings and she picks up to say hello, I advised Marta to take a piece of Connor's food and toss it on his bed or in his crate. Once Connor starts to move toward the bed or crate when he hears the phone ring (as it will become a cue for going to that spot to get food), Marta can gradually work on delaying the reinforcement for a few seconds at a time so that eventually Connor can go to his spot and wait quietly for a good bit of time. In addition, I suggested Marta consider purchasing two or three special 'telephone time toys.' Gimborn white sterilized bones are a good option, as the hollow middle can be stuffed with a small bit of food and will keep Connor happily occupied. After loads of repetitions, Connor is sure to get the idea that running to his bed or crate is the best thing to do when the phone rings because he may get a tasty treat or special chew toy."

In a July 24, 2016 article on the website *Dogs.About.com*, Amy Bender writes that there are some keys to successfully training an older dog, especially one who has been adopted from a shelter. They may have baggage that needs to be overcome, so it's important to be patient. "An adult dog comes with his own history, which can make him nervous about his new surroundings. Don't give up on your new dog after only a few days. Your adult dog may need a period of adjustment, which can take anywhere from a few days to a month or so. Once your adult dog realizes he has found his forever home, he will soon settle into being part of the family," writes Amy.

Some animal experts believe in crate training a dog and not assuming it is housebroken, especially when it first arrives in a new setting. "I believe you should treat your adult dog just as you would a new puppy," writes Amy. "Keep him confined when you are not able to supervise him, and when you release him from the crate, take him immediately to the place outside where you want him to relieve himself. The good news is that adult dogs have more control over their bladders and bowels than young puppies. The house-training process usually goes much more quickly with adult dogs than with puppies or adolescent dogs that don't have this control yet."

Amy writes that people should never underestimate the ability of an older dog to learn new things. And there are many professional trainers and classes for adult dogs. Classes provide the added benefit of allowing older dogs to become better socialized by meeting and playing with other dogs. "Because you probably don't know for sure the type of experience your adult dog has had with training in the past, positive reinforcement methods are your best bet," Amy writes. "Using treats and praise is an effective training method for dogs of all ages and breeds. Keeping things fun and upbeat, rather than punishing your adult dog, is also a great way to strengthen the bond between you and your dog."

But there are still rules of the road that older dogs must follow to be successful in their new homes.

Amy continues, "An adult dog may have been able to do things in his previous home that you don't want to him to do in yours, such as jumping on guests or lying on the furniture. Start teaching your adult dog the rules for your home right now. It may take some work at the beginning, but teaching your adult dog basic commands and working on solving his behavior problems from day one means your dog will soon settle into being a happy and healthy part of your family."

Dr. Shawn Dunn knows how loving and being around animals can make the difference in a person's health and well-being. "It is a known scientific fact that petting a dog or cat will decrease your blood pressure," Shawn said. "We have seen that people in nursing homes or hospitals benefit greatly from visits from service animals and especially their own pets. Our pets give us a reason to live, when sometimes so many have no other reason. Animals have also literally saved people from serious depression and have gotten them out of their homes and back into the world. I believe no child should grow up without a pet, and they should learn the responsibilities of caring for one at an early age."

Of course, not all pets are created equal. "The truth is, there are many animals that—while they provide emotional support and love—still may require a bit more care than their owners initially anticipated," said Shawn. "People too often get these cute little things and don't have the means to care for them. The sad result is that they often times end up in shelters or sanctuaries."

Shawn noted that many people would have a hard time bringing exotic or unusual animals into their homes but added that animals in sanctuaries—whether birds of prey, potbelly pigs, horses, or parrots—can still be positively influenced by the power of regular human/animal interactions.

Shawn is also an advocate for giving shelter dogs and cats a permanent home. While they may not be as malleable as puppies or kittens, they still can be successfully trained and integrated into their new surroundings. She has worked with her own animals on doing just that. "Knowing in advance the obstacles you may run into, especially when you bring an older animal into the home or one with disabilities, is critical. I always tell people that spray bottles (when you have a cat and bird situation or an aggressive dog) are your friend," Shawn said.

Shawn also recommends doing your homework when it comes to learning what type of animal is best for you and your family. "It is especially critical to know the different animal breeds and make the best choice for your own living situation. For example, a person who lives in an apartment in the city might not want to get a dog that needs a lot of physical exercise and stimulation. Knowing in advance what meets your needs will assure you and your animal will live in harmony," Shawn said.

Just like us, animals love their special treats. "Unlike the food we love, animals shouldn't be tempted by pizza or cookies, just the treats they crave the most and are good for their health. They can be used not just as a reward but also as a welcome distraction," Shawn said. Along with a good meal or treat, positive reinforcement and a happy environment are two of the most important aspects of getting the most out of the animal in your life. "I just love the phrase 'party animals,' not because I'm a big partier myself, but because I believe that everything should be made into a fun thing," Shawn said. "That would include the most hated of all grooming activities—nail trimming. Lots of cuddles and great treats create a bond between you and your animal. There is nothing more special for you or your pet than looking each other in the eyes. Positive reinforcement is the ticket."

When your dog runs from you and won't come, it might be time to get back to a routine of obedience training. Dogs want and need guidance. "One of my patients, Jessi, is an example of an owner who can't correct her dogs because she loves them too much and doesn't want to hurt their feelings, thus, her dogs are completely unruly when she's around," Shawn said. "They act like angels when they're with me, though. The alpha personality comes into play here, but I told Jessi, 'You are the alpha, not your dog!'"

"In addition," she said, "certain behaviors need to be assessed and corrected, like having your dog jump on you when you don't want them to. I see this all the time, and I tell my patients that if you want to discourage this behavior, and not have your guests be bombarded by your jumping dog as well, you need to discourage your pet from doing this by not giving him attention or praise until he stops jumping. Obedience classes can give more specifics on how to accomplish this, and I recommend starting the classes as soon as you can. It creates a wonderful bond between you and your pet, and oftentimes people will realize the amazing athletic abilities of their dogs and go into agility classes—which are such great fun for both the dog and their human."

According to Shawn, some of the most important obedience training commands include: come, sit, stay, down, and no. "When my pets hear me actually say 'no,' in a firm voice, they all freeze to see who is creating an infraction. This has stopped a lot of dog fights—especially when two alpha dogs find themselves living together against their will. My favorite though is kisses. Each dog learns that command right off the bat, and it's a happy joyful time, especially when I get home from work. Also, I encourage my dogs to bark on command. It really helps when you have a new addition that is wandering off and you want to get their attention. I have my other dogs bark, and the new pet invariably comes running back."

For those who have many different animal species in the home, Shawn recommends treating them equally. "I have dogs, cats, horses, and a bird. I treat all the indoor pets the same. My bird can walk around on the floor and share a bowl of vanilla ice cream with any one of my dogs. She can land on any dog and three of the cats without any problem; they think she's a dog too. However, one of my new rescue cats still has what I call the hunt in her, and that's where the spray bottle comes in. When I see her stalking the bird, who is flying around free when I'm home, she gets a spray from across the room. When I feed treats, each animal gets a treat and they all have to be getting along and not acting aggressively. This method is really helping me stop the food aggression between a new, older rescue dog that my daughter recently brought home and my thirteen-year-old alpha female terrier, who is the indoor animal matriarch of the family," said Shawn. "We did have an incident, once, where the new dog attacked her and grabbed her by the neck. I immediately yelled no and pinned the new dog by the scruff, just as a mother dog would do when correcting her puppies. I do believe in pinning a dog for aggressive behavior that could result in injury or worse. It often gets their attention. Afterward, things go right back to normal and no grudge is ever held."

Shawn also strongly suggests that people who are beginning to house-break a dog never get mad, yell, or rub their dog's nose in messes that might occur. "The dog probably has no idea why you're mad, and this results in nothing but the dog being afraid of you," said Shawn. "Instead, with puppies and older dogs, I take them out constantly, and when they go to the bathroom outside I make such a big fuss over them that I'd be embarrassed for anyone to drive by and see me. If you can actually catch them in the act of eliminating in the house, run, pick them up and say no, and rush them outside and finish off with big-time praise. I realize not everyone will have the time for this and, as a result, may need to use a crate for house-training. I think that's fine, but once they're trained, I believe dogs should have the run of the house. Make sure there are plenty of chew toys to distract them from chewing on things that aren't meant to be chewed."

Shawn said that one important thing to keep in mind is that dogs may not have full control of their bladder until six months of age, so don't be discouraged if the housebreaking takes longer than you anticipate. "If your dog has diarrhea in the house, they can't help that and the cause of diarrhea should be investigated. Always consult with your vet if your dog suddenly has a change in his elimination habits—if he has trouble holding it, is urinating in odd spots or where he sleeps, has difficulty urinating, has changes in his stool, etc. You never know when a medical problem may be causing the issue at hand," said Shawn.

Even if you do your homework, give lots of love, take your dog to obedience training, and provide a safe, happy and structured home, a few unexpected issues may still arise. The good news is that with a bit of preparation and trial and error to see what works best, many of those pitfalls can be successfully overcome. "I tell my pet owners to prepare a checklist and add items as time goes on," Shawn said. "Some of those are: preparing your dog for vet visits; scheduling vet visits; keeping a list of preventive medications; keeping a grooming routine; handling every part of your dog or cat by playing with its ears, toes, tails, belly; and rewarding it with positivity and playfulness when it accepts all of your annoying habits, such as touching the animal in places that it may at first find to be out of its comfort zone. I make everything a game. Nail clippings happen like this in my house: I get out the clippers and the container of cat treats. The animals see this and always give me a skeptical look. I never call them to me for something they don't particularly like—even baths. Instead, I pick them up and take them to the clipping area. After each paw is done they get a cat treat—seems special for some reason. I speak calmly and praise them when they hold still, and if they resist, I say a firm no; once they are holding still again, I return to the calm and praise. I do the same with each animal, and after each is done, they get a big dog treat. Once all the animals are done, everyone gets another treat, and they all run around like crazy as if they just had a bath. I run around with them, telling them how wonderful they are."

Shawn added that some people may find this difficult because the size of an animal may make it difficult to restrain. It is always good to get a lesson from your veterinarian, and then you'll also know how far down to cut without hitting the quick—the fleshy part under the nail.

Lastly, if you are going to own a pet, you need to get over keeping your home in tip-top shape. It's just not going to happen. "Nice furniture just doesn't stay nice if you choose to have pets, so you just deal with it," Shawn said. "Shedding is a fact of life. I tell my patients' owners to groom them on a regular basis and quit complaining about all the hair. Everyone who sees me out in public wearing a black shirt full of hair knows I have animals in my life. I wear that fur-laden shirt as a badge of honor!"

EPILOGUE

"Our task must be to free ourselves . . . by widening our circle of compassion to embrace all living creatures and the whole of nature and its beauty."

—Albert Einstein

ANIMALS HAVE HELPED HUMAN BEINGS SINCE THE BEGINNING OF TIME become more productive, happy, and safe. They have guarded our homes and flocks, helped us open doors, helped us safely cross streets, alerted us to danger, apprehended bad guys, and comforted and cajoled us in times of trouble. They have even given their lives in an effort to save our nation's bravest from enemies—both foreign and domestic.

So it is more than fitting that their stories be memorialized. Many heartwarming and insightful books have been written about police and military dogs. They serve as testimonials to the training and dedication of the people who do this work and the dogs who are heroes in their own right. We are thankful to those authors who have taken the time to tell their dramatic stories so beautifully. As we have found in the writing of this book, many other animal species have helped veterans and warfighters recover from their physical and invisible injuries. A red-tailed hawk on a veteran's arm can transform his life. A cat can mitigate loss and grief. A potbelly pig renews a sense of belonging and being needed. A horse can offer calm in an emotional storm. And dogs—well they are simply man's best friend and can be as close as family members for wounded veterans.

One of the most crucial lessons we have learned is the importance of animal adoption. Why pay for something so precious and life altering when adoption is a far more affordable option? Abandoned and abused animals deserve a permanent home of their own, and they have found that and more with so many of our nation's veterans. When veterans adopt shelter animals, something magical happens. They can look into each other's eyes and inherently know they are not strangers, sharing a bond like no other.

Sanctuaries, too, play an important role in the lives of animals and veterans. They provide shelter where wounded, abused, or abandoned animals can live out their lives with safety, security, and an abundance of love. These wonderful places are havens for healing, both for the animals saved and the veterans who come for solace.

The work of rescue and sanctuary programs that have opened their arms to veterans has been dynamic and transformational. It will be fascinating to see, as some of the national studies conclude, the statistical confirmation of the healing power of animals for veterans, especially those with PTSD. Of course, these studies will confirm what many already know about the power of the bonds between animals and humans. They grow to be lasting and inseparable. "You can't have one without the other," as Sammy Cahn wrote in the hit song "Love and Marriage." Just ask Tyler, Jimmy, Shanda, Leslie, Justin, Paul, Aaron, Patrick, Jonathan, Tom, Stefanie, Shawn, Molly, Debi, and Mandi. They will tell you, in no uncertain terms, how lost they would be without the animals in their lives. Our sincerest hope is that you, the reader, will not only be moved by their adventures together but also advocate on behalf of all those who have served our great nation and the animals who stand steadfastly by their side.

ABOUT THE AUTHORS

Dava Guerin

Dava Guerin is the coauthor, along with Kevin Ferris, of *Unbreakable Bonds: The Mighty Moms and Wounded Warriors of Walter Reed*, released with rave reviews by Skyhorse Publishing in 2014. Guerin also coauthored two memoirs: *Keep Chopping Wood* with Mike Hardwick and *Presidents, Kings and Convicts* with former member of Congress Bob Clement (D-TN). She is also a Washington, DC–based communications consultant and writer and was the former communications director for the US Association of Former Members of Congress in Washington, DC. She was president of Guerin Public Relations, Inc., a full-service communications firm for more than twenty years; was people editor of *Local Living Magazine* and *Bucks Living Magazine*; and worked in senior-level positions for Ketchum Public Relations and the Philadelphia Convention and Visitors Bureau.

With more than twenty years in the marketing communications and public relations fields, Guerin has worked with numerous US presidents and managed visits for world leaders, US politicians, and entertainers. She continues to support former First Lady Barbara Bush and the Barbara Bush Foundation for Family Literacy. She has also managed national and international public relations programs for many Fortune 500 companies and professional sports teams; provided media credentialing and media management for the 2000 Republican National Convention, the President's Summit for America's Future, We the People 200, the Congressional Medal of Honor Society, LIVE8, and the Philadelphia Liberty Medal; and she was editor of the 2000 Republican National Convention's *2000 Official Delegate and Media Guide*. Her freelance work has appeared in many national media outlets including *The Hill*, *American Legion Magazine*, the *Philadelphia Inquirer*,

Washington Examiner, and many others. She has appeared on FOX News, 6ABC, NBC10, and KYW News radio, among others. She is an advocate for wounded warriors and their families, supports the Elizabeth Dole Foundation and the Gary Sinise Foundation, as well as helps families of wounded warriors directly.

Guerin graduated Summa Cum Laude with a master of education degree in organizational behavior from Temple University, and she graduated from Goddard College with a bachelor of arts degree in English and literature. Guerin also attended Rutgers University and the University of London's summer program focusing on history and literature. She was past president of the Philadelphia chapter of American Women in Radio and Television, is on the advisory board of the Tug McGraw Foundation, and has supported many nonprofit organizations that focus on literacy and veteran's issues.

She resides with her husband, mother, and two Labradoodles in Berlin, Maryland.

Author Dava Guerin with her Australian Labradoodle Tinkie. *Photo by Terry Bivens*

Dava's Australian Labradoodles, Tinkie and J.P. Morgan. *Photo by Terry Bivens*

Kevin Ferris

Kevin Ferris is the coauthor, with Dava Guerin, of *Unbreakable Bonds: The Mighty Moms and Wounded Warriors of Walter Reed* (Skyhorse 2014). He is a columnist and commentary editor at the *Philadelphia Inquirer*, and his freelance work has appeared in the *Weekly Standard*, the *Wall Street Journal*, the *Christian Science Monitor*, and *American Legion* magazine. He has two children and lives in West Chester, Pennsylvania, with an Irish setter named Samson.

Photo credit Tania Gail Ciolko